"If you've ever wondered why the Gospels are so  this book is for you! Clifton Black navigates the comp Synoptic Gospels without ever losing sight of their sub depth and good humor, Black draws readers into each sion of Jesus' message."

—Susan E. Hylen, Almar H. Shatford Professor of New Testament,
Candler School of Theology, Emory University

"As one of the many students who has had the privilege to learn the Gospels in the classroom of C. Clifton Black, I can attest that this volume has all the humor, verve, and faithfulness of his matchless persona. A perfect volume for students, *A Three-Dimensional Jesus* distills what really matters in Synoptic studies and presents it with clarity that arises from years of faithful and honest friendship with these writings. Rich historical data provide a sense of the ancient ethos. Geographical rootedness allows the imagination to locate the stories in real places. Visual aids in both charts and artwork stimulate the mind for maximal apprehension. Conversations with a wide range of Gospels scholars stretch the reader to see different fruitful ways of studying these texts. Black frees the reader to admit with him that there are many things we do not know about these accounts of Jesus; but that lack, instead of inhibiting, actually empowers faithful response to the good news proclaimed therein."

—Amy Peeler, Professor of New Testament, Wheaton College

"C. Clifton Black first sparked my scholarly interest in the Gospels decades ago when I was a master's student in one of his classes. To this day I know of no better guide to these texts. Here he offers an introduction to the first three Gospels that is informed by high-level scholarship but is also accessible to nonspecialists. In witty prose he walks the reader through the major themes of these texts, highlighting the distinctive ways each proclaims the good news of Jesus Christ. If you've been looking for a measured, informed, and practical guide to the Synoptic Gospels, look no further. This is your book."

—David F. Watson, Academic Dean and Vice President for Academic Affairs,
and Professor of New Testament, United Theological Seminary

"In *A Three-Dimensional Jesus*, Clifton Black shares his love of reading the Gospels in engaging, memorable ways. Using a wide variety of illustrations drawn from television, classical music, and art, as well as a review of Roman history featuring 'Big Julie and the Imperials' and interspersed conversations with other teacher-scholars, he invites readers to delight in encountering Jesus and the Synoptic Gospels in all their varied dimensions."

—Laura C. Sweat Holmes, Professor of New Testament,
Wesley Theological Seminary

"C. Clifton Black's *A Three-Dimensional Jesus* is an informed and engaging introduction to the Synoptic Gospels. It is written in a style that is accessible to students, pastors, and laypeople. The reader encounters careful and balanced analyses and is enriched by insightful conversations with scholars, preachers, and art and music historians—an important reminder that Scripture must be read in community. I am excited to see this book and highly recommend it."

—Robert E. Moses, Associate Professor of Religion,
High Point University

"C. Clifton Black is a winsome and learned guide; he will take you on a delightful and stimulating tour through the Synoptic Gospels while inviting you to eavesdrop on conversations with a host of friends (who also happen to be experts) along the way. If you are interested in discovering or rediscovering the worlds of Matthew, Mark, and Luke in all their complexity—from political settings to preaching challenges—this book is for you."

—Rebekah Eklund, Associate Professor of Theology,
Loyola University Maryland

"In a world where no one knows what is true and most intelligence seems artificial, C. Clifton Black enters the fray with an impassioned and well-tempered reading of the Synoptic Gospels. With precious insights and deft prose on every page, Black offers an inspiring reading of the Synoptics while showing his work in such a way that the reader is not just entertained but also informed and empowered. Punctuated with anecdotes, interviews, and other witticisms, this book is not your typical introduction to the Synoptics; it is an invitation to think about the Gospels and the Christian faith in a new way."

—Micah D. Kiel, Professor of Theology, St. Ambrose University

"Clifton Black has written an invaluable resource for studying the Synoptic Gospels for students at every level. The present volume reflects the culmination of lifelong study, combining cutting-edge research with Black's contagious enthusiasm to read Matthew, Mark, and Luke with a stubborn, insatiable curiosity."

—J. P. O'Connor, Associate Professor of New Testament,
Northwest University

A Three-Dimensional Jesus

A Three-Dimensional Jesus

An Introduction to the Synoptic Gospels

C. Clifton Black

WESTMINSTER
JOHN KNOX PRESS
LOUISVILLE · KENTUCKY

Book design by Sharon Adams
Cover design by Marc Witaker / MTWdesign.net

Library of Congress Cataloging-in-Publication Data is on file
at the Library of Congress, Washington, D.C.

ISBN: 9780664265526

Most Westminster John Knox Press books are available at special quantity discounts when purchased in bulk by corporations, organizations, and special-interest groups. For more information, please e-mail SpecialSales@wjkbooks.com.

This book is dedicated to my students at

Duke University (1984–85),

The University of Rochester (1986–89),

Colgate Rochester Divinity School/Bexley Hall/Crozer Theological Seminary (1987–89),

Perkins School of Theology, Southern Methodist University (1989–99),

Princeton Theological Seminary (1999–2024),

with gratitude for teaching me how to teach.

Contents

List of Figures:
Photographs, Illustrations, Tables

Permissions for Use

The author and publisher express sincere appreciation to the following agencies for their kind permission to reproduce excerpts from several previously published works:

Preface

This book aims to introduce its readers to the New Testament's first three Gospels. It's safe to say that I've read no books more often than these. Oddly, for over six decades, not once have I tired of them. Just the opposite: the longer I've read them, the more they've fascinated, comforted, disturbed, calmed, provoked, and perplexed me. I wish this book were better. I'm certain it would be worse if the Gospels did not still keep from me secrets I cannot unravel. That fact is demonstrated whenever I enter a classroom: invariably a perceptive student will ask a question about the Gospels' interpretation that I cannot answer. Drawing on a nimble command of my intellectual powers, I declare, "I don't know." Throughout this book that confession recurs. As I've aged, I find myself making it more often—not only of the Gospels, but of just about everything else.

But take heart: we needn't know everything about the Gospels to profit by reading them. It's ignorance that maintains our humility, returns us to study, and helps us to spot frauds whose flimflam is exposed by reassertion of their oh-so-certain understanding.

A Three-Dimensional Jesus is an invitation: by no means a comprehensive account, but a friendly word of welcome. If this little book could pull the chain that opened the floodgates of one reader's imagination to blurt out, "What a weird, wondrous world Mark (or Matthew or Luke) has opened before me," I would be as happy as a clam. There I go again. How happy *is* a clam? What do we know of the emotional life of crustaceans? For all I know, they may be tired of all that sand up their bivalves.

Dr. Bridgett Green was the editor who soft-soaped me into this project. Departing for a time to join with the faculty of Austin Presbyterian Theological Seminary before returning to Westminster John Knox Press, she can sidestep blame for the outcome. No less charming but less fortunate is her successor at WJK, Ms. Julie Mullins, who has suffered me much while suffering much. Alice astutely asked, "What is the good of a book without pictures and conversation?" (Lewis Carroll, *Alice's Adventures in Wonderland* [1865]). Both are profuse in this book. For much of the former (my photographs), the subvention of travel to Israel, Palestine, and

Jordan in December 2019, and the luxury of a year's sabbatical in 2019–20, I thank the Trustees and President of Princeton Seminary. For invaluable help in confirming copyright clearances, I thank Michele Blum, overseer of rights and permissions at WJK, and Leslie Garrote, editorial intern at WJK and PhD candidate at Baylor University's Department of Religious Studies. JoAnn Sikkes at BookComp, Inc., composited and typeset a busy book with flair. The copyediting by S. David Garber and proofreading by Bob Land have been unimpeachable. I am grateful to Jen Weers, who prepared the subject index, and to Elise Hess for the index of Scripture and ancient sources. As always, Dan Braden supervised the entire production with consummate professionalism and good humor.

For this book's sparkling conversations on a potpourri of topics, I am indebted to Dale Allison, Marianne Blickenstaff, Alan Culpepper, Anna Marley, Markus Rathey, Barbara Reid, Elizabeth Shively, John Thompson, and William Willimon. All gave me precious gifts of their time and expertise.

Kaitlynn C. Merckling, matriculant for the PhD in New Testament at Princeton, supported me in countless ways as my research assistant. She is the latest, probably last, among a cadre of graduate students, now colleagues, who across two decades have cared for my books as though they were their own: David J. Downs (currently of Keble College, Oxford University), Melanie A. Howard (Fresno Pacific University), Micah D. Kiel (St. Ambrose University), Kara J. Lyons-Pardue (Point Loma Nazarene University), Devlin R. McGuire (Biblical Seminary of Colombia in Medellín), M. J. P. O'Connor (Northwest University), Callie Plunket-Brewton (Trinity Episcopal Church, Florence, Alabama), and Laura Sweat Holmes (Wesley Theological Seminary). With pride and affection I thank them all.

As ever, Harriet Black stood beside me while I pounded my head against cinderblocks. So she has done for forty-five years and counting.

"Let us be grateful to the people who make us happy; they are the charming gardeners who make our souls blossom." Marcel Proust wrote a lot more than this in his seven-volume *À la recherche du temps perdu* (1913–27), but nothing better.

C. C. B.
The Feast of All Saints
1 November 2022
Princeton, New Jersey

Abbreviations

ANCIENT SOURCES

Aesop	*Life of Aesop*
A.J.	Flavius Josephus (37–ca. 100), *Jewish Antiquities* (Lat., *Antiquitates judaicae*)
Amph.	Plautus (ca. 254–154 BCE), *Amphitruo*
Ann.	Tacitus (ca. 56–120), *Annals*
Ap.	Flavius Josephus, *Against Apion*
Ass	Apuleius (ca. 142–ca. 170), *The Golden Ass*
Ast.	*Oracles of Astrampsychus* [a pseudonym] (ca. 4th c. CE)
Aug.	Suetonius (ca. 69–122), *Life of Augustus*
b.	Babylonian Talmud (preceding the title of a tractate; ca. 5th c. CE)
B.J.	Josephus, *The Jewish War* (*Bellum judaicum*)
Cal.	Suetonius, *Life of Caligula*
Carm. Astrol.	Dorotheus of Sidon (late 1st c. CE), *Carmen Astrologicum* (*Astrological Song*)
CD	*See* DSS
CIL	*Corpus Inscriptionum Latinarum* (Berlin, 1863–)
Civ.	Augustine of Hippo, *The City of God* (Lat., *De civitate Dei*)
Claud.	Suetonius, *Life of Claudius*
Decal.	Philo of Alexandria (ca. 20 BCE–50 CE), *On the Decalogue*
Dial.	Seneca the Younger (ca. 4 BCE–65 CE), *Dialogues*
Dom.	Suetonius, *Life of Domitian*
Dreams	Artemidorus (2nd c. CE), *The Interpretation of Dreams*
DSS	Dead Sea Scrolls (ca. 200 BCE–100 CE)
	CD Damascus Document
	1QM War Scroll
	1QS Manual of Discipline
Embassy	Philo of Alexandria, *The Embassy to Gaius*
Ep.	Cicero (106–43 BCE), *Epistles*
First Apol.	Justin Martyr (100–165), *First Apology*

Gold	Plautus, *Pot of Gold* (*Aulularia*)
Gos. Thom.	*Gospel of Thomas*
Gov.	Salvian (ca. 405–ca. 495), *On the Government of God*
Haer.	Irenaeus (ca. 130–ca. 202), *Against Heresies* (*Adversus haereses*)
Hist.	Cassius Dio (ca. 155–ca. 235), *Roman History*
Hist. eccl.	Eusebius (ca. 260–ca. 340), *Church History* (*Historia ecclesiastica*)
Jul.	Suetonius, *Life of Julius Caesar*
Law	Philo of Alexandria, *Allegories of the Law*
Let.	Pliny the Younger (61–ca. 113), *Letters*
Lives	Plutarch (ca. 46–ca. 120), *Parallel Lives*
LXX	Septuagint (ca. 200 BCE—50 CE)
m.	Mishnah (preceding the title of a tractate; ca. 3rd c. CE)
Med.	Marcus Aurelius Antoninus (121–180), *Meditations*
Metam.	Ovid (43 BCE–18 CE), *Metamorphoses*
Mor.	Plutarch, *Morals* (*Moralia*)
Mos.	Philo of Alexandria, *Life of Moses*
Names	Philo of Alexandria, *On the Translation of Names*
Nat.	Pliny the Elder (ca. 23–79), *Natural History*
Nero	Suetonius, *Life of Nero*
1QM	*See* DSS
1QS	*See* DSS
OTP	*Old Testament Pseudepigrapha* [ca. 200 BCE–300 CE]. Edited by James H. Charlesworth. 2 vols. New York: Doubleday, 1983, 1985
Pesaḥ.	Pesaḥim (tractate of the Mishnah and Talmud)
P.Oxy.	*The Oxyrhynchus Papyri*. London, 1898–.
Pur.	Empedocles (ca. 494–434 BCE), *Purifications*
Rab.	Cicero, *On Behalf of Gaius Rabirius*
Sat.	Juvenal (ca. 50–150), *Satires*
Satyr.	*Satyricon* (authorship uncertain; late 1st c. CE)
Smyrn.	Ignatius of Antioch (d. 108/140), *Epistle to the Smyrnaeans*
Tib.	Suetonius, *Life of Tiberius*
Titus	Suetonius, *Life of Titus*
Verres	Cicero, *Against Gaius Verres*
Vesp.	Suetonius, *Life of Vespasian*
Vita	Josephus, *Life of Flavius Josephus*

MODERN SOURCES

AB	Anchor Bible
ANET	*The Ancient Near East Today*

ANTC	Abingdon New Testament Commentary
BZNW	Beihefte zur Zeitschrift für die neutestamentliche Wissenschaft und die Kunde der älteren Kirche
ICC	International Critical Commentary
IRUSC	Interpretation Resources for the Use of Scripture in the Church
JBL	*Journal of Biblical Literature*
JRBI	*BACH: Journal of the Riemenschneider Bach Institute*
JRS	*Journal of Roman Studies*
JSNTSup	Supplements to Journal of the Study of the New Testament
KJV	King James Version (1611)
LEC	Library of Early Christianity
LJS	Lives of Jesus Series
LNTS	Library of New Testament Studies
NCB	New Century Bible
NEB	New English Bible (1970)
NIV	New International Version (1973)
NovTSup	Supplements to Novum Testamentum
NRSV	New Revised Standard Version (1989)
NTL	New Testament Library
NTT	New Testament Theology
RC	*Religion Compass*
RSV	Revised Standard Version (1952)
SANT	Studien zum Alten und Neuen Testaments
SNTSMS	Society for New Testament Studies Monograph Series
SPNT	Studies on Personalities of the New Testament
TEV	Today's English Version (1976) = Good News Bible/Translation

OTHER SIGLA

BCE	before the Common Era (= BC)
c.	century
ca.	around, approximately (Lat., *circa*)
CE	the Common Era (= AD)
cf.	compare (Lat., *confer*)
chap(s).	chapter(s)
CTS	Latin: Custodia Terrae Sanctae (Custody of the Holy Land)
ed(s).	edited by, edition, editor(s)
e.g.	for example (Lat., *exempli gratia*)
esp.	especially
et al.	*et alii*, and others

fig.	figure
Gk.	(in) Greek language
HB	Hebrew Bible
Heb.	(in) Hebrew language
idem	author of a work just named (Lat., "the same")
i.e.	that is (Lat., *id est*)
L	Hypothetical Source for Luke
Lat.	(in) Latin language
lit.	literally
M	Hypothetical Source for Matthew
MS(S)	manuscript(s)
N.B.	note well (Lat., *nota bene*)
no(s).	numbers
NT	New Testament
orig.	original
OT	Old Testament
Q	Hypothetical Source for Matthew and Luke
//	parallel with
rev.	revised
trans.	translated by, translator(s), translation
v(v).	verse(s)
vol(s).	volume(s)

The Quotable Synoptics

With a deep bow of appreciation for Bernard Levin, who did the same for Shakespeare.[1]

If you are able to read **the signs of the times**, you are quoting the Synoptics. If you are **a prophet without honour**, for whom there is **no room in the inn**, you are quoting the Synoptics. If you are **the salt of the earth** and among **the meek** who **shall inherit the earth** with all its **gold, and frankincense, and myrrh**, you are quoting the Synoptics. If you **turn the other cheek, go the** second **mile**, don't **let your left hand know what your right hand is doing**, know better than to throw **pearls before swine**, and can assay **one pearl of great price** with **faith** that **moves a mountain**, you are quoting the Synoptics. If you **render to Caesar the things that are Caesar's** but can distinguish **God and mammon** because **no man can serve two masters**, or if you **have washed your hands, saying, I am innocent of one jot or one tittle** that could lead to **hellfire**, then you are quoting the Synoptics as you smell **the lilies of the field** and would as **a** good **Samaritan go and do likewise.** *But*—if you are **the blind leading the blind** and **strain out a gnat while swallowing a camel**; if you are **wolves in sheep's clothing**, living in **a den of thieves** or **a house divided against itself** because you **take the sword**, you shall **die by the sword**, even though you are quoting the Synoptics, **Physician, heal thyself, O ye of little faith: he with ears to hear, let him hear** that **blessed are the peacemakers** and **by their fruits ye shall know them. Get thee behind me, Satan; for many are called, but few are chosen,** and **many that are first shall be last and the last shall be first** at **the eleventh hour,** when **the sheep** are divided **from the goats** and **even a camel** can go **through the eye of a needle** while quoting the Synoptics. **Well done, good and faithful servant: what therefore God hath joined together, let not man put asunder. Shake off the dust of your feet:** only **seek, and ye shall find** that you are quoting the Synoptics.

---

1. Bernard Levin, *Enthusiasms: Art, Literature, Music, Food, Walking* (London: Jonathan Cape, 1983), 167–68.

1

The Gospels

A Curtain-Raiser

Extended stories about Jesus in the New Testament (NT) are traditionally called "Gospels" (with a capital *G*). Around 155 CE Justin Martyr (ca. 100–ca. 165), an early Christian apologist, clearly and evidently for the first time on record used *euangelion* to describe a literary composition of the good news of Jesus' life, death, and resurrection (*First Apol.* 55). So far, so good.

From that simple observation erupts a lava of questions whose answers range among straightforward, unexpected, complicated, or downright impossible to reply with confidence. For clarity's sake, let's identify some of them right now.

- ♦ What does the term "gospel" mean? What bells chimed when first-century Jews and Gentiles (non-Jews) heard that term?
- ♦ Who wrote the Gospels?
- ♦ Where did the Gospels originate?
- ♦ What traditions did their authors probably use in compiling them?
- ♦ Why were the Gospels written?
- ♦ What literary genre in antiquity do the Gospels most closely resemble?
- ♦ This book's subtitle refers to "the Synoptic Gospels." What are they?
- ♦ What is the relationship among these "Synoptic Gospels"?
- ♦ We know of many Gospels that never made it into the NT. Why not?
- ♦ Geographically, where are the events narrated in the Gospels set?
- ♦ Within the NT's Gospels, who are the characters that we regularly meet?
- ♦ As the Gospels were transmitted by early Christians in the first and second centuries CE, what sorts of people in the Roman Empire would likely have heard or read them?

Reading these items, some of you may already be "sighing deeply in your spirits" (cf. Mark 8:12). Trust me. Each of these questions is important. Some are fascinating; many are elusive. If we don't consider them at least briefly from the beginning, the rest of this book will make little sense. So let's roll up our sleeves and get started.

WHAT DOES THE TERM "GOSPEL" MEAN?

"Gospel," a "good spiel," translates the Greek word *euangelion* into English as "good news." Convert "u" to "v," abbreviate, and you have "evangel." A reporter of good news is an "evangelist," the term that biblical scholars use in referring to the authors of the NT Gospels: Matthew, Mark, Luke, and John. In the middle and late first century CE, many NT writers use "gospel" (with a lowercase *g*) to refer, not to a book, but to *a message*: the proclamation of salvation, conceived as liberation from sin, brokenness, and estrangement from God. God reveals this good news through Jesus' life, death, and resurrection (Mark 1:1; Rom 1:1–4). This we observe in Matthew 11:4–5: "Jesus answered, 'Go back and tell John what you are hearing and seeing: the blind can see, the lame can walk, the lepers are made clean, the deaf hear, the dead are raised to life, and the good news is preached [*euangelizontai*] to the poor'" (TEV).

Early Christians' adoption of the word *euangelion* arose from at least two cultural traditions. In the Roman Empire,[1] the term had acquired religious significance with reference to Augustus, whose accession to the throne and subsequent decrees were propagandized as "glad tidings" or "gospels":

> A savior for us and our descendants, [Augustus] will make wars to cease and order all things well. Through his appearance Caesar has exceeded the hopes of all former *good messages* [*euangelia*]. . . . For the world the birthday of the god [Caesar] was the beginning of his *good message* [*euangelion*]."[2]

Although none of the evangelists presents Jesus in direct opposition to Caesar, they remembered that Jesus had preserved Jewish monotheism by differentiating Caesar from God (Matt 22:15–22//Mark 12:13–17//Luke 20:20–26). By adopting the term *euangelion*, early Christians may have quietly challenged any Roman emperor's claim to be a "savior" through military victories.[3] Instead, they identified Jesus, even at his birth, as "a Savior, who is the Messiah, the Lord" (Luke 2:11; see also 1:68–69; 2:29–32).

---

1. Dating this ancient empire is difficult. A Roman Republic, in place as early as the sixth century BCE, was consolidated under the emperor Augustus by 27 BCE, split into Western and Eastern sectors around 395 CE, fell apart in the West around 480 after conquest by Germanic tribes, and came to an end in the East on May 29, 1453, when Ottoman Turks under Mehmed II conquered Constantinople. For more information on Roman emperors during the time of Jesus and the evangelists, see chap. 4 below.

2. Quoted by Frederick W. Danker, *Jesus and the New Age according to St. Luke: A Commentary on the Third Gospel* (St. Louis: Clayton Publishing House, 1972), 24; Helmut Koester, *Ancient Christian Gospels: Their History and Development* (Philadelphia: Trinity Press International, 1990), 3–4.

3. "Savior" (Gk. *sōtēr*) was applied to all sorts of authorities and estimable personalities in antiquity: not only rulers, but also physicians, statesmen, officials, and philosophers. In the OT it usually refers to Israel's God (e.g., Pss 24:5; 27:9 [26:9 LXX]; Mic 7:7), a meaning carried over into the NT (1 Tim 1:1; 2:3; 4:10; Titus 1:3; 2:10; 3:4; Jude 25). Jesus is revered as Savior in Luke 2:11; John 4:42; Acts 13:23; Eph 5:23; Phil 3:20; 2 Tim 1:10; Titus 1:4; 2:13; 3:6; 1 John 4:14; 2 Pet 1:1; 3:2.

Also underlying "the good news" in the NT is a tradition in the Septuagint (LXX), a translation of the Hebrew Bible (HB)[4] into Greek that appears to have originated as early as the second century BCE. There the basic meaning of *euangelion* is a "happy report" (2 Sam 18:27). "The good news" acquires another connotation from the prophetic book of Isaiah, which proclaims "joyful tidings" of Israel's liberation from Babylonian captivity, facilitated by Cyrus the Great, king of Persia (539 BCE):

> How beautiful on the mountains
>   are the feet of those who bring *good news*,
> who proclaim peace,
>   who bring *good tidings*,
>   who proclaim salvation,
> who say to Zion,
>   "Your God reigns."
> (Isa 52:7 NIV, emphasis added; also see 40:9; 61:1–2a)

The apostle Paul, a first-century Hellenistic Jew, refers to the "gospel" as orally communicated or "preached" (Rom 1:15; 10:15; 15:20; 1 Cor 1:17; 9:16). At its simplest "the good news" is identified with "Jesus Christ, raised from the dead, a descendant of David" (2 Tim 2:8; see also Rom 15:16; 1 Cor 15:16). Paul refers to "the good news" not just as words but as *a dynamic event*, the exercise of God's might for human and cosmic restoration: "For I am not ashamed of the gospel; it is the power of God for salvation to everyone who has faith" (Rom 1:16; cf. 1 Thess 1:5). Early Christians who trusted this "good news" quickly came to consider it a norm for proper conduct: "Only live as citizens in a manner worthy of the gospel of Christ" (Phil 1:27; see also Gal 2:14). God's gospel had and has power to elicit courage amid suffering (Mark 8:35; 1 Thess 2:2) and requires obedience by its believers (Heb 4:6; 1 Pet 4:17). This gospel's proclamation transcends time and space (Eph 1:13; Col 1:5; 1 Pet 1:12; Rev 14:6).

WHO WROTE THE GOSPELS FOUND IN THE NEW TESTAMENT?

On its face, this appears to be a silly question. There's a twofold reason why it's not. First: within the texts of the Gospels themselves, all are anonymous. But what about their titles, "According to Matthew" and the like? That's the second point

4. The Hebrew Bible (*miqra*, "that which is read") is a canonical collection of Hebrew books, traditionally consisting of teaching, or Law (*Torah*); Prophets (*Nevi'im*); and Writings (*Ketuvim*). During the Middle Ages the entire corpus came to be known by the acronym *Tanakh*: $T + N + K$. The Christian Bible incorporates these books as its "Old Testament" (OT). The precise number of books in the OT varies among Eastern Orthodox, Roman Catholic, and Protestant Christians.

to note. Our earliest Greek manuscripts with such titles cannot be dated earlier than 200 CE, a century or longer after these Gospels were almost surely written.[5] So where *did* these names come from?

The oldest tradition describing the composition of Mark and Matthew is from Papias (ca. 60–130), Bishop of Hierapolis (6 miles northeast of Laodicea, in modern-day Turkey; cf. Col 4:13), recorded by Eusebius of Caesarea (ca. 260–ca. 340; *Hist. eccl.* 3.39.15–16):

> Now this is what [John] the elder used to say: "Mark became Peter's interpreter and wrote accurately whatever he remembered, but not in order, of the things said or done by the Lord." For he had neither heard the Lord, nor had he followed him, but later on, as I said, [followed Peter], who used to offer the teachings in anecdotal form [alternatively: "as need arose"], but not making, as it were, a systematic arrangement of the Lord's oracles, so that Mark did not miss the mark in thus writing down individual items as he remembered them. For to one thing he gave forethought: to leave out nothing of what he had heard and to falsify nothing in them. . . . And about Matthew, this was said: "Matthew systematically arranged the oracles in the Hebrew language, and each interpreted them as he was able."

The earliest tradition about Luke's Gospel is recorded in the Muratorian Canon, the oldest extant list of NT writings, which, though we can't be sure, may have originated in Rome as early as 180:

> The third Gospel book [was] that according to Luke. After Christ's ascension this physician Luke, whom Paul had taken with him as an expert in the way [of the teaching], wrote it under his own name in accordance with his own thinking. Yet neither did he himself see the Lord in the flesh. Therefore, as he was able to ascertain it, he begins to tell the story from the birth of John [the Baptist] (lines 2–8; cf. Col 4:14)

Bishop Irenaeus of Lyons (ca. 130–200) offers the earliest reference to the Evangelist John, as quoted by Eusebius (*Hist. eccl.* 3.23.3–4):

> In the second book of his work, *Against Heresies* [2.22.5], [Irenaeus] writes as follows: "And all the elders who associated with John the disciple of the Lord in Asia bear witness that John delivered the Gospel to them. For he remained among them until the time of [the Emperor] Trajan [98–117]; . . . and John is a faithful witness of the apostolic tradition."

---

5. For more on this subject, see Martin Hengel, *Studies in the Gospel of Mark*, trans. John Bowden (Philadelphia: Fortress Press, 1985), 65–74; Graham N. Stanton, *Jesus and Gospel* (Cambridge: Cambridge University Press, 2004), 63–91.

The interpretation of these witnesses is difficult.[6] Any English translation masks Greek words whose connotations are uncertain. These traditions are practically impossible to verify and, in some cases, are contradicted by others. Sometimes what's stated doesn't tally with the evidence in front of us. Matthew—at least the Gospel we have—was indisputably written in Greek and not Hebrew, was not a translation of a Semitic original, and (as we soon shall see) seems dependent on Mark's Gospel to an extraordinary degree. If the author of Matthew's Gospel was a follower of Jesus, why would that evangelist have depended so heavily on a secondhand source?[7] Remember the critical point: *in none of these Gospels does an author identify himself.* Their various titles were not applied to the Gospels until the early third century, when widespread adoption of a fourfold Gospel canon made it necessary to differentiate them. Moreover, the testimonies I have quoted are notable for their reserve: Papias and the Muratorian Canon attribute their traditions to predecessors and come clean that neither Mark nor Luke was an eyewitness (which Luke 1:2–3 concedes). All are more focused on providing a "faithful witness to the apostolic tradition" and less concerned about specific writers who may finally have composed them.

Twenty-first-century readers in the West are preoccupied by literary authorship; first-century church leaders invested far more confidence in oral reports from trustworthy informants. Papias insisted, "I was of the opinion that things out of books do not profit me so much as what comes from a living and abiding voice" (*Hist. eccl.* 3.39.4). Papias, Irenaeus, and others wanted trustworthy accounts about Jesus, and that's what the evangelists intend to provide. If the author of the Second Gospel[8] (for instance) cared nothing about identifying himself, why should we be obsessed by that?

WHERE DID THE GOSPELS ORIGINATE?

Once again, certainty is impossible. Strong arguments have been made for Matthew's origin in Syria, particularly in the city of Antioch, whose ruins today lie near

6. Detailed analyses of two of these testimonies are offered by C. Clifton Black, *Mark: Images of an Apostolic Interpreter*, SPNT (Columbia: University of South Carolina Press, 1994), 77–191; and R. Alan Culpepper, *John the Son of Zebedee: The Life of a Legend*, SPNT (Columbia: University of South Carolina Press, 1994), 107–86. On the traditions surrounding Matthew, consult W. D. Davies and Dale C. Allison Jr., *A Critical and Exegetical Commentary on the Gospel according to Saint Matthew*, ICC (Edinburgh: T&T Clark, 2004), 1:7–58; regarding Luke, see Joseph A. Fitzmyer, *The Gospel according to Luke I–IX: Introduction, Translation, and Notes*, AB 28 (Garden City, NY: Doubleday & Co., 1981), 35–53.

7. Matthew the tax collector in Matt 9:9 is identified as Levi in Mark 2:14 and Luke 5:27. In oral traditions inherited by the evangelists, events were remembered even though names often varied. See also Matt 8:28//Mark 5:1//Luke 8:26.

8. By scholarly convention Matthew, Mark, Luke, and John are referred to as the First, Second, Third, and Fourth Gospels, their canonical sequence, irrespective of the most probable dates when they were written: Mark, shortly before or after 70; Matthew, ca. 80–90; Luke, ca. 80–90; John, ca. 100. All these dates are matters of educated guesswork.

Antakya, Turkey. Antioch figures prominently in the book of Acts (11:19–30), and Ignatius, an early bishop of Antioch who died sometime in the second century CE, alludes to Matthew (1:18; 3:15; *Smyrn.* 1.1). Rome persists in patristic anecdotes about the creation of Mark's Gospel. From what we can piece together of early Roman Christianity, Mark's origin there is plausible but impossible to verify. Luke's Gospel appears intended for Gentiles in a predominantly Gentile setting, but there's no scholarly consensus on its birthplace.[9] Ephesus, Alexandria, and Antioch have been proposed as places for the Fourth Gospel's origin, yet "it is impossible to make out a satisfactory and conclusive case for any of [these] three great cities."[10] As with authorship, so too with provenance: we needn't despair over our insuperable ignorance because none of the Gospels' interpretation depends on fixing their origins.

ON WHAT TRADITIONS DID THE EVANGELISTS RELY IN COMPILING THEIR GOSPELS?

Since we have identified so much that we *don't* know, it may come as a relief to note something that no serious scholar doubts: that the sayings and stories of Jesus, collected in the Gospels, at first circulated orally. Our best evidence for that lies in Paul's Letters, written in 50–57, sometime between fifteen and thirty-five years before the Gospels were composed.[11]

By the early 50s, about twenty years after Jesus' ministry, Paul knows that Jesus

- ◆ was Jewish: born under the law (Gal 4:4), of David's lineage (Rom 1:3);
- ◆ had more than one brother (1 Cor 9:5), one of whom was named James (15:7; Gal 1:19; 2:9, 12);
- ◆ had a close entourage of disciples, including Cephas, or Peter,[12] and John (Gal 2:1–14);
- ◆ voluntarily gave his life for the sins of his followers (1 Cor 15:3; Gal 1:4), which they interpreted as fulfillment of God's will for the world's salvation (2 Cor 5:19; Phil 2:8) in accordance with Jewish Scripture (1 Cor 15:3);
- ◆ was, by decree of "the rulers of this age" (1 Cor 2:8), executed by crucifixion (1 Cor 1:17–25; Gal 3:1), and his remains were buried (1 Cor 15:4; Rom 6:4); yet
- ◆ was raised from death on the third day and appeared to Cephas, the Twelve, and to many other believers (1 Cor 15:4–8).

9. See Davies and Allison, *Saint Matthew*, 1:138–47; Black, *Apostolic Interpreter*, 224–59; Fitzmyer, *Luke I–IX*, 53–59.

10. C. K. Barrett, *The Gospel according to St. John: An Introduction with Commentary and Notes on the Greek Text*, 2nd ed. (Philadelphia: Westminster Press, 1978), 131.

11. Whether any of the Gospels depended on Paul's Letters is, however, a disputed matter that we cannot resolve here.

12. *Cephas* is the Aramaic form of the Greek term *Petros*: "Rock." In colloquial English, Jesus nicknamed Simon "Rocky" (Matt 10:2//Mark 3:16//Luke 6:14; John 1:42).

In addition, Paul occasionally cites sayings of "the Lord" (Jesus) to bolster points he wants to make on diverse topics: marriage and divorce (1 Cor 7:10–11; cf. Matt 19:6, 9//Mark 10:8–9, 11–12//Luke 16:18), recompense for the gospel's proclamation (1 Cor 9:14; cf. Matt 10:10//Luke 10:7), and the benefit of breaking bread and drinking wine in memory of his death for their sake, "the new covenant in my blood" (1 Cor 11:23–25; cf. Matt 26:26–28//Mark 14:22–24// Luke 22:17–20). Some of Paul's counsels echo those of Jesus without explicit attribution to him (Rom 12:14; cf. Matt 5:44//Luke 6:27; Rom 14:14; cf. Matt 15:10//Mark 7:14).

From this evidence it reasonably follows that others like Paul, who were not among Jesus' earliest disciples, transmitted traditions about him that were received from those who had been early followers. These remembrances took various forms: sayings of different kinds, including parables (e.g., Luke 15:1–32); miracle stories, especially of healings (Matt 17:14–18//Mark 9:14–27//Luke 9:37–42); legends, like the birth of Jesus (Matt 1:18–2:23; Luke 1:26–2:40) and the death of his predecessor, John the Baptist (Matt 6:14–29//Mark 6:14–29); marvelous epiphanies, like Jesus' transfiguration (Matt 17:1–8//Mark 9:2–8// Luke 9:28–36). Most likely the greatest of all Jesus-traditions, perhaps the earliest to be remembered, was the passion narrative: the story of the events leading to his arrest, trial, crucifixion, death, and resurrection (Matt 26:1–28:1–8//Mark 14:1–16:8//Luke 22:1–24:53//John 12:1–8; 13:21–30, 36–38; 18:1–20:29). How Jesus died, and the astonishing aftermath, generated pressure to remember his teaching and events earlier in his life.[13]

WHY WERE THE GOSPELS WRITTEN?

The answer to this question should become clearer in the chapters that follow. Generally speaking, however, all the Gospels share some similar raisons d'être:

♦ *to remember Jesus:* This is assumed in the preceding section. Papias favored "what comes from a living and abiding voice" (*Hist. eccl.* 3.39); but when death silenced the voices of Jesus' earliest witnesses, memoirs had to be written to stabilize oral traditions.
♦ *to come to terms with the delay of the risen Jesus' return in glory:* As we shall consider in a later chapter, Jews regarded resurrection as an end-time event. Paul believed that Jesus would return suddenly and soon, "like a thief in the night" (1 Thess 5:2), come to a world whose "present form . . . is passing

13. The classic studies of the traditions behind the Gospels remain worth reading: Martin Dibelius, *From Tradition to Gospel*, trans. Bertram Lee Woolf (New York: Charles Scribner's Sons, 1919); Rudolf Bultmann, *History of the Synoptic Tradition*, trans. John Marsh, rev. ed. (New York: Harper & Row, 1968); Vincent Taylor, *The Formation of the Gospel Tradition*, 2nd ed. (New York: St. Martin's Press, 1957).

away" (1 Cor 7:29–31). As decades passed, Jesus' adherents were compelled to reconsider the imminence of "the day of the Lord" (1 Thess 4:13–5:11; 2 Pet 3:3–11). Jesus himself was remembered as warning his followers that not even the Son of God nor the angels in heaven know the exact day and hour (Matt 24:36//Mark 13:32). In the meantime:

♦ *to help early Christians understand their identity as communities formed around a crucified and risen Lord:* Their problems were many. Jesus' earliest followers were Jews. How were rural, Palestinian traditions to be translated into language that an increasing number of urban Gentiles could understand? How were both Jewish and Gentile disciples to structure their communities as followers faithful to Jesus' instructions? How were first-century Christians to interpret and respond to persecution, whether by their own families (Mark 13:12–13), fellow Jews (John 9:22; 12:42; 16:2), or Gentile authorities (Luke 21:12–15)? Therefore,

♦ *to reawaken and to fortify faith* are clear motivations in all the Gospels. While their contents may have converted some non-Christians, all these writings are confessional, assuming that their readers share their authors' basic beliefs about Jesus. Across generations, such faith needed to be strengthened and put into concrete action. That fundamental obligation leads directly into the next issue.

WHAT KIND OF LITERATURE IS A GOSPEL?

Believe it or not, NT scholars still cannot agree on that question. It didn't distress the NT's evangelists. Matthew introduces his work as a "book" (*biblos*); Luke, as a "narrative" (*diēgēsis*). Mark alone opens, "The beginning of the good news" (*euangelion*), but it's not at all clear that he refers to a literary artifact: he could as easily be referring to "glad tidings." What perplexes scholars is the Gospels' literary genre, and genres are mixtures of form (a work's style and structure), content, and function. In simple terms, when ancient readers or listeners encountered Matthew, Mark, or Luke, what did they think they were reading or hearing?

♦ "Sage sayings," like Aesop's fables (maybe 6th c. BCE) or later rabbinic aphorisms (codified in the Mishnah, early 3rd c. CE)? The Gospels contain such (like the Golden Rule: Matt 7:12//Luke 6:31),[14] but they also include a lot of material that cannot be so categorized.
♦ "Tales of Jewish martyrs" like Daniel (6:1–28) or Eleazar (2 Macc 6:18–31; 4 Macc 5:1–7:23, ca. 150 BCE–200 CE)? The passion narrative can be read in this way; again, however, there's more to the Gospels than that.
♦ "Encomia": praise of celebrated personages, like Philo of Alexandria's *Life of Moses* (mid-first c. CE)? Certainly the evangelists are well disposed to Jesus,

14. This precept is widespread in Jewish literature, as illustrated in Sir 31:15, "Judge your neighbors' feelings by your own, and in every matter be thoughtful" (RSV; ca. 175 BCE). Virtually all religious traditions uphold such a sentiment: "Do not impose on others what you do not yourself desire" (*Sayings of Confucius* [ca. 480 BCE] 15.24, trans D. C. Lau [New York: Penguin Books, 1979]).

but they don't heap praise on their subject as Philo does on his (Moses, the "lover of virtue," whose mind was purified of all passions: *Names* 37; *Law* 3.45, 48).

♦ Apocalyptic? All the Gospels are colored by end-time thinking, stressing God's intervention in the last days. Still, Luke would never be confused with the NT's Revelation to John.

♦ Greek tragedy or comedy? The Gospels may incorporate aspects of both, but they are not constructed like Sophocles' *Oedipus the King* (ca. 430 BCE) or Aristophanes' *The Clouds* (ca. 420 BCE).

Nowadays most, though not all, scholars classify the Gospels as specimens of *ancient biographies*.[15] Even that doesn't settle the matter because this genre was broad, absorptive of briefer literary categories, and in diverse ways bent, turned, and twisted by different ancient authors. Still, more than anything else the Gospels look and sound like ancient biographies: historically stylized prose narratives of an individual's life.[16] That fairly covers the Gospels' form and content. Their function is the proclamation of particular religious beliefs about their subject, Jesus, and the moral character shaped by those beliefs. It's hard to find an ancient biography that doesn't suggest to its readers an ethical takeaway of some kind. The Greek philosopher Plutarch (ca. 45–120 CE) compares his work as a biographer to that of a portrait painter who tries to capture "the signs of the soul," whether good or bad, of influential personages (*Lives* 1.2–3).

In a letter to a fledgling band of Christians written in the early 50s, Paul sang back to them what may well have been a hymn in honor of Christ, whose verses poetize the essence of who he was, what he did, how God responded to him, and the import of it all for everyone:

Have this mind among yourselves, which is yours in Christ Jesus,
　who, though he was in the form of God,
　　did not count equality with God a thing to be grasped,
　but emptied himself, taking the form of a servant, being born in the likeness of men.
　And being found in human form he humbled himself and became obedient unto death,
　　even death on a cross.

15. This position was influentially articulated by Clyde Weber Votaw, *The Gospels and Contemporary Biographies in the Greco-Roman World* (Philadelphia: Fortress Press, 1970; comprising essays first published in 1915). More recently, David E Aune, *The New Testament in Its Literary Environment*, LEC (Philadelphia: Westminster Press, 1987); most exhaustively, Richard Burridge, *What Are the Gospels? A Comparison with Graeco-Roman Biographies*, 3rd ed. (Waco, TX: Baylor University Press, 2018).

16. Like most ancient biographies, the Gospels presuppose some familiarity with their subjects, are selective in their reports, can be chronologically and geographically nonspecific, and are often vague about cause and effect in a person's life. In all these respects they differ from modern biographies, which play by different rules. To ask the Gospels to render comprehensive, well-rounded, unbiased lives of Jesus is unfair to their authors and inevitably disappointing to us as readers. The problem is not with the Gospels: it's with our unreasonable expectations of them.

> Therefore God has highly exalted him
>   and bestowed on him the name which is above every name,
>   that at the name of Jesus every knee should bow,
>   in heaven and on earth and under the earth,
>   and every tongue confess
>   that Jesus Christ is Lord, to the glory of God the Father.
>
> (Phil 2:5–11 RSV)

In different ways all the Gospels expand these declarations into gripping narratives.

A significant implication of understanding the Gospels in this way is the need to read them *bifocally*, as their authors surely intended: the Gospels are stories of Jesus framed to address the real-life concerns of early Christian communities. The Jesus they remembered is the living Lord, who speaks to his churches even now, as the earliest witnesses died, as the early Christian movement evolved, as they struggled to hold on to their Jewish heritage, as they drifted off course and required correction, as they underwent persecution, as they awaited Jesus' return for a much longer time than they had originally anticipated.

An analogy from recent American history may help us understand something of what the evangelists were doing. How does one explain the extraordinary popularity of the television series *M*A*S*H* (1972–83), whose final episode (February 28, 1983) remains the most-watched dramatic finale in TV history? Why, almost four decades later, does *M*A*S*H* remain a staple of international viewing, available on Netflix and other media providers? Did and does it satisfy some insatiable appetite to learn about the lives of doctors, nurses, and patients of a Mobile Army Surgical Hospital, stationed in Uijeongbu from 1950 to 1953? Hardly. Most viewers know and care as much about the Korean Conflict as they do the Peloponnesian War.

The answer: Vietnam. That conflict in southeast Asia (1955–75) overlapped the series' first three years and featured the return of wounded, traumatized American soldiers to civilian life. For a decade, families in the United States tuned in to the evening news on one of only three commercial stations and watched on-site coverage of a real, bloody war that was destroying not just a nation's but also a world's fathers and mothers, sons and daughters. Then, once a week, they gathered around *M*A*S*H* to try to make sense out of the deadliest absurdity they were living. Because human beings *do* have a strange appetite for war, that series still resonates with the tragic farce of patching up soldiers to send them back onto front lines again, to be blown apart.

That's what I mean by reading the Gospels bifocally. In each, *two stories are unfolding simultaneously*: stories of Jesus, and stories of his followers four or five decades later. In the chapters that follow, we shall observe how three evangelists proclaimed faith, wrestled with faith, and guided their churches by remembering what Jesus and his earliest disciples had said and done.

HOW ARE THE SYNOPTIC GOSPELS INTERRELATED?

Three of the NT's Gospels may be conveniently viewed alongside one another: Matthew, Mark, and Luke. Because their narrative presentations of Jesus are consistent and coherent, though not identical and interchangeable, scholars refer to them as the Synoptic Gospels (Gk. *opsis* [seen] + *syn* [in company with]).

Much similarity among the Synoptics may be seen in parallel passages of Jesus' words.

Matthew 7:7–8	Luke 11:9–10
Ask, and it will be given you; seek and you will find; knock, and it will be opened to you. For every one who asks receives, and he who seeks finds, and to him who knocks it will be opened. (RSV)	And I tell you, Ask, and it will be given you; seek, and you will find; knock, and it will be opened to you. For every one who asks receives, and he who seeks finds, and to him who knocks it will be opened. (RSV)

Matthew 13:12	Mark 4:25	Luke 19:26
For to those who have, more will be given, and they will have an abundance; but from those who have nothing, even what they have will be taken away. (NRSV)	For to those who have, more will be given; and from those who have nothing, even what they have will be taken away. (NRSV)	I tell you, to all those who have, more will be given; but from those who have nothing, even what they have will be taken away. (NRSV)

Though they appear in different parts of these Gospels, these sayings are in verbatim agreement, not only in English but also in the Greek being translated. Note that the first set of sayings have no parallel in Mark. There are other permutations: material shared only by Matthew (15:21–28) and Mark (7:24–30), or only by Mark (1:21–28) and Luke (Luke 4:31–37), as well as material that appears in only one of these Gospels (Matt 17:24–27; Mark 4:26–29; Luke 7:11–17).

For you math lovers and statisticians, we can climb more deeply down into the weeds.

1. Of Mark's 662 verses, 609 are paralleled in Matthew. In other words: give or take a minor verbal variation, 90 percent of what one finds in Mark appears also in Matthew.
2. Of Matthew's 1,069 verses, 523 are paralleled in Mark. Give or take minor variations, 50 percent of what one finds in Matthew appears also in Mark.
3. Of Mark's 662 verses, 357 are paralleled in Luke; 55 percent of Mark's content may also be found in Luke.
4. Of Luke's 1,150 verses, 325 are paralleled in Mark; 40 percent of Luke's content appears also in Mark.
5. Within these parallel verses exists *a high degree of verbatim agreement* in Greek. There are a few minor instances of agreements of Matthew and Luke

with Mark that deviate from the Markan material, either stylistically or substantively.[17]

6. *A high degree of agreement in the sequence of passages* exists among these parallels. In material shared by all three, Matthew and Luke typically agree with each other's sequence of presentation only insofar as they agree with Mark's. Conversely, when either Matthew or Luke diverge from Mark's ordering of material, either Matthew or Luke deviates from the other's sequence. The chart on p. 13 (fig. 1) may help you in visualizing this. Matching texts are indicated with chapter-and-verse references.

We arrive, then, at an important conclusion: in both the wording of passages and their narrative arrangement, very seldom do Matthew and Luke agree with each other without also agreeing with Mark. In these three Gospels' interrelationships, *Mark appears to be the middle term or common factor.* That said, Matthew and Luke also share material with each other that Mark lacks, though this material is not arranged with the close agreement in narrative sequence that they share with Mark. (Hypotheses for these shared sources will be explored in the charts on the following pages.) And each of the three Gospels, especially Matthew and Luke, contains some material absent from the other two.

Possible Solutions of the Synoptic Problem

With that, we have identified not only the Synoptics, but also the problem attached to them. *Some kind* of relationship exists among Matthew, Mark, and Luke. For centuries careful and curious readers have tried to account for that relationship.

First, we can rule out correspondences of oral tradition before any of the Gospels were committed to writing. As I have mentioned, most scholars assume that such oral tradition circulated during the years immediately after Jesus. Among Palestinian Jewish Christians, most likely it would have originated in Aramaic, but verbatim agreements among the Synoptics are *in Greek.* A good example is Matthew 7:7–8//Luke 11:9–10, quoted above in parallel columns. Look again at the words underlined. Either Matthew is using Luke's wording, Luke is using Matthew's wording, or both are drawing on the wording of a common source. However you slice it, the relationship among the Synoptics is primarily *literary,* based on written material.[18] One or more of these Gospels is using another as a source.

---

17. An example: In Matt 26:68 and Luke 22:64, Jesus' accusers ask an identically worded question: "Who is it that struck you?" Mark does not reproduce that question. In context, however, it makes better sense of their challenge, "Prophesy!" (Mark 14:65).

18. Adverbs like "primarily" are weasel words but in this case necessary. Even if their relationship is basically literary, that would not preclude the continuing influence of oral modifications of the documents until they reached a level of fixity several centuries later. Common sense suggests that such influence was in play, inhibiting absolute verbatim agreements.

Fig. 1. A Comparison of the Structure of the Synoptic Narratives

Matthew	Mark	Luke
1:1–2:23 (Infancy Narratives)	– –	1:1–2:52 (Infancy Narratives)
3:1–4:25	1:1–39	3:1–4:44
– –	– –	5:1–11
5:1–7:29 (First Discourse: *The Sermon on the Mount*)	– –	– –
8:1–4	1:40–45	5:12–16
8:5–34	– –	– –
9:1–17	2:1–22	5:17–39
9:18–10:4	– –	– –
10:5–42 (Second Discourse: *Missionary Instructions*)	– –	– –
11:1–30	– –	– –
12:1–21	2:23–3:19	6:1–19
– –	– –	6:20–8:3 (The "Small Insertion," including *The Sermon on the Plain*, 6:20–49)
12:22–50	3:20–35	– –
13:1–52 (Third Discourse: *Parables of the Kingdom and the Church*)	4:1–34	8:4–21
– –	4:35–5:43	8:22–56
13:53–17:27	6:1–9:32	9:1–45 (excluding Mark 6:45–8:26: The "Great Omission")
18:1–35 (Fourth Discourse: *Instructions for Church Life and Discipline*)	9:33–50	9:46–50
– –	– –	9:51–18:14 (Special *Lukan Travel Narrative*: The "Great Insertion")
19:1–24:3	10:1–13:4	18:15–21:7
24:4–25:46 (Fifth Discourse: *Eschatology and the Church*)	13:5–37	21:8–38
26:1–28:8 (Passion Narrative)	14:1–16:8 (Passion Narrative)	22:1–24:11 (Passion Narrative)
28:9–20 (Resurrection Appearances)	– –	24:13–53 (Resurrection Appearances)

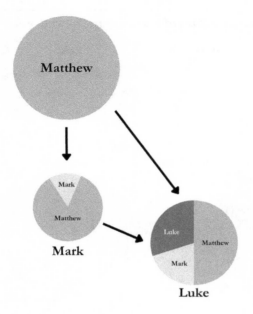

Fig. 2. The Augustinian hypothesis: Matthew was the earliest Gospel, on which first Mark and then Luke depended. Luke was also dependent on Matthew and to a lesser degree on Mark. Diagram courtesy of M. J. P. O'Connor.

If Mark is the point of intersection between Matthew and Luke, one may hypothesize at least a dozen possibilities for how the three Gospels relate to one another. The four most prevalent in NT scholarship[19] are schematized in Figures 2, 3, 4, and 5.[20] All these hypotheses are logically possible. Not all are equally plausible.

1. The Augustinian Hypothesis

The first hypothesis, often called Augustinian because it was assumed by Augustine of Hippo (354–430), is the least satisfying. It accounts for Mark and Luke's verbal agreement with each other, as well as Luke's agreement with both Mark and Matthew. (Luke used both sources.)

This hypothesis explains little else: (a) When all three Gospels agree, why does Luke tend to follow Mark's wording, not Matthew's, even when Matthew's version is linguistically and syntactically superior? (b) About 40 percent of Matthew's Sermon on the Mount (5:1–7:29) is reproduced in Luke's Sermon on the Plain (6:20–49); the remaining 60 percent of Matthew's Sermon on the Mount is scattered throughout Luke. Why would Luke, which presents itself as "an orderly account" (1:3), break up Matthew's neatly arranged blocks of Jesus' teaching?[21]

19. The hypothesis of Luke → Mark → Matthew is most unlikely, since Luke lacks 45 percent of Mark's content.

20. In Figs. 2–5, Matthean material is indicated in gray, Markan material in palest gray, Lukan material in darkest gray. Black is for Q, an entity to which I shall soon introduce you.

21. If these blocks have slipped from your mind, return to fig. 1 and note Matthew's five great discourses.

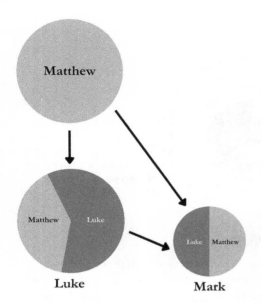

Fig. 3. The Griesbach hypothesis: Matthew was the earliest Gospel, on which Luke depended; Mark is a compression of both Matthew and Luke. Diagram courtesy of M. J. P. O'Connor.

(c) Why do Luke's infancy narratives (1:5–2:52) and post-resurrection stories (24:15–33) apparently show the author as being unaware of Matthew's (1:1–2:23; 28:11–20)? (d) If Mark used Matthew, why did Mark omit Matthew's stories of Jesus' birth and postmortem appearances and the majority of Jesus' teaching?

2. The Griesbach Hypothesis

The second hypothesis, which often travels under the name of its proponent Johann Jakob Griesbach (1745–1812), has in its favor three strengths. (a) It justifies Matthew and Luke's minor agreements in wording against Mark. (Luke follows Matthew's lead.) (b) It explains some odd characteristics of Mark vis-à-vis the other Synoptics: in preserving some passages missing from one of his sources, sometimes Mark follows Matthew (Mark 7:24–30//Matt 15:21–28), yet at other times Luke (Mark 1:21–28//Luke 4:31–37). (c) Most important: this hypothesis does not require the assumption of any lost sources outside of the three Gospels to interpret the Synoptics' relationships (which the third hypothesis, to be presented, does involve): that which appears in Matthew and Luke but not in Mark was simply ignored or excised by Mark. The weaknesses of this "two-Gospel hypothesis" as a source for Mark are the same that plague the Augustinian conjecture. How does one explain Mark's excision of so much Matthean and Lukan material, especially that which is congenial with Mark's point of view (e.g., Jesus as teacher; John as Jesus' precursor)? And why would Mark, whose Greek is by far the least polished of the three, deliberately muddle Matthew's clear Greek and Luke's elegant Greek?

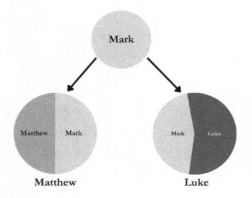

Fig. 4. The hypothesis of Markan priority: Mark was the earliest Gospel, on which Matthew and Luke depended apart from each other. Diagram courtesy of M. J. P. O'Connor.

3. The Hypothesis of Markan Priority

The strength of the third hypothesis, which assumes Mark's compositional priority, is this: if we assume that Matthew and Luke used Mark, it's usually easy to understand *how* they used it and *why* they changed it in the ways they did. Stylistically, they clean up Mark's blunders. Theologically, they clarify a lot that Mark leaves obscure. Narratively, they fill a lot of gaps. Where they forge into territory Mark hasn't covered, Matthew and Luke take very different shapes. For instance, Mark lacks both a story of Jesus' birth as well as a reunion of the risen Lord with his disciples. Matthew and Luke append both, drawing on different traditions available to each evangelist.

The greatest weakness in the hypothesis of Markan priority is that it cannot account for the plethora of Jesus' teaching, absent from Mark, which Matthew and Luke share. In Mark you won't find most of the content in Matthew's Sermon on the Mount (5:1–7:29), much of which is paralleled in Luke's Sermon on the Plain (6:20–49).[22] To explain that, most scholars postulate the existence of a written source of Jesus' sayings, a source that no longer exists but from which both Matthew and Luke drew, probably independently of each other.[23] Scholars have tagged this hypothetical sayings-source as Q: not in homage to James Bond's gadget master, but because *Quelle* is the German word for "source." Compilations of Q material reveal some consistent themes, coherently developed.[24] It's not an unreasonable conjecture, but it sticks in the craw of advocates of the

22. Matthew 5:13 and 15 have rough parallels in, respectively, Mark 9:50 and 4:21. See also Matt 5:23–24, 29–30//Mark 11:25; 9:43–48; Matt 6:12, 14–15//Mark 11:25; Matt 7:2//Mark 4:24–25.

23. Why? Because Luke radically diverges from Matthew's sequence of these sayings, though not from Matthew's ordering of Markan material. Moreover, Matthew clumps many sayings of Jesus together. Luke, for no apparent reason, disseminates them throughout his Gospel.

24. See Robert A. Spivey, D. Moody Smith, and C. Clifton Black, *Anatomy of the New Testament*, 8th ed. (Minneapolis: Fortress Press, 2019), 112–13.

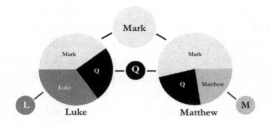

Fig. 5. A four-source theory. Independently of each other, Matthew and Luke drew upon Mark, Q, and one source unique to each. Diagram courtesy of Melanie A. Howard.

Griesbach hypothesis, who favor their argument's apparent simplicity. Even those who accept Q's existence need to keep firmly in mind that it is a *theoretical* entity.[25]

4. The Four-Source Hypothesis

For over a century most scholars have accepted the theory of two sources, Mark and Q, to resolve the Synoptic Problem and explain the convergences and divergences among three Gospels that are so similar. If we assume that Mark was the earliest Gospel—and I do, as do most scholars—then, to account for the material unique to Matthew (M) or to Luke (L), one must expand the two sources (Mark and Q) to four. Proportionately, the result is depicted in figure 5.

No solution of the Synoptic problem satisfactorily accounts for all its intricacies. If the bar is set that high, no solution ever will. We can speak only of hypotheses and probabilities, not of knockdown proof. At this writing and for the foreseeable future, the two-source (or four-source) theory seems to me and most scholars the best, or least problematic, to explain the Synoptics' interrelationships.

WHAT ABOUT THE GOSPEL ACCORDING TO JOHN?

With the other three, the NT's Fourth Gospel shares a broad narrative outline about Jesus: rather early, he is baptized (John 1:29–34) and calls disciples (1:35–51); eventually he dies by crucifixion and is raised from death (12:1–21:25). John contains other specific stories with parallels in Matthew, Mark, and Luke: among others, Jesus' feeding of five thousand (John 6:1–15; cf. Matt 14:15–21//Mark 6:35–44//Luke 9:12–17) and his expulsion of moneychangers from the temple (John 2:13–22; cf. Matt 21:12–13//Mark 11:15–19//Luke 19:45–48).

Even so, the differences between John and the other Gospels far outrun their likenesses. In the Synoptics, Jesus' ministry, localized in Galilee and its environs, apparently spans about a year. In John, Jesus travels to Jerusalem (in Judea) for

---

25. *The Critical Edition of Q,* ed. James M. Robinson, Paul Hoffmann, and John S. Kloppenborg, Hermeneia (Minneapolis: Fortress Press, 2000), is 691 pages long: no mean feat for a commentary on a document we do not have, whose existence is only postulated.

at least three annual feasts (2:13; 5:1 [?]; 7:1–52; 11:55–12:19).[26] The sheer content of John diverges from that of the others. Of John's ninety-three constituent passages, only twenty-five have clear Synoptic parallels. Put differently, 73 percent of John's Gospel has no material counterpart in the other NT Gospels. The Synoptics' Jesus speaks as a Jew of God's inbreaking kingdom (Matt 4:17// Mark 1:14–15//Luke 4:43); the Johannine Jesus accepts others' acknowledgment of him as king (John 1:49–50; 12:13, 15; 18:37) and even declares himself "Christ" (John 17:3). In the Fourth Gospel, Jesus speaks in Christian terms about himself (cf. John 14:6 with Acts 4:12).

For these and other reasons, John is not considered a Synoptic Gospel. Not more than 27 percent of it can be tracked alongside Matthew, Mark, or Luke. More often than not, its contents and plotline simply veer away from all the others, as though it were drawing from a distinctive tradition that occasionally intersected with theirs.[27] That's why this book does not linger on John, even though it has proved as fundamental as Matthew, Mark, and Luke in shaping the church's evolving theology and practice.

WHAT ABOUT OTHER ANCIENT GOSPELS NOT IN THE NEW TESTAMENT?

Even more maverick than John are written materials about Jesus that were multiply generated in the church's first four centuries. We know of about fifty such documents. Some have survived as fragments, others as whole books. Still others we know only because they were quoted by such early Christian writers as Clement (ca. 150–ca. 215) and Origen of Alexandria (ca. 185–ca. 253), Epiphanius of Salamis (ca. 315–403), and Jerome (ca. 345–420). In terms of genre, they roam the literary map, with legends, dialogues, and revelatory discourses. Some are anonymous; others are attributed to Christian apostles (like Peter), holy women (like Mary, the mother of Jesus), arch heretics, and even OT figures (Eve). One of the most intriguing is the *Gospel of Thomas*, written in Coptic (Egyptian), perhaps of Syrian origin in the mid-second century CE. Lacking any narrative framework, *Thomas* is a serial presentation of 114 purportedly "secret sayings": some are strikingly close to what we find in the Synoptics; others are rather bizarre.

---

26. How old was Jesus when he died? Christian tradition blended his three-year ministry in John with Luke's claim (3:23) that Jesus was about thirty years old when beginning his ministry: 30 + 3 = 33. Nowhere in the NT are these inferences added up.

27. The NT's four Gospels ride more closely together in the passion narrative: of John's twenty-five passages in that section, fourteen (56 percent) have Synoptic parallels while eleven (44 percent) do not.

Jesus said, "Look, the sower went out, he filled his hand [and] cast [the seeds]. Some fell upon the road; the birds came [and] gathered them. Others fell upon rock, and struck no root in the ground, nor did they produce any ears. And others fell on the thorns; they choked the seeds, and the worms ate them. And others fell on the good earth, and it produced good fruit: it yielded sixty per measure and one hundred twenty per measure." (*Gos. Thom.* 9; cf. Matt 13:3–9//Mark 4:3–9//Luke 8:4–8)[28]

Jesus said to them: "When you make the two one, and when you make the inside as the outside, and the upper as the lower, and when you make the male and the female into a single one, so that the male is not male and the female is not female, and when you make eyes in place of an eye, and a hand in place of a hand, and a foot in place of a foot, and an image in place of an image, then shall you enter [the kingdom]." (*Gos. Thom.* 22)[29]

That second saying may have been profoundly meaningful for the community to whom it was addressed, but it flunked two important tests for eventual inclusion in the NT. (1) It was too eccentric for most Christians. (2) It didn't sound like Jesus as they remembered him (cf. Mark 10:6; Gen 1:27).

Another option available to early disciples was the *Diatessaron* (Gk. "through [the] four"), a collected combination of the NT's Gospels attributed to Tatian the Assyrian (or Syrian, ca. 120–ca. 180 CE) around the year 170 CE. Although its original text has not survived, we know enough about it from Eusebius (*Hist. eccl.* 4.29.6) to suss out its character: a harmonized amalgamation of Matthew, Mark, Luke, and John—the Cuisinart version, as it were. It was immensely popular in the Syriac church, which reckoned it scriptural right down to the fifth century. In the end most Christians worldwide concluded that each NT Gospel should have its peculiar say, placed alongside each other. Had they not so decided, this book could offer you only a one-dimensional Jesus. But Tatian's creation still lingers in our imaginations when we accidentally blend the Gospels into a singular form or when we watch practically any movie ever made about Jesus. Invariably and deliberately, the screenwriters create their own *Diatessaron*s.

A SENSE OF PLACE

When reading the Synoptics, we step into a strange world and a culture unlike our own in many respects. Yet many of the places Jesus and his disciples frequented

28. See R. McL. Wilson, trans. of *Thomas*, in *New Testament Apocrypha*, vol. 1, *Gospels and Related Writings*, rev. ed. Wilhelm Schneemelcher (Louisville, KY: Westminster/John Knox Press, 1991), 118.
29. Wilson, *Gospels and Related Writings*, 120. To this the only sensible reply of the disciples I can imagine would be, "Yeah, that's just what we were thinking, but we wanted to hear it from you."

Fig. 6. Map of Israel in the first century CE.

may still be visited. Because all the Gospels present them on the stage of world history as they knew it, not far away in some celestial Olympus, we honor the evangelists when we consider biblical geography. To that end, I direct your attention to figure 6. On this map you can find places whose names I'll set in **boldface** (below).

The Roman Empire partitioned Israel into numerous territories with porous boundaries. Moving clockwise, from north to south and back, these included **Syro-Phoenicia** (Mark 7:26); **Ituraea**, **Abilene**, and **Trachonitis** (Luke 3:1);

the **Decapolis** ("Ten Towns": Matt 4:25; Mark 5:20; 7:31); **Idumea** (Mark 3:8); **Judea** (Matt 2:1, 5, 22; Mark 3:8; 10:1; Luke 1:5, 65); **Samaria** (Luke 17:11); and **Galilee** (Matt 4:15, 18, 23, 25; Mark 1:9, 28, 39; 9:30; Luke 1:26; 2:4, 39; 4:31; 5:17). Matthew (4:25; 19:1) and Mark (3:8; 10:1) refer to an indeterminate region "beyond the **Jordan [River]**."

Galilee (Matt 4:12//Mark 1:14//Luke 4:14; and elsewhere) was a hub for intersecting Palestinian ports and caravan routes through Syria, Jerusalem, and Egypt. Adjacent to the Decapolis (Mark 5:20; 7:31), Galileans were more familiar with Gentile languages and customs than were Judeans (cf. Matt 4:15), who in turn eyed Galilee with suspicion for its adulterated Judaism. Galilee was an agrarian wonderland: fertile soil, more abundant pastures than in Syria or Judea, lucrative exports of olives and grain and wines, and a fishing industry based on the freshwater **Sea of Galilee** or Tiberias (modern-day Lake Kinneret: Matt 4:18; 15:29; Mark 1:16–20; 7:31). While most Galileans probably eked out a hand-to-mouth existence comparable to America's southern sharecroppers during the Great Depression, a few wealthy families owned imperially regulated estates in Galilee and other regions. (At one time Herod the Great, whom we'll meet in chap. 3, may have acquired about two-thirds of Judea, the province to the south [*A.J.* 15.342–64].) **Nazareth**, an agricultural village in Lower Galilee, is remembered as Jesus' hometown (Matt 21:11; 27:71; Mark 1:9, 24; 10:47; 16:6; Luke 4:16, 34; 18:37), as well as that of Joseph (Matt 2:23; Luke 2:4, 39) and Mary (Luke 1:26; 2:39). Jesus ministered mainly in neighboring villages near the Sea of Galilee: **Capernaum**, on the lake's northwestern shore, which the evangelists present as something like Jesus' base of operations (Matt 4:13; 9:1; 11:23; Mark 2:1; Luke 4:31); **Chorazin** (Matt 11:21; Luke 10:13–15), about three miles north of Capernaum; **Nain**, nine miles southeast of Nazareth (Luke 7:11–17); and **Bethsaida** (Mark 8:22–26; Luke 9:10–11), whose precise location is uncertain but located by some on Tiberias's northern shoreline.

On the Mediterranean's eastern coast in Phoenicia, **Tyre**, touting itself as the world's oldest continuously inhabited city, and **Sidon**, to its north, are identified as scenes of Jesus' mighty works (Matt 11:21–22; 15:21; Mark 7:24; Luke 10:13–14). The same is claimed for one of the Decapolis's ten cities, **Gerasa** (Mark 5:1–20// Luke 8:26–39: modern-day Jerash, Jordan). **Gadara**, another member of the Decapolis that neighbors modern Umm Qais, is the place Matthew 8:28–34 identifies for Jesus' healing of two demoniacs. At **Caesarea Philippi**, south of Mount Hermon, Peter confesses his belief in Jesus' messiahship (Matt 16:13–20//Mark 8:27–30). Unlike Matthew (10:5), Luke situates some of Jesus' ministry (17:11) and that of his envoys (9:52) in the province of Samaria, a district that continues to maintain a dissident Jewish identity centered on Mount Gerizim (John 4:1–30).

Connecting Galilee and Judea is the **Jordan River**, which flows roughly from north to south from southeastern Syria, crosses the modern-day Hula Valley,

Fig. 7. The Jordan River remains a site for Christians' baptism and renewal of their baptism. Photograph by Clifton Black.

north of the Sea of Galilee, and drains into the Dead Sea in Judea. For Jews, just north of the Dead Sea is the traditional site of crossing into the promised land (Josh 3:15–17); for Christians, it the place of Jesus' baptism by John (Matt 3:13–17//Mark 1:9–11//Luke 3:3).

The southern district of Judea—specifically, **Jerusalem** and its environs—is the locale for the Synoptics' passion narratives. (In Luke 9:51–18:14 much of Jesus' ministry happens en route to Jerusalem.) This district's limestone canyons made travel difficult, though the arable soil of its hill country remains good for fruit trees and vineyards. Traditionally its severe eastern wilderness was regarded as a place of testing (2 Sam 15–16; *B.J.* 6.326, 351, 366), as it was for John the Baptist and Jesus (Matt 3–4). Probably because of its association with King David (Mic 5:2), the divergent nativity stories in Matthew (1:18–2:23) and Luke (2:1–39) locate Jesus' birth in **Bethlehem**, six miles south of Jerusalem. **Jericho**, a Palestinian town in the landlocked territory of the West Bank, is remembered as a site for Jesus' healing of the blind (Matt 20:29–34//Mark 10:46–52//Luke 18:35–43); in Luke it is also the home of Zacchaeus, a tax collector honored by Jesus (19:1–10). Bethphage, which the evangelists identify as near **Bethany** (Matt 21:1//Mark 11:1//Luke 19:29), is the hamlet where Jesus dispatches disciples to secure a colt

Fig. 8. The Old City of Jerusalem, viewed from the Mount of Olives to the east, with the Dome of the Rock, an Islamic sanctuary, in the center. Photograph by Clifton Black.

for his entry into Jerusalem. Overlooking the eastern side of Jerusalem's Old City, the Mount of Olives is the setting for Jesus' somber discourse with his disciples regarding the city's imminent destruction and its aftermath (Matt 24:3–14//Mark 13:3–39). Luke identifies that slope as the place of Jesus' prayer before his arrest (22:39–54); Matthew (26:36–56) and Mark (14:32–52) pinpoint those events at Gethsemane, a park at the foot of Mount Olivet. The exact site of Jesus' crucifixion, Golgotha (Matt 27:33//Mark 15:22) or "Skull Place" (Gk. *kranion*, Luke 23:33), remains disputed. Hebrews 13:12 indicates that it was outside the wall of the Old City. The fourth-century Church of the Holy Sepulchre, the traditional site of Jesus' death, sits today within Jerusalem's Old City Walls, though the walls may have been differently contoured in the first century. Likewise, we're unsure of the precise location of **Emmaus**, where Luke 24:13–32 describes a dramatic appearance of the risen Jesus to some disciples at supper. (Its location on the map, northwest of Jerusalem, is a guess.)

The Jerusalem temple, the cultic heart of Jews across the centuries and a center of Jesus' teaching in Matthew (21:12–23:39), Mark (11:1–12:44), and Luke (19:45–21:4), is no more. Only a portion of its Western Wall remains after its demolition by the Romans in 70 during a disastrous Jewish uprising. In its place since the seventh century has stood the Dome of the Rock, the Islamic shrine commemorating Muhammad's night journey to heaven, according to early interpretation (ca. 621).

THE CAST OF CHARACTERS

In all four of the NT's Gospels, particular figures recur and interact in complicated ways. Each merits attention, beginning with the most central. All of the NT's Gospels invite an encounter with Jesus of Nazareth: a real, distinct, historical figure. Yet none of them is preoccupied by chronological, psychological, or purely factual interests; all are dominated by their religious and theological perspectives. Jews and Muslims, agnostics and atheists, can (and usually do) concede the existence of the Jesus of history. Only Christians acknowledge this Jesus as the Christ of faith.

The Historical Jesus

A Conversation with Dale Allison Jr.

Dale C. Allison Jr. (PhD, Duke) is the Richard J. Dearborn Professor of New Testament at Princeton Theological Seminary. His academic research is focused on the historical Jesus, the Gospel of Matthew, Q, early Jewish and Christian eschatology, inner-biblical exegesis, the history of the interpretation and application of biblical texts, and the Jewish Pseudepigrapha.[30]

CCB: As a historian, do you find some claims about Jesus made in the Gospels rather incredible? Why or why not?

DCA: I believe that human experience is teeming with puzzling anomalies and, indeed, fantastic absurdities. The world is not a reasonable place, where everything has a reasonable explanation. So the catch for me is almost always not the claim but the evidence. And there are episodes in the canonical Gospels for which the evidence is indeed meager. Peter's walking on the water in Matthew 14:28–29 is an example.

CCB: "There are more things in heaven and earth, Horatio, / Than are dreamt of in [our] philosophy" (Hamlet 1.5.67–68). May I assume that you would not dismiss out of hand the historicity of some miracle stories in the Gospels?

---

30. This and all conversations with other scholars in this volume have been edited and compressed for brevity and clarity.

DCA: It would not surprise me if Peter and a few others really did witness Jesus transfigured in light (Matt 17:1–7//Mark 9:2–8//Luke 9:28–36), or if some of his healings involved more than psychosomatic factors. I am also fairly confident that Jesus was able once in a while to have a sense of what would happen before it happened.

CCB: What was Jesus "up to"? Do you think historians can recover what was important to him?

DCA: I don't believe he was a monomaniac. He must have been "up to" several things, just as each Gospel is "up to" several things. In this they represent him accurately. In general, however, I think that the summaries of the evangelists, such as Mark 1:14–15 and Matthew 4:23–25, give us a decent sense of what he was about. Beyond that, if I had to bet, I'd wager as Johannes Weiss (1863–1914)[31] and Albert Schweitzer (1875–1965)[32] thought: he hoped early on for a movement of widespread repentance that would usher in the eschatological kingdom of God. Yet repentance on a sufficient scale did not, to his satisfaction, eventuate. Partly as a consequence, he went up to Jerusalem, still hoping that the kingdom might come in its fullness, yet resigned to martyrdom.

CCB: How badly did Matthew, Mark, or Luke distort Jesus' ministry? What did they get right about him?

DCA: I think that the best way of getting at the historical Jesus is to read Matthew, Mark, and Luke, albeit with critical commentaries at hand. On the recurrent themes and motifs, they cannot be far off. Or if they are, then the sources have suffered a catastrophic memory loss, and we can't make up the lack.

CCB: What other recurring themes or motifs, yet unmentioned, do you think should be noticed?

DCA: A sense that something new is at hand: God depicted as Father, hostility to wealth, extraordinary requests and difficult demands, and conflict with religious authorities. Intention is what matters most: special regard for the unfortunate, loving and serving and forgiving others, and suffering and persecution for his disciples. I also believe that Jesus thought he was Somebody. Misleading is Rudolf Bultmann's famous dictum that, with Easter, "The proclaimer became

---

31. Johannes Weiss, *Jesus' Proclamation of the Kingdom of God*, ed. Richard Hyde Hiers and David Larrimore Holland, LJS (Philadelphia: Fortress Press, 1971).

32. Albert Schweitzer, *The Quest of the Historical Jesus: A Critical Study of Its Progress from Reimarus to Wrede*, trans. W. Montgomery, ed. John Bowden (Minneapolis: Fortress Press, 2001).

the proclaimed."[33] Jesus was the center of his own eschatological scenario, and he thought of himself as *messias designatus*, Messiah-in-waiting.

CCB: Why should we try to reconstruct Jesus historically? Why not take the Gospels at face value?

DCA: I don't take any important text at face value. And I don't understand how anyone, after the Deists,[34] can take any religious text at face value. Would one ask this about the Book of Mormon? Or the Qur'an? In the end, I am a modern person as well as a Christian. Both doubt and faith run deep within me. Moreover, just as I care about what really happened in the cases of Socrates, Augustine, Muhammad, Luther, Lincoln, and my own father—nobody asks why I care in those cases—I care about what really happened with Jesus. Theologians who don't care are a mystery to me.

CCB: I take your point. As you know, some skeptics argue that all historical reconstructions are flawed, maybe doomed, by the historians' own biases and blind spots. What's your response to such arguments?

DCA: I agree: all historical reconstructions are flawed. This, however, does not mean they are doomed. That would be skepticism run amok. We should do our best, despite all our failings. This isn't any different from trying to live a good life: we do our best even though we constantly fail and fall short.

CCB: What books about Jesus do you recommend to serious students as trustworthy and helpful?

DCA: I would say: Go and read some old books—David Friedrich Strauss, *The Life of Jesus Critically Examined* (German original, 1840),[35] Schweitzer's *The Quest of the Historical Jesus*,[36] C. H. Dodd's *The Parables of the Kingdom*,[37]

---

33. Rudolf Bultmann, *Theology of the New Testament*, trans. Kendrick Grobel, 2 vols. in 1 (Waco, TX: Baylor University Press, 2007), 1:33.

34. Deists expounded a philosophical view, which took hold in France and Great Britain during the Enlightenment and relied on reason alone, discounting divine revelation as a source of religious knowledge.

35. David Friedrich Strauss, *The Life of Jesus Critically Examined*, trans. George Eliot (Mary Ann Evans; in 1846), from the 4th German ed. (1840), ed. Peter C. Hodgson, LJS (Philadelphia: Fortress Press, 1972).

36. Albert Schweitzer, *The Quest of the Historical Jesus* (German original, 1906), 2nd English ed. (New York: Macmillan Co., 1922).

37. C. H. Dodd, *The Parables of the Kingdom* (original, London: Nisbet & Co., 1935), 2nd ed. (New York: Charles Scribner's Sons, 1961).

and Joachim Jeremias's *The Parables of Jesus*.[38] Then read through Gerd Theissen and Annette Merz's *The Historical Jesus: A Comprehensive Guide*.[39] If you study these five books carefully, you'll be able to understand most everything else, including the up-to-date stuff.

CCB: On both counts, I concur. Thank you very much, Dale.

To Professor Allison's remarks, I add that the so-called "historical Jesus" is no less a literary construct than that of the NT's evangelists. The difference between them: the Gospels' authors interpret Jesus religiously, from the standpoint of Christian faith, dilating on developments that occurred in the decades between his life and their compositions. Historians attempt scholarly retrievals of what lies beneath the Gospels' surfaces, often by peeling away the evangelists' interpretations. How wide is the gap between the historians' Jesus and that of the evangelists? Not so vast, in Professor Allison's view. I agree—but others do not. The question has been disputed across three centuries of NT scholarship. It will never be resolved.

Now let's turn to the characters in the Gospels with whom Jesus mixes it up.

"Who *Are* Those Guys?"

—Paul Newman to Robert Redford in
Butch Cassidy and the Sundance Kid (1969)[40]

In the Gospels, Jesus addresses himself to various Jewish contemporaries. Often they are not identified beyond their assemblage in "crowds" or "multitudes" (e.g., Matt 4:25; Mark 10:1; Luke 5:15). Sometimes, however, his interlocutors are named in ways that correspond with the terminology of first-century historians like Flavius Josephus (ca. 37–ca. 100). The evangelists assumed that these groups Jesus addresses were familiar to their listeners. To us they are not. It behooves us to know something about them—even if, alongside expert historians, we haven't as much hard, reliable information as we would like.

The **Sadducees** (Matt 16:11; Mark 12:18//Luke 20:27) evidently comprised a priestly aristocracy in the second century BCE until 70 CE. Their origins are fuzzy but may be traceable to the Zadokites (Ezek 40:45–46; Ezra 7:2), a family descended from Zadok, the first high priest in Solomon's temple (2 Sam 8:16–18; 1 Kgs 2:35).

---

38. Joachim Jeremias, *The Parables of Jesus*, trans. S. H. Hooke, 2nd ed. (New York: Charles Scribner's Sons, 1972).

39. Translated by John Bowden (Minneapolis: Fortress Press, 1998).

40. Reprinted in William Goldman, *Adventures in the Screen Trade: A Personal View of Hollywood and Screenwriting* (New York: Warner Books, 1983), 361, 364, 371, 376.

Of the principal Jewish sects during Jesus' day, the Sadducees were the most religiously and politically conservative (*B.J.* 2.8.2–14; *A.J.* 18.1.2–17). More so than others, they collaborated with their imperial overlords in the administration of Israel's cities. In that respect they may have resembled **Herodians** (Matt 22:16//Mark 12:13; Mark 3:6; *A.J.* 14.15.10), partisans of the Herodian dynasty. (See "A Horde of Herods" in chap. 3.) The Sadducees may also have enjoyed a dominant position in the **Sanhedrin** (Matt 26:59//Mark 14:55//Luke 22:66; Acts 4–5), a tribunal of about seventy Jewish elders whose judicial authority the Romans permitted as a sop to subjugated Jews. (Thus, for example, the Synoptics describe Jesus' arraignment by chief priests before being remanded to the custody of an imperial prefect: Matt 26:59–68; 27:1–2//Mark 14:55–65; 15:1//Luke 22:66–71; 23:1.) Religiously the Sadducees tended to accept as authoritative only the written Torah, the HB's first five books;[41] they refused to accept apocalyptic beliefs, like resurrection, which had no basis in those writings; and they presided over sacrificial worship in the temple (*A.J.* 13.297). The latter may have been their undoing: when Titus's Roman legions razed Herod's second temple in 70, there was no longer a center for cultic sacrifice and, therefore, no raison d'être for the Sadducees themselves.

The single most influential Jewish sect during the late first century and beyond was the **Pharisees**, whose name may have been derived from the Hebrew term *pārašîm*, "separatists." Compared with the Sadducees, the Pharisees were less politically connected with the Romans and religiously more liberal. They embraced a wider range of Scripture as authoritative (Law, Prophets, and Writings) and beliefs (like resurrection) contained within some of them. For them Torah was not merely what had been committed to writing but also included its traditional interpretations, which were oral and unwritten in the first century (*A.J.* 13.5.9; 18.1.2; *Vita* 10). Essentially, the Pharisees comprised a lay reform movement within first-century Judaism, which advocated devotion to Torah in all seasons of life. For that they accrued a high degree of popular respect (*A.J.* 18.15). After the temple and its high priesthood collapsed in 70, the Pharisees were instrumental in shifting Judaism's center of gravity away from the sacrificial cultus and onto the law, where it remains to this day. The reason for that enduring influence is that the rabbinic tradition, whose legal interpretation was codified in the third-century Mishnah and the fourth- and fifth-century Talmuds, is descended from the Pharisaic point of view.

In Matthew (5:20; 26:57), Mark (2:16; 10:33), and Luke (9:22; 15:2), **scribes** are associated with both Sadducees and Pharisees as antagonists of Jesus. This group is hard to pin down. The term's etymology in both Hebrew (*sōpēr*) and Greek (*grammateus*) suggests a "secretary," whose service could range from that of a recorder to a cabinet officer (in a synagogue; cf. "Secretary of the Treasury"). Sirach 38:24–39:11 (2nd c. BCE) characterizes a scribe as an educated expert in

41. These are Genesis, Exodus, Leviticus, Numbers, and Deuteronomy.

Fig. 9. The Western Wall, all that remains of Herod's temple in Jerusalem. Notice those in prayer, bowed against the wall. The kiosks on the concourse are not concession stands but lending libraries of Jewish prayer books and copies of the Talmud. Photograph by Clifton Black.

Torah and an adviser to the governing classes. In Josephus (*B.J.* 1.26.3; 5.13.1), Acts (19:35), and *2 Baruch* (9:1–10:4; ca. 100), scribes refer to community leaders of varying social status.

Josephus also refers to a third "school" of first-century Jews (*B.J.* 2.8.2–13), unmentioned in the NT but important for rounding out our knowledge. These are the **Essenes**, a radically separatist, ascetic community (1QS 1.11–12; 5.1–8; CD 12.1–2), datable to the second century BCE, which despised what they considered a corrupt administration of Jerusalem's temple and sought to purify itself perfectly (1QS 6.2–5; CD 10.14–12.6; *J.W.* 2.123). Led by an unidentified figure they regarded as "the Righteous Teacher" (CD 1.1–2.13), many Essenes withdrew to the wilderness, awaiting their vindication by God and retribution for practically everyone else (CD 4.2–6.11; 1QM). Although biblical scholars are not of one mind in this matter (or any matter, for that matter), many believe that a group of Essenes were settled in Qumran, on the Dead Sea's northwestern shore, and left behind the famous Scrolls first discovered between late 1946 and early 1947 and still being unearthed. Josephus suggests that this group dissolved under Roman assault by the end of the Jewish revolt in 66–73 (*B.J.* 2.152–53).

Fig. 10. The author in the Dead Sea, unsuccessfully searching for scrolls. Archaeologists must exercise patience and prepare themselves for disappointment. Photograph courtesy of Gretchen Sausville.

Josephus names a "fourth philosophy," Jewish revolutionaries against the Roman Empire (*A.J.* 1.6; 17.271–72; 18.1.6; *B.J.* 2.8.1; cf. Acts 5:36–37), whose origins can be traced as far back as the Maccabeans' successful revolt against the Syrian dynasty of the Seleucids (167–63 BCE). Mark (15:7) and Luke (23:18–19) refer to Barabbas as one such murderous insurrectionist. By the 60s CE these rebels had loosely coalesced into militant resisters known as **Zealots** (*B.J.* 2.162–562) and the **Sicarii** (dagger men; *B.J.* 2.425–29). Such forces of resistance against Rome holed up, almost a thousand strong, in the fortress mesa at **Masada** and, in 73 or 74, committed mass suicide rather than be conquered, raped, and enslaved by the Romans after a year-long siege.

One figure, often on the stage of all the Gospels, deserves special recognition.

John the Baptist

John the prophet was not an American Baptist, Southern Baptist, or a member of any of the Protestant groups descended from seventeenth-century Separatists from the Church of England. A first-century Jew, John is identified in the

Fig. 11. A view of Masada from its base, facing southeast. Photograph by Clifton Black.

Synoptics as either "the baptist" (*ho baptistēs*, a title: Matt 16:14//Mark 8:28// Luke 9:19) or "the baptizer" (*ho baptizōn*, a nickname: Mark 1:4). Our primary, first-century sources for information about him are a brief passage in Josephus's *Jewish Antiquities* and the NT's four Gospels and Acts of the Apostles. As with Jesus, John's portrayal in these sources is based on historical fact but colored by each author's point of view.

1. Josephus's *Antiquities*

The portrait of John in Josephus's *Antiquities* (18.116–19) is set within a larger narrative intended by that historian to interpret his fellow Jews to his Roman patrons. In Josephus's report, John was "a good man" who had urged his fellow Jews to practice justice toward one another and piety toward God. Those who complied with John were baptized by him, "a consecration of the body suggesting that the soul had already been thoroughly cleansed by righteous conduct" (18.117). So popular was John that Herod Antipas, governor of Galilee and Perea (Luke 3:1), feared his leading a revolt. "[Herod] decided it advantageous to make a preemptive strike and be rid of [John], rather than wait for an upheaval, get entangled in a messy situation, then see his mistake" (18.119). John was arrested, transferred to Fortress **Machaerus**, east of the Dead Sea (see fig. 6), and executed. Some Jews interpreted the punishing defeat of Herod's army by King Aretas IV of Petra (18.109–15) as divine judgment on Herod Antipas for killing John (18.116).

That's the Baptist as Josephus presents him. How do the NT's evangelists characterize him? In general they are less concerned with John's potentially volatile popularity and more interested in his role as a prophetic foil for Jesus (cf. Mal 4:5).

2. Mark

In Mark, John is an ascetic prophet, living in the wilderness. In costume and conduct he is likened to the ninth-century BCE prophet Elijah (1:6; cf. 2 Kgs 1:8; Mark 9:11–13). He preached that his fellow Jews should repent and be baptized for their sins' forgiveness (Mark 1:4–5). Among those whom he baptized was Jesus (1:9–11). John had predicted the coming of one far mightier than he (1:7–8). Mark portrays a national repentance movement fostered by John (1:5), who enjoyed a following of disciples (2:18; 6:29) and a ministry of magnitude comparable to that of Jesus' (6:14–16; 8:28), who began his own work after John's arrest (1:14; cf. Matt 4:12; 11:2–6; Luke 3:20).[42] Jerusalem's authorities were aware of his reputation as a prophet (11:30–33). Mark attributes his death to criticism of Herod Antipas's marriage to his sister-in-law. Antipas feared John. Outmaneuvered by his wife, Antipas executed John (6:17–28).

3. Matthew

Matthew follows Mark's lead, amplifying some details. John is flatly identified with Elijah (17:9–13) and explicitly points to Jesus as Scripture's fulfillment (3:3). Although their ministries dovetail, with both preaching repentance on the threshold of the kingdom's coming (3:2; 4:17), John implicitly regards Jesus as sinless and must be cajoled by Jesus into baptizing him (3:13–17). Jesus valorizes John's ministry (11:9–14) while esteeming his own followers even more highly (11:11). Anticipating Jesus' vituperation against scribes and Pharisees (23:1–36), John castigates Pharisees, Sadducees, and Jerusalem's Jewish authorities (3:7–10; 21:32). After his imprisonment, John expresses doubts about Jesus' messiahship, evidently based on premises different from Jesus' own (11:2–6). The manner of John's death is similar to what we find in Mark, save for the detail that Herod wanted to execute him because "[the people] took him to be a prophet" (14:5). Here Matthew is closer to Josephus, although Matthew replicates John's accusing Herod of incest (14:3–4; cf. Mark 6:17–18).

---

42. For reasons soon to be considered, the Fourth Gospel presents overlapping ministries of John and Jesus. Although we cannot be sure, that may have been the case. While the Fourth Gospel's subordination of the Baptist to Jesus is more over-the-top than what we find in the Synoptics, the latter firmly locate John in a lower rank..

4. Luke

Like Mark and Matthew, Luke correlates the ministries of John and Jesus, subordinating John to Jesus. Both qualities surface in Luke's infancy narrative, which, as we shall see, presents parallel circumstances for the births of (kinsmen) John and Jesus (1:5–25//1:26–35; 1:46–56//1:57–80) while elevating Jesus' status. John is conceived by a postmenopausal mother (1:8–25); Jesus is conceived by Mary through the power of the Holy Spirit (1:34–35). In utero, John extols pregnant Mary (1:41, 44). He is a prophet like Elijah (1:17, 76), while Jesus is the Son of God and Messiah (1:32–35; 3:15–17). Conceding that Jesus was baptized (3:21–22), Luke does not describe John's baptism of Jesus; in fact, Luke refers to John's imprisonment immediately *before* Jesus' baptism (3:20–21). Though both John and Jesus are in Herod's sights (3:18–20; 13:31–33), Luke does not recount John's execution by Herod, perhaps to stay focused on the unique importance of Jesus' suffering and death (24:26–27; cf. 9:9). Characteristic of Luke, John's critique of his countrymen is widened to include the wealthy, tax collectors, and soldiers (3:10–14; cf. 6:24–25; 7:1–10, 29–30; 15:1). In Luke, John appears as a transitional figure between the era of the Law and the Prophets (16:16) and the era bringing the surprising presence of God's kingdom in Jesus (17:20–21). Luke perpetuates this idea in what is considered his second volume, Acts (1:4, 22; 11:16; 13:24–25; 18:25; 19:4).

5. John

The Fourth Gospel's depiction of John repeatedly hammers the claim in 1:6: "[John] was not the light but came to bear witness to the light [namely, Jesus: 1:9]"). In this Gospel, John's duty is twofold: to testify to his own insignificance (1:15, 19–28, 30; 3:28–30) and to Jesus' superior standing (1:23, 29, 31–36; 5:33, 35; 10:41). After his imprisonment (3:24), John rejoices to learn that Jesus is attracting more disciples than John (3:26–30; 4:1); some of his own disciples had already begun following Jesus, whom they rightly recognized as the Messiah (1:35–42). So persistent is the Fourth Evangelist in putting John in his proper place, insisting that John did so himself, that it has led scholars to wonder if competition between the two teachers and their entourages had occurred.[43] In subtler ways, Matthew and Luke bespeak the same concern to relativize John's significance, though a rivalry between him and Jesus is less evident in the Synoptics (Matt 11:11–15// Luke 7:28–30).

Among twenty-first-century scholars, the historical figure of John has enjoyed reappraisal. Judiciously weighing the evidence, Joel Marcus has concluded that the Gospels' portraits of John contain more than a kernel of veracity, that at least

---

43. There's a hint of such in Acts 19:1–7. Down to the present day the Mandaeans, whose origins are elusive, venerate John the Baptist as the ultimate prophet.

some of Jesus' own teaching was likely derived from John's, and that serious com-petition probably existed between the followers of John and Jesus.[44] In the Gospels that contest, predictably, is always resolved in Jesus' favor.

THE AUDIENCE

To whom did Jesus preach and, some fifty years later, to whom did the evangelists write?

Just Folks

I'm Nobody! Who are you?
Are you nobody, too?

—Emily Dickinson[45]

The total population of the Roman Empire—spanning 2.5 million square miles, including Palestine, with over 6,000 square miles—is unknown. Robert Knapp[46] speculates a figure of 50 or 60 million. Of that guesstimate, less than half of 1 per-cent, 100,000 to 200,000 people, belonged to one of the three wealthiest orders that governed everyone else—except for the Roman emperor, who occupied a league of one. Owing to ancestry and assets, **the senatorial order**, which was not always the richest, comprised the highest political and social rank. Beneath that, members of **the equestrian order** tended to acquire wealth, not senatorial status and power. Elites in these richest ordines, some 5,000 adult men, were con-centrated in Rome. The far less affluent **decurial order** governed the empire's remaining town and cities. Only some 40,000 adult males, in whom was concen-trated over 89 percent of the empire's wealth, made up the decurial order and controlled everything for the remaining 99.5 percent.

44. Joel Marcus, *John the Baptist in History and Theology*, SPNT (Columbia: University of South Caro-lina Press, 2018).

45. I beg the reader's indulgence for a relevant digression. In "Emily Dickinson Escapes," *Boston Review: A Political and Literary Forum* (February 21, 2020), https://bostonreview.net/arts-society/lynne-feeley-emily-dickinson-escapes, Lynne Feeley traces six images of the poet (1830–86) across seven decades of commentary: the disappointed lover (in Dickinson's *Love Poems and Others* [Mt. Vernon, VA: Peter Pauper Press, 1952]), domestic Vesuvius (in Adrienne Rich's "Vesuvius at Home," 1975), poet-scholar (Susan Howe, 1985), passionate feminist (Martha Nell Smith, 1992; Ellen Louise Hart, 1998), warrior against patriarchy (Alena Smith, 2019), ambitious professional sensitive to her genius (Martha Ackmann, 2020). My point: even with refined tools of historical and sociological analysis, modern biographers tend to recast their more recent subjects in the light of their own eras' preoccupations. So do the authors of today's lives of Jesus. And, using very different conceptual tools at their disposal, so did the evangelists.

46. *Invisible Romans* (Cambridge, MA: Harvard University Press, 2011), 103. In what follows my debt to Knapp is considerable.

Much farther down the socioeconomic ladder stood the empire's **freedmen** (formerly slaves). At worst, these folk could be confident of daily bread; at best, their resources allowed them leisure to pursue political or social interests. Freedmen comprised top soldiers, modest farmers, artisans and merchants, along with retainers who supplied their needs: architects, physicians, and professional teachers. By their cooperative labors these men and their families, about 25 percent of the total population, stabilized the empire's day-to-day operation and evidently thought well of themselves. Lucius Nerusius Mithres, a small-town merchant in Italy, left behind this inscription: "I sold people useful goods; my honesty was acclaimed everywhere; I paid my taxes, was fair and straightforward in my dealings, helped as many as I could, and was highly regarded among my friends" (*CIL* 9.4796). Their principal goal was financial security; their persistent concerns, death and disease, were unpredictable and omnipresent (*Dreams* 2.1, 59). They enjoyed socializing in public entertainments, including civic associations, public baths (*CIL* 6.15258), and executions (*Metam.* 10.29–34). Religious ceremonies were popular (*Metam.* 11.8–18). Theological niceties were ignored, but attacks on divine patronage that could jeopardize finance were not taken lightly (Acts 19:23–41). Especially for those who enjoyed free birth without legal constraints or financial liabilities, it's not surprising that dominance in the usually monogamous household was an overriding virtue for freedmen; subjugation was a shameful stigma.

The **wives** of these ordinary men had no legal standing, couldn't vote, and enjoyed little education. Their principal occupation was the household's efficient maintenance: supplying food and clothing, brokering intrafamily tensions, and child-rearing. Procreation, which assured the family's posterity, was the overriding purpose of marital sex. An epitaph by a certain Claudia asserts what she believed important for passersby to know of her life: she loved her husband and bore him two children; she managed the home; she weaved wool; "her conversation was lovely; her bearing, graceful" (*CIL* 6.15346). Ordinary women also worked outside the home as midwives, nurses, clothiers, cleaning ladies, fortune tellers, and priestesses; these jobs kept them connected with other women. Surprisingly, some traveled quite a bit on family visits or business trips (*P.Oxy.* 14.1773; Acts 16:14; 18:1–3). At home or abroad, abusive violence against them was not uncommon (*Dreams* 2.48; *Satyr.* 74–75; *CIL* 13.2182). Though undeniably disadvantaged,[47] not all of society's cards were stacked against them. A woman bringing to marriage a dowry from her father would exercise some leverage over the husband, who hoped to inherit its resources at her death but forfeited them back to her father in case of divorce (*Gold* 475–77).

---

47. See Susan E. Hylen, *Women in the New Testament World* (New York: Oxford University Press, 2019).

Fig. 12. A mother breast-feeding a baby in the presence of the father. Detail from the marble sarcophagus of Marcus Cornelius Statius, who died as a young child. Origin unknown. Housed in the Louvre Museum, Paris. Image courtesy of Marie Lan-Nguyen (2009).

For Egypt during the imperial period, Jane Rowlandson calculates that about one-third of rural landowners were women, who collected rent on perhaps as much as one-quarter of their holdings.[48] Even though the courts were closed to them, women could finesse legal complaints through family members. Insofar as possible, ordinary men and women alike avoided the judicial system, which was controlled by elite men both clumsy and corrupt (Luke 18:1–8; Jas 2:6; *Metam.* 10.33).

Fifty percent of the imperial population were **the poor**: free men and women who lived hand to mouth, with barely enough to survive day by day. Upward mobility was impossible; their lot, predetermined and impossible to change; their preoccupation, staying alive (*Carm. Astrol.* 1.22–24). Unless they happened to serve as tenants of others' farms (Matt 21:33–41), temporary charity from their peers was their only safety net, which extended no farther than their bene-factors' meager resources (cf. Luke 11:5–8). Artemidorus, a professional dream interpreter, ranks the poor among society's dregs: "They are like the worthless,

48. Jane Rowlandson, ed., *Women and Society in Greek and Roman Egypt: A Sourcebook* (Cambridge: Cambridge University Press, 1998), nos. 169–73.

obscure places into which shit and other waste are thrown, or anything else of inconsequence" (*Dreams* 2.9).

By comparison, **slaves**[49] constituted 15 percent or less of the population and tended not to teeter on starvation's edge. Their purse (*peculium*) belonged to their masters, but some slaves amassed sums, which they spent at their own discretion (*CIL* 11.6314; *Amph.* 539). Still, enslavement—whether by captivity in war, kidnapping through piracy, birth into a slave family, or abandonment by freedmen— was miserable. "Great gods! What wretched, pitiable creatures!" (*Metam.* 9.12). Abuse, both physical and mental, was calculated to buckle a slave to the master's will and expected, even sanctioned, with small hope of practical remedy (*Satyr.* 45; *Civ.* 11.16). Since there was no downside to capability, slaves tended to comply. Insecurity was a constant obsession and wore many haunting guises: "How can I come to terms with my master? Will I be sold? If so, what of my family, from which I'll be split? What are the chances of my being freed? If I try to escape, will I be caught?" (*Ast.*). To cope with such anxieties while prudentially accommodating oneself to current circumstances, resistance occurred in various forms: simple self-assertion, which masters expected (*Aesop*); theft and property damage (*Gov.* 4.3.13–18); murder (*CIL* 13.7070); most commonly, flight. Unless the master had branded his human property, fugitive slaves could blend into crowds (*Let.* 10.29–30). The best means of escape was manumission (1 Cor 7:21b), a possibility that masters offered slaves as incentive to cooperate. In his *Life*, Aesop repeatedly petitions his master Xanthus for his freedom; Xanthus repeatedly promises to free Aesop, then reneges. Beyond the fact that slavery in antiquity was not racially based, the biggest difference between the institution then and in recent times was any sense of its intrinsic evil. Slavery was so deeply lodged into the first-century social economy that its abolition was inconceivable to both master and slave alike. If a slave was released, the elite might look down their noses at such newly made freedmen, while ex-slaves could take pride in the competence or good conduct that had earned them their freedom (*CIL* 6.9222; *Satyr.* 57).

To fill out this sketch, others deserve mention. Freedmen serving as **soldiers** relinquished civilian freedom but—if they survived war and disease—received regular pay, food, housing, training, and in some cases veterans' benefits: a fair exchange in a world rife with economic uncertainty. **Gladiators**, male and female (*CIL* 14.5381), enjoyed notoriety for bravery and sexual prowess but, predictably, died at a younger age than their contemporaries. Some **prostitutes**, female and male, opted for an occupation with steady income; others were forced into that

---

49. At this writing the trend is to refer to members of this group as "enslaved persons," lest human beings be diminished in essence to a particular trait. I consider this tendency noble in our day but anachronistic and historically misleading. During the imperial era slaves *were* essentialized: people were regarded as chattel, as property other than real estate. "The past is a foreign country: They do things differently there" (L. P. Hartley, *The Go-Between* [New York: New York Review Books, 2002], 17).

through slavery or to feed a starving family.[50] They broke no laws, but most were exploited by rapists and pimps, whose take on a trick was outrageously high. Those who resorted to **banditry** or **piracy** were real desperadoes: the poor's poorest, the oppressed's most heinously exploited (*Metam.* 7.4). If apprehended for severe crimes, they usually suffered death by crucifixion or mauling in the arena: a considerable deterrent but an acceptable risk for those who believed they had nothing to lose.

To summarize: for 99 percent of Jesus' and the evangelists' audiences, "Life," sighed Woody Allen, "is full of misery, loneliness, and suffering—and it's all over much too soon."

CONCLUSION

We owe an unpayable debt of gratitude to the NT's evangelists, all of whom probably did their work in the last three decades of the first century. By applying pen to papyrus, they made sure that the earliest remembrances of Jesus would not be lost. They assured—and warned—Christians that faith in Jesus would be regulated, not held hostage to ecstatic visions or private insights. By these authors' efforts, Jesus of Nazareth remained the central figure with whom Christians would have to come to grips in construing their understanding of God. Within four centuries the church across the world reached the practical decision, later legalized, that no single Gospel, nor jumble of several, would suffice for Christian faith. The figure of Jesus was too large, too complex, for any such reduction. A multidimensional Jesus demanded a multidimensional interpretation. It is to three of those cardinal presentations that this book is devoted, with highest esteem.

---

50. Rebecca Fleming, "Quae corpore quaestum facit ['She Who Makes Money from Her Body']: The Sexual Economy of Female Prostitution in the Roman Empire," *JRS* 89 (1999): 38–61.

THE CONVERSATION CONTINUES

Humbled by Our Predecessors

A Conversation with John L. Thompson

John L. Thompson (PhD, Duke), the Gaylen and Susan Byker Professor Emeritus of Reformed Theology at Fuller Theological Seminary, taught historical theology at Fuller for thirty years (1989–2019). An ordained minister of the Presbyterian Church (U.S.A.) and an internationally recognized specialist in the writings of the Protestant reformer John Calvin, he has concentrated on the history of biblical interpretation with a particular interest in gender issues in Jewish and Christian Scripture and tradition.

CCB: John, the history of biblical interpretation is a gargantuan subject, about which you know a lot, I know a smidgen, and this book's readers may know nothing. Let's begin with a basic question. In broad strokes, how would you characterize the differences between the ways modern scholars typically read Christian Scripture and the techniques employed by its interpreters throughout most of Christian history?

JLT: Neither modern scholars nor ancient writers are all alike. They come in different flavors. Some modern scholars approach the biblical text as an object, a religious artifact from the past to be analyzed. Indeed, some regard it as a dangerous artifact that has done more harm than good; by deconstructing that text, they hope to neutralize its injurious effect. Yet other modern scholars not only want to address the text but also to feel personally addressed by it, as a word that comes to them not merely by means of human invention or artifice. The contrast between these two ways of regarding the Bible—as an abstract object, external to oneself, thus opposed to a voice that genuinely addresses the reader—was famously distinguished by the theologian Karl Barth (1886–1968) in his commentary on Romans (1919; 2nd ed., 1921).[51]

While many practitioners of historical criticism try to get behind the text in order to recover the culture that produced it, scholars of earlier centuries attempted to understand the world depicted or created by the text, with the aim of entering that world: a world, they believed, that is governed or guided by that text's divine author. Ancient commentators regarded Scripture

---

51. Karl Barth, *The Epistle to the Romans*, trans. Edwyn C. Hoskins, from the 6th German ed. (1928; London: Oxford University Press, 1933).

as inspired; for them, the principal implication of inspiration is that this text must have import, not only within its own narrative world, but a meaning that endures to the present day, addressing us in our created goodness and existential brokenness.

CCB: We'll return to the subject of inspiration presently. Before doing so, let's narrow the focus. When, say, Origen of Alexandria (ca. 184–ca. 283) interpreted the Gospels, how did he go about it? What was he trying to accomplish?

JLT: Origen was enthusiastic about biblical allegory. He found Christ in the OT in many texts that we would scarcely regard as messianic predictions. Wherever he found Christ, explicit or implied, his interpretation ran like this: because Christ is the head of the church and members of the church make up the body of Christ, then, in some way, anything that applies to Christ also applies, by extension, to his body, the church, as well as to individual members, the Christians who make up that body. Like many of the ancient church's interpreters, Origen also believed that almost every biblical text is liable to have multiple layers of meaning: (1) the literal sense, the *body* of the text; (2) a moral sense or some derivative lesson, the *soul* of the text; and (3) implications about the beatific life to come, the *spirit* of the text. John Cassian (ca. 360–ca. 435) refined this approach by speaking of *four* senses of Scripture. For him, Scripture tells us not only about (1) the history of God's ways with God's people, the literal or historical reading. It also informs us of (2) what we should believe, the allegorical sense; (3) what we should do, the moral sense; and (4) what we should hope for, the mystical sense. This "fourfold rule" could be difficult to apply to every text in Scripture, but the general inclination was much emulated in subsequent centuries. Theologians like Thomas Aquinas (1225–74) insisted that every spiritual reading of Scripture must be based in some text that literally teaches these other meanings.

CCB: Did biblical interpretation change across time amid the church's convulsions? Are there big differences in the Gospels' interpretation between Cassian during the patristic era and Martin Luther (1483–1546) or John Calvin (1509–64) during the Protestant Reformation?

JLT: It would be misleading to say that major convulsions of the church *caused* changes in scriptural interpretation. It's commonplace to point up a difference between the Antiochene and Alexandrian approaches to exegesis: Alexandrians liked allegory; Antiochenes preferred the ancient equivalent of literal interpretation without excluding the text's spiritual implications. The distinction between these two "schools" is real but often overdrawn or caricatured. And the differences were more a matter of regional patterns, perhaps cultural variations, and less the precipitates of major church crises.

The Protestant Reformation both influenced and was influenced by changes in thinking about how to read the Bible. Luther and his followers regarded Scripture as having been obscured both by spurious human traditions, sanctioned by papal authority, and by the deterioration of medieval preaching, which critically weakened popular understandings of the gospel and salvation. For these reasons Protestants discounted a good deal of ecclesiastical tradition and tried to reevaluate the proper shape of Christian beliefs and practices in the light of "Scripture alone"—though this slogan, too, can be misleading.

The Reformation benefited from a prior movement within the Renaissance known as Christian humanism: itself a tradition, marked above all by a drive to retrieve purer forms of both Christian and non-Christian texts and by recovering long-lost linguistic capability in such languages as Greek and Hebrew. This new learning came of age right as movable type and the printing press arrived on the scene. Soon, cheaply published pamphlets provided an immense amount of tinder and kindling, to which Luther and many others applied the spark. The widespread dissemination of texts and renewed concern for their interpretation coincided almost perfectly with Protestant interests and approaches to Scripture.

CCB: Let's fast-forward by a century or two. What impact did the Age of Enlightenment have on the Gospels' interpretation?

JLT: The European Enlightenment was a watershed. The influence of printed publications and Christian humanism increased exponentially from the sixteenth century to the seventeenth. "Backgrounds" of the Bible as well as intense scrutiny of ancient languages garnered the attention of scholars, sometimes leaving parish pastors and priests far behind. The seventeenth century marked the beginning of "critical" study of the Bible, producing massive multivolume compilations of commentary drawn from scores of respected biblical exegetes. But the material that was excerpted and gathered in these compendia was often atomized: reduced to snippets of lexical or grammatical or geographical or linguistic minutiae, with less interest in the Bible's overarching narrative or practical application. Sometimes knowledge of critical background contributed not to piety but to skepticism. The later seventeenth century saw a resurgence of an extremely low Christology, which doubted the existence of the Trinity and the possibility of miracles, depicting Jesus as an inspired religious teacher at best. Regarding Christ as a notable human teacher while granting his divinity as, at most, an honorific title became standard practice as the European Enlightenment gained traction.

CCB: Now to the subject of scriptural inspiration. To this day, Christians have never agreed on what it means. What has it meant in the history of Christianity? How, do you think, we might most helpfully think of inspiration now?

JLT: "Inspiration" is a term derived from the NT (2 Tim 3:16) to describe writings of the OT but was easily generalized to include the NT as well. Various NT texts envision inspiration as assuring the reliability of the message if not the words in the Bible, as well as guaranteeing a fixed interpretation of the texts and their message. But it's true that teachers throughout the church's history have differed over the mechanism and character of inspiration. Does it pertain to the text's general meaning, or is every word inspired? Was the text shaped by the human author, or was it dictated word by word? The answers tend to say more about the interpreter and don't always illumine the text very much.

Similar observations can be made about other terms that Christians have fought over, like infallibility and inerrancy. Even among advocates for inerrancy, for instance, a great diversity of theologies emerges from a supposedly inerrant biblical text—differences about eschatology, church polity, war and peace, the place of women, charismatic gifts, and so on. This is one reason why I have found greater satisfaction in studying how particular theologians and pastors depict Scripture in particular contexts than in analyzing theories of inspiration or inerrancy. The task of the pastor and theologian is to contextualize ancient writings in ways that both address and challenge the church in new contexts that are constantly evolving.

CCB: Has historical criticism—studying the biblical text's historical meaning in its original context—been a gift to the church or a blessing only to other historical critics, inside or outside the church?

JLT: "Historical criticism" needs to be defined with some care. Sometimes commentators prior to the seventeenth century are described as "precritical," but they were by no means uncritical. Neither were they uninterested in history that illumines the world of the text, and even what may be going on in the context that produced a Gospel or any particular book.

Historical criticism in its later forms has sometimes given rise to an ingrained wariness about the Bible. This is called a hermeneutic of suspicion: studying how a text reveals the partisan interests of the writer who produced it. I think suspicion can be an intriguing tool, but I'm struck by how unfairly it's often wielded. The philosopher Paul Ricouer (1913–2005) said that a hermeneutic of suspicion should be directed, in the first place, at the interpreter: how am *I* misrepresenting the text? It ought to be obvious that every text has an agenda and every author a reason for writing, and not every agenda or reason is necessarily pure in heart. But readers also have their agendas, and texts suffer distortion from biased readings. Indeed, our readings of past interpretations are themselves often dismissive, chopping ancient or medieval or Reformation commentaries into shallow sound bites.

I think that earlier commentators would have been delighted to learn some of the insights that have been gleaned under the large umbrella of historical criticism. But some historical critics believe that a practiced faith precludes objectivity. Traditional commentators would vigorously dissent! So when historical criticism approaches the Bible sympathetically, premodern interpreters would likely have welcomed it. But when historical criticism is used as a weapon against the text, premodern interpreters would have turned away.

CCB: And so do I. What do you appreciate about the ways premodern interpreters read the Bible? Are there things they still have to teach us?

JLT: I think they should not be simply parroted wholesale. Calvin contextualized the scriptural message in a manner suitable for the sixteenth century, but the sixteenth century is now half a millennium removed from us. By the same token, one of the great risks of interpretation in our own day is that of presentism: the prejudice that only what is modern or current can possibly have anything to say to us. And so we often vilify the past as backward thinking, repressive, the bastion of elite privilege. But a fair and careful reading of premodern commentaries reveals, not only foibles, but also some stunning commitments to inclusion, social justice, care for the poor and refugees, and surprising sympathy for the marginalized figures who appear with regularity in the Bible itself. Sometimes we may discover that biblical interpreters of the Christian past embody and advocate our own favorite virtues with a greater intensity and discipleship than we ourselves manifest. We may even find ourselves appropriately threatened when we encounter, in the past, greater learning, greater integrity, and even greater godliness than our own. But I consider it to be a very good day when I find myself humble before those gone before me.

CCB: I can imagine no better note on which to end our conversation. Thank you, Professor Thompson.

2

Jesus according to Mark

A Veiled Unveiling

"[A] beginning of the good news of Jesus Christ [the Son of God]": so Mark opens. In chapter 1 we considered the meaning of "good news" (Gk. *euangelion*). I've bracketed "Son of God" here because some ancient Greek texts of Mark include that appositive while others do not. That leaves us with "Christ," or "Messiah" (*christos*), a title ascribed to Jesus, not his last name.

The Hebrew term *meshiach* (or *māšîaḥ*) means "anointed." In the OT it refers to Israel's prophets (1 Chr 16:22; Ps 105:15), priests (Exod 40:15; Lev 4:3, 5, 16; 16:32) or high priests (Num 35:26), kings real (1 Kgs 19:15–16; 2 Kgs 9:3, 6, 12; Ps 2:2) or idealized (1 Sam 2:10; Dan 9:25–26), and even the Persian potentate Cyrus: after conquering Babylon in 539 BCE, he permitted exiled Israelites to return home (Isa 45:1). In itself there's nothing eschatological (having to do with the end times) about *meshiach* or *christos*. In the first century CE, some other Jewish books envision an ideal king of the ancient Davidic dynasty who will judge the wicked and restore Israel's righteous remnant: "After the times have come of which I have spoken to you, when the nations are moved and the time of my Anointed One comes, he will call all nations, and some of them he will spare, and others he will kill" (*2 Baruch* 72:3).[1] Perhaps riffing on "the Ancient of Days" mentioned in Daniel 7:9–10, *1 Enoch* imagines a heavenly, preexistent "Elect One" (48:10; 62:5; 69:27). During the third century BCE to the first century CE, ascetic Jews who composed the DSS (CD 12.23; 1QSa 2.11–23) expected messiahs of both Aaron (a priest) and of Israel (a king)—the first, to purify Jerusalem's temple and its worship; the second, to liberate Israel from foreign occupation—as well as a righteous teacher "at the end of days" (CD 6.7–11). Daniel (ca. 164 BCE)

---

1. Translated by A. F. J. Klijn, "2 Syriac Apocalypse of Baruch," in *OTP* 1:645. For other examples of a messianic figure like this, see *4 Ezra* 11–12 in *OTP* 1:548–51.

Fig. 13. Mark's Gospel Outlined and Summarized

1:1–13	Prologue: Jesus, the Spirit, and their precursors
Contents:	Introduction (1:1), scriptural context (1:2–3), the ministry of John the Baptist (1:4–8), the divine acclamation of Jesus as God's son at his baptism (1:9–11), and Jesus' temptation (1:12–13)
1:14–15	*Transitional summary:* John's arrest and the opening announcement of Jesus' ministry
1:16–3:6	First major section: Jesus' authority and its resultant opposition
Contents:	The beginning of the Galilean ministry: Jesus' summons of his first disciples (1:16–20), a series of healings, evoking immense popularity (1:21–45), a series of five controversy stories (2:1–3:6)
3:7–12	*Transitional summary:* Jesus withdraws, yet attracts followers from all points of the compass radiating from Galilee, and silences unclean spirits from broadcasting his identity as "Son of God."
3:13–6:6a	Second major section: Jesus' parabolic ministry among "insiders" and "outsiders"
Contents:	A complex of material dealing with genuine and spurious discipleship (3:13–35), Jesus' teaching in parables (4:1–34), a series of four miracles (4:35–5:43), and his rejection in his homeland (6:1–6a)
6:6b	*Transitional summary:* Continuation of Jesus' teaching in villages
6:7–8:21	Third major section: Outreach to Gentiles and the disciples' increasing blindness
Contents:	The dispatch of the Twelve (6:7–13), Herod's execution of John (6:14–29), a complex of material concentrated on Jesus' feeding of five thousand (6:30–56), Jesus' rejection of "the tradition of the elders" on defilement (7:1–23), healings beyond Galilee (7:24–37), a complex of material centered on Jesus' feeding of four thousand (8:1–21)
8:22–26	*Transitional anecdote: Jesus gives a blind man sight.*
8:27–10:45	Fourth major section: Christology and discipleship in the light of Jesus' suffering
Contents:	Teaching on discipleship spun out of Peter's confession (8:27–9:1), Jesus' transfiguration (9:2–13) and healing of an epileptic child (9:14–29), and a recurring pattern of passion predictions, misunderstandings by the disciples, and teaching on the true discipleship (9:30–10:45)
10:46–52	*Transitional anecdote: Jesus gives a blind man sight.*
11:1–13:37	Fifth major section: The week in Jerusalem before Jesus' arrest and crucifixion
Contents:	A cycle of episodes involving the temple and prayer (11:1–33), overlapping a second collection of five controversy stories (11:27–12:34); Jesus' corrective teaching (12:35–44) and a discourse on the end of days, delivered to four disciples on the Mount of Olives (13:1–37)
14:1–15:47	Sixth major section: The passion narrative
Contents:	The plot to capture Jesus (14:1–11), his Last Supper with the Twelve (14:12–25) and prediction of their defection (14:26–31), his anguish and their faltering in Gethsemane (14:32–42), his betrayal (14:43–52), trials (14:53–15:15), humiliation, crucifixion, death (15:16–41), and burial (15:42–47)
16:1–8	Epilogue: The discovery of the empty tomb

expresses an apocalyptic hope for Israel's national restoration without mentioning a messiah (10:20–21). The main takeaway here: not all Jews living before and during Jesus' time harbored end-time aspirations of religious and political renewal. If they did, they didn't agree among themselves whether Israel's restoration would rely on a messiah. If they did believe that, they didn't agree on what that messiah would look like.[2] Some, like Rabbi Akiva in 132 CE, endorsed a contemporary revolutionary, Simon Bar Kokhba, as a militant messiah who would free Israel from Roman imperialism.[3] They were sadly mistaken.

Apart from inferences drawn from Paul's Letters, written in the mid-first century CE by a Hellenistic Jew who regarded Jesus as the Christ (e.g., Rom 1:1; 1 Cor 1:1; 1 Thess 1:1), it is anyone's guess what messianic connotations colored the traditions Mark inherited.[4] Even more speculative is what such an idea might have meant to the Gentiles among Mark's listeners before or after 70. We do not know the answers; to understand this Gospel, we don't need to know that. Like other ancient writers, Mark is interested in showing, not telling, how a term so ambiguous as *christos* should be understood. Like all the evangelists, Mark has no intention of *proving* that Jesus is the Christ. From the start, his Gospel *assumes* that to be true, and his audience is expected to accept it. In Mark, the Second Gospel, "Messiah" does not define Jesus: *Jesus* redefines "Messiah."

And that's where the wicket gets sticky because Mark's depiction of Jesus as Christ is so bizarre. The only characters in this Gospel who so declare him—his disciple, Simon Peter, and his adversary, Jerusalem's high priest—are either hushed (8:29–30) or don't believe it (14:61–63). Unclean spirits that recognize Jesus as "God's Holy One" or "the Son of [the Most High] God" are gagged before their exorcism (1:23–26; 3:11–12; 5:7a). Even if they weren't, who would credit the testimony of those believed to be demon-possessed? Jesus' primary ministries in Mark are healings, often of demoniacs (1:21–28, 39; 5:1–20; 7:24–30; 9:14–29), and teaching, usually in parables (3:23; 4:1–34). Neither proves his messiahship, as Mark makes clear. Nobody in this Gospel witnesses Jesus' ministry, drops to their knees, and acclaims him the Messiah based on what's been seen or heard. Jesus' instruction is so obscure that his closest followers cannot understand it (4:13; 6:52; 8:14–21; 9:32) and, when clear, is flatly rejected by friend and foe alike (2:1–3:6; 10:2–31; 12:1–12; 14:26–31). The same with his mighty works: after he feeds a grand total of nine thousand people with a dozen loaves and some sardines (6:30–44; 8:1–10), pious Pharisees demand Jesus to show a sign

2. For more information consult John J. Collins, *The Scepter and the Star: The Messiahs of the Dead Sea Scrolls and Other Ancient Literature* (New York: Doubleday & Co., 1995).

3. Documented in the Jerusalem Talmud's tractate *Ta'anit* 4.68d.

4. In 1 Cor 15:3–7 Paul clearly identifies items of traditional preaching about Jesus that he received from others, then delivered to his audiences. Whether Mark knew and used Paul's letters is a highly controversial question in current NT studies.

from heaven (8:11–13). What more could possibly convince them? Jesus drives out demons right and left; from that, Jerusalem's scribes conclude that he's in league with Satan and his family thinks he's crazy (3:21–22, 31). His ministry ends in disgrace and the *ne plus ultra* of executions: crucifixion (14:27–37). What kind of messiah is *that*?

What to Look For in Mark

1. *A narrative roller-coaster:* the story hurtles its readers along, "immediately" (the Greek adverb *euthys*, which first appears in 1:10, then 40 other times), with harsh jolts, hairpin curves, and, in amusement-park lingo, "an aggressive thrill factor." You can read this Gospel in an hour. Do it. You'll see what I mean.

2. *An apocalyptic clash* between good and evil (1:12–13, 21–28; 4:13–20), between faith and fear (4:31–6:6a; 9:19–24), between diabolic forces that have commandeered this world and the God who intends to restore creation (3:19b–30; 6:14–44; 7:24–8:10; 9:9–29; 13:1–37).

3. The *unfathomable mystery* of God's kingdom and the Messiah whom God has sent to inaugurate it. The mystery of the kingdom is given to Jesus' followers (4:11), who, despite having it explained to them (4:34), do not understand it (4:41; 6:52; 8:1–21; 10:35–42). Meanwhile, swarms of needy and mostly nameless nobodies recognize his power to rescue them (1:40; 2:1–12; 3:7–8; 5:22–29; 6:53–56; 7:24–35; 8:22–26; 9:14–29; 10:46–52). Jesus is truly the Christ, God's anointed redeemer (1:1, 11; 8:29; 9:2–8, 41). Satan's minions recognize him as their prime adversary (1:24; 3:11; 5:5–7); Jesus repeatedly quashes these declarations of his identity and mighty works (1:25, 34b, 43; 3:12; 5:43; 7:24, 36a; 8:26, 30; 9:9; 11:33), "but the more he stifled them, the more eagerly they proclaimed it" (7:36; cf. 1:28, 45). Mark resolutely sustains this tension between secrecy and disclosure. Guess what? He never resolves it.

4. *The compassion of Jesus* (6:34; 8:2) *to suffer and die for others* (8:31–32; 9:31; 10:33–34, 45; 14:48–49; 15:6–15). Understanding Jesus is no prerequisite for being healed by him.

5. *The cost of discipleship to Jesus, the failure of his uncomprehending disciples, and God's dedication to restore them, no matter what.* Mark's definition of discipleship is crystallized in 8:34: "If any want to become my followers, let them deny themselves and take up their cross and follow me." Following their

teacher, Jesus' disciples will suffer betrayal, persecution, even death for others' sake (8:35–38; 10:29–30; 13:9–13). Their conduct should tally with Jesus' own (6:7–13; 10:39b–40; 13:32–37); faithful subservience is their appropriate rank (9:33–37; 10:31, 42–44; 11:22–26). Although the Twelve relinquish much (1:16–20; 2:14; 10:28), in Mark's account they end up miserable failures (14:17–21, 29–31, 37–41b, 50–51, 66–72), just as Jesus predicts (14:27). Their disloyalty is no match for Jesus' and God's fidelity to them (10:29–30; 13:11, 13b, 26–27; 14:28; 16:7).

A PARABOLIC KINGDOM

Now after John was arrested, Jesus came into Galilee,
    preaching God's good news and saying,
"The time has been fulfilled,
    and the kingdom of God is on the threshold;
turn around and trust the good news."
                        —Mark 1:14–15

These are the first words spoken by Jesus in Mark. We might then expect explicit instruction from Jesus about how the clock has reached this climactic hour and the content of both God's good news and his kingdom. Instead we are plunged headlong into a fast-paced account of Jesus' recruitment of his closest followers (1:16–20, filled out in 3:13–19a), his exorcism of diabolical spirits from those pitifully possessed (1:21–28, 34, 39), his sympathetic cures of multitudes suffering diverse diseases (1:30–31, 40–45; 3:1–5), and the geographical spread of many others who seek his healing (1:28, 32–33, 36–39; 2:1–5, 10–12; 3:7–8), coupled with an escalating antagonism from religious authorities (2:1–3:6) and even his own family, who (by 3:19b–35) interpret his ministry as either crazed or inspired by Satan (contrast 1:9–11). As early as 3:6 a plot is being hatched to destroy the one whom Satan's demons, the unclean spirits, recognize as their enemy; Jesus quickly silences them (1:34; 3:11–12). Even those who recognize in him a healer like none other (1:27; 2:12) have begun to hem him in (1:45), practically starving and nearly crushing him (3:9–10, 20). In short, Mark litters his narrative with jagged puzzle pieces left for the reader to begin assembling them. God's kingdom is breaking in—"fresh wine" is flowing into fresh containers (2:22)—even if its beneficiaries don't entirely understand it and its adversaries are blind to it. Finally, at chapter 4, Jesus offers a lengthy yet oblique description of what that kingdom is like, which raises as many questions as it answers. At this point, therefore, it behooves us to pause and consider two critical issues: What is meant by "the kingdom of God"? Why does Jesus interpret it parabolically?

Fig. 14. Listing on the Sea of Galilee, also known as Lake Tiberias (John 21:1) or Kinneret, as the sun begins to set on a December evening. Photograph by Clifton Black.

The Kingdom of God

The OT's hymns of praise frequently acclaim "the LORD is king" or "the LORD reigns" (e.g., 1 Chr 16:31; Pss 10:16; 96:10; 146:10). Curiously, the phrase "the kingdom of God" (Gk. *hē basileia tou theou*) never occurs in the HB, though something close—"the kingdom of the LORD"—appears once (1 Chr 28:5). In the *Psalms of Solomon*, a collection of Hellenistic Jewish hymns written, perhaps, in the late first century CE, "the kingdom of God" is synonymous with God's strength, endless mercy, and eternal standing over the nations.

By contrast, God's *basileia*—which may be translated as "kingdom," "reign," "sovereignty," or "dominion"—is the constant refrain of Jesus' message in the Synoptics. The term appears 51 times in Matthew; 18 times in Mark; 49 times in Luke. Nowhere does Jesus define this kingdom. Instead, he alludes to it in coherent ways.

1. *The kingdom originates from God alone.* God prepares (Matt 20:23//Mark 10:40; Matt 25:34), gives (Matt 21:43; Luke 12:32; Matt 7:7//Luke 11:9), or bequeaths (Matt 5:3//Luke 6:20; Matt 19:14; Mark 10:14; Luke 18:16) the kingdom to

those who yearn for (Matt 6:33//Luke 12:31; Matt 7:7–8//Luke 11:9–10), accept (Mark 10:15//Luke 18:17), or inherit it (Matt 25:34).

2. *God's sovereignty is unlike any in this world*, in which tyrants throw their weight around the poor *schlimazels*[5] beneath them (Matt 20:25–27//Mark 10:43–44//Luke 22:25–27).

3. *God's dominion transcends its time and space.* Jesus never localizes it in Jerusalem or anywhere else on Israel's map.

4. The kingdom's reciprocal energies are *justice and mercy*. Built into God's supreme dominion is a pressure for righteousness (*dikaiosynē*): integrity, justice, a power to restore everything thrown out of joint beyond human capacity to repair (Matt 12:41//Luke 11:32; Matt 11:29–30). Accordingly, Jesus' disciples tend the sick, feed the hungry, give drink to the thirsty, offer hospitality to strangers, clothe the naked, forgive debtors, and visit the imprisoned (Matt 25:35–39, 42–43; Mark 11:25; Luke 17:3–4). Those regarded as morally defective—tax collectors on the imperial payroll (Matt 9:10–11//Mark 2:15–16//Luke 5:29–30), indigent johnnies-come-lately (Matt 20:1–16), lost sheep and lost children (Matt 18:10–14; Luke 15:1–32), the flagrantly sinful (Matt 9:10–11; Matt 11:19//Luke 7:34)—receive from Jesus special attention, to the predictable dismay of the pious. The currency of the kingdom is restoration, not retribution, because the kingdom's citizenry comprises forgiven sinners (Matt 9:13//Luke 5:32) who have repented, or turned toward, God (Matt 4:17//Mark 1:15). For this reason, God's *basileia* is the subject of "glad tidings," "good news," or "gospel" (*euangelizesthai*; Mark 1:14–15; Luke 4:43; 9:2).

5. *God's kingdom overlaps both present and future.* In all its fullness, God's earthly reign is expected in the future (Matt 8:11//Luke 13:28–29; Mark 14:25//Matt 26:29). And yet "the time"—*ho kairos*, the critical moment, the golden season— "has now been fulfilled, and the kingdom of God has drawn near," "on the verge," or "is at hand [*ēngiken*]" (Mark 1:15//Matt 4:17).

6. *Jesus himself*, what he does and what he says, *is the reliable index to the kingdom's character.* "If by the finger of God I drive out demons, then the kingdom of God has come to you" (Luke 11:20//Matt 12:28). Jesus' parables of the kingdom explode this world's values, rattle it in ways startling and repulsive, and begin the liberation of creation for its true destiny, as God intends. By the Father's decision and the Son's compliance, Jesus already activates the impact of a reign yet to be fully realized on earth (Matt 11:25–26//Luke 10:21–22; Luke 12:49–51//Matt 10:34). For the Synoptic evangelists, *the kingdom of God is where Jesus Christ is.*

---

5. In Yiddish, *schlimazels* are not the same as *schlemiels*. A *schlemiel* habitually spills chicken soup, which invariably slops over a *schlimazel*. But I'm a goyish schnook (Gentile dolt). So to me you should listen?

To sum up this commotion of notions: the kingdom of God refers to God's eternal sovereignty over all, now invading human history in a unique emissary, Jesus. "Go and tell John what you have seen and heard: the blind receive their sight, the lame walk, the lepers are cleansed, the deaf hear, the dead are raised, the poor have good news brought to them" (Luke 7:22//Matt 11:5 NRSV).

Because God's sovereignty, expressed in the idea of God's kingdom, is roughly comparable to everyday experience yet unlike any government this world knows, its truth can only be expressed off-kilter: in parables.

Would You Believe It?

Part I: The Parables

All the Synoptics confirm Jesus' proclamation of God's kingdom in parabolic form (Gk. *para* + *bolē* = something "thrown alongside"). Almost nine decades ago in *The Parables of the Kingdom* (1935), the celebrated Welsh biblical scholar C. H. Dodd (1884–1973) framed a definition so comprehensive, concise, and incisive that most of the Gospels' interpreters still quote it: "At its simplest the parable is a metaphor or simile, drawn from nature or common life, arresting the hearer by its vividness and strangeness, and leaving the mind in sufficient doubt about its precise application to tease it into active thought."[6] Let's analyze Dodd's definition.

1. Parables plunge us into a sea of *metaphor*, images that allude to more than they articulate on the surface.

2. Parables are usually rooted in *everyday life*.

3. Parables are *vivid and strange*. Images collide and stories twist, often in unexpected ways.

4. Parables *tease*, provoking listeners to wonder just what the teller is driving at. A juxtaposition sparks questions without answering them. "I heard what he said. What does *that* mean?"

Jesus' parables do not adhere to a single, rigid form. Some are simple similes, *a* likened to *b*: "The kingdom of heaven is like treasure hidden in a field, which a man discovered and covered up" (Matt 13:44).[7] When that comparison is stretched to suggest a course of action, "then with delight he goes and sells all that he has and buys that field," we veer toward an "example-story." Some parables are shaped as quizzical aphorisms: "If Satan also is divided

---

6. C. H. Dodd, *The Parables of the Kingdom* (London: Nisbet & Co., 1935), 5.

7. As a pious Jew avoids pronouncing the divine name, "the kingdom of heaven" is Matthew's typical circumlocution for referring to "the kingdom of God." The two expressions are interchangeable.

against himself, how will his kingdom keep standing?" (Luke 11:18//Matt 12:26// Mark 3:26). Some of Jesus' most memorable parables are stories that conclude with either an explicit moral (the neighborly Samaritan in Luke 10:29–37) or a frightening finale (postmortem solace for the poor and misery for the rich: Luke 16:19–31). Rarely in the Synoptics does Jesus interpret his parables (Matt 13:18–23//Mark 4:13–20//Luke 8:11–15). The evangelists may have created or adapted such explanations of some parables, where these interpretations do appear, for their churches' benefit (e.g., Matt 13:36–43).

Jesus was not antiquity's only parable spinner: Aesop, Aristotle, and the rabbis used such devices.[8] The OT is a treasury of figurative discourse. In Hebrew *měšālîm* refers to riddles or dark sayings: "I shall open my mouth in a *māšāl*; / I shall utter dark sayings from of old" (Ps 78:2). "Wickedness proceedeth from the wicked" (1 Sam 24:13 KJV) is an old aphorism; Babylon's invasion of Judah as a forest fire kindled by "the LORD" is a parable speeding toward allegory (Ezek 20:45–49; cf. Mark 12:1–12). Nathan's *māšāl* of the ewe lamb (2 Sam 12:1b–4) builds to an exquisite conviction of its listener, King David—"Gotcha!" (2 Sam 12:5–14)—that is similar to Jesus' own *měšālîm*.

Reading the Synoptics, you might ask (and if you don't, I will): "Do the parables in each Gospel have a coloring distinctive to that evangelist?" All of Mark's parables, save one (the secretly growing grain: 4:26–29), are found in Matthew and Luke. Collectively, they register the unforeseen character of God's kingdom (4:3–9, 30–32) and assurance of its judgment (12:1–12; 13:28–29). Parables unique to Matthew's Gospel are stark and garish, even scary. Houses built on sand fall to pieces (7:26–27). An unclean spirit is evicted from somebody who just resumes housekeeping with seven spirits more and worse (12:43–45). Good and bad fish are sorted, sheep and goats are separated: the good are saved, the rotten pitched into fiery furnaces (13:47–50; 25:31–46). Many parables unique to Luke revolve around debts and their forgiveness (7:41–43; 16:1–8; 18:10–14), recovery of lost valuables (15:8–10; 15:11–32; 16:1–8), misplaced confidence in worldly possessions (12:16–21; 16:19–31), the demands of discipleship (14:28–30; 14:31–33), and extreme reversals in status (16:19–31; 18:10–14). Although the conclusions of parables in Mark and Matthew are usually "rounded off," many of Luke's parables are open-ended. In Luke, we never learn whether a rich fool died on the very night he was confronted with his mortality (12:16–21), if a sterile fig tree bore fruit the next year (13:6–9), or if an elder son accepted his father's invitation to celebrate his prodigal brother's homecoming (15:25–32).

8. See David R. Cartlidge and David L. Dungan, *Documents for the Study of the Gospels* (Minneapolis: Fortress Press, 2015), 137–49.

So much for Mark 4:1–34's background. Now pay attention to its careful structure:

Fig. 15. Arrangement of the Parables in Mark 4

A. Introduction (vv. 1–2)
   B. The sower (vv. 3–9)
      C. The parables' purpose: mystery given or withheld (vv. 10–12)
         D. The sower explained (vv. 13–20)
      C'. The parables' purpose: disclosure and secrecy (vv. 21–25)
   B'. The growing seed (vv. 26–29) and the mustard seed (vv. 30–32)
A'. Conclusion (vv. 33–34)[9]

This text and its context swing between poles of publicity and privacy, distance and proximity, parables and explanation (vv. 1–2, 10, 33–34). The heart of the section, vv. 13–20, explains the sower parable by allegorizing it (vv. 3–9). This interpretation may have originated among early Christians, reflecting on their missionary hardships and the difficulty of discipleship (cf. 2 Cor 4:7–12). The "seed" in Jesus' original parable (Mark 4:5, 7, 8) is inconsistently interpreted as "the word" (i.e., the gospel: vv. 14, 15b) and various responses to its proclamation (vv. 15a, 16–20). Consider this: Mark 4:13–20 is a précis of the entire Gospel of Mark, which recounts the vicissitudes of Jesus' ministry in the face of satanic temptation (1:13, 15; 8:33), his disciples' temporary affirmation but apostasy under fire (4:16–17; 9:42–47; 14:27), and this world's lures of wealth and prestige (4:18–19; cf. 9:33–37; 10:17–27). At the end, in spite of everything, good soil bears astonishing fruit (4:20): Jesus is vindicated by his resurrection (14:28; 16:6–7).

Taken together, the three parables in chapter 4—the sower (4:3–9), the growing seed (4:26–29), and the mustard seed (4:30–32)—liken God's kingdom (v. 11) to seeds whose dismal origins, from random sowing or minute size, yield astonishing outcomes: a hundredfold produce (v. 8), automatic growth (v. 28), "the greatest of all shrubs" (v. 32). Fertility and fruitlessness are common metaphors in Jewish and early Christian apocalypticism (1 Cor 3:6–8; *2 Esd* 4:26–32), even as roosting in large branches (Mark 4:32) suggests the protection of God's elect (Ezek 17:23; 31:6; Dan 4:12, 21) and as sickle and harvest (Mark 4:29) refer to final judgment (Joel 3:13a; Rev 14:14–20; a figure persisting in the metaphor of Death as "the Grim Reaper"). The scarlet thread running through Jesus' parables in Mark 4 is the claim that God's sovereignty preposterously frustrates human expectations. Although 75 percent of a planter's effort is wasted, 25 percent takes root, for no

---

9. The technical term for this crosswise arrangement is a chiasmus: a rhetorical figure in which terms or concepts are unfolded in one order and then in inverse order.

Fig. 16. Even today, just outside Capernaum, one finds blended soil, some barren, some fruitful. Photograph by Clifton Black.

apparent reason, and thrives with incredible prolificacy. A seed explodes and its fruit matures, without any cultivation. The tiniest seed yields the largest vegetable (*to lachanōn*, 4:32)—not a sequoia, but a zucchini leafy enough for nesting. Such images may stupefy rather than clarify—which in itself is an absurd sort of clarification. God's kingdom does not operate in accordance with received opinion and the violence of this world's principalities. At every point God's kingdom confounds conventional wisdom, turns it around, and defies it again.

The best evidence for this reading lies in Jesus' baffling reason for his parabolic speech (Mark 4:10–12): namely, to teach in parables with the intent to *confound* his listeners. In both the OT and NT (Dan 2:18–30; Rom 11:25; 1 Cor 4:1; Eph 3:3–9; Rev 10:7), the "secret" or "mystery" (*to mystērion*, Mark 4:11) refers to God's cosmic purposes, graciously unveiled to a select few. Things temporarily hidden are meant for disclosure (4:21–22). That revelation, however, is shrouded in paradoxical concealment, a deafening and blinding, which the parables themselves are intended to inflict (v. 12).[10] Like other NT authors (John 12:40; Acts 28:26–27), Mark adapts Isaiah 6:9–10 to interpret the gospel's rejection: preaching the word

---

10. See Laura C. Sweat, *The Theological Role of Paradox in the Gospel of Mark*, LNTS 492 (London: Bloomsbury/T&T Clark, 2015).

both provides *and* deprives the good news to those mysteriously disposed to receive or to refuse (Mark 4:24–25).

From the Classroom: A True Story

A certain NT professor directed the class's attention to the plain meaning of Mark 4:11–12: Jesus taught in parables, not to clarify, but to confuse. A student slammed down one hand as she raised the other.

"I **HATE** that. It makes no sense that Jesus would do such a thing."

The professor replied, "Is your mind hardened to that possibility?"

"Yes!"

"Congratulations!" said the professor. "You have demonstrated the power of Mark's Gospel over his readers twenty centuries after it was written."

If some among Jesus' listeners enjoy even a shred of insight into his teaching, such is God's gift (cf. Dan 2:19; Rom 16:25; Eph 3:3–5), not the product of their education, industry, or cleverness. Even more confounding: "those outside" (Mark 4:11) can be those, like his family, who are closest to Jesus (3:21, 31–32). Parables told as his listeners "were able to hear it" (4:33) are equivocal; the Twelve, to whom everything is explained (v. 34), persist in misunderstanding (v. 13; 6:52; 7:18a; 8:17, 21; 14:68). Mark never resolves this discord: he sustains it. And for good reason. Commonplace puzzles can be figured out. Divine mystery, never.

A PARABOLIC MESSIAH

We opened this chapter with Mark's initial claim: Jesus is the Christ, the Messiah (1:1). Not until halfway into this Gospel does the evangelist return to this pronouncement, now made by one of Jesus' twelve closest followers, Simon Peter (8:29). Only here in this Gospel does a disciple of Jesus ever claim that Jesus is the Christ. Jesus' response with a stern command (*epetimēsen*) is jarring: "Shut up!" His disciples are to say nothing about him to anyone (8:30). That is in character with Jesus' typical insistence that his identity and authority be buttoned up (1:34; 3:12; 5:43a; 7:36a). Mark 8:29–30 is the instance par excellence of what NT scholars have often identified as "the Messianic Secret,"[11] though "Messianic silence" or

---

11. Though its argument is flawed, William Wrede's *The Messianic Secret*, trans. J. C. G. Greig (from German orig., 1901; London: James Clarke, 1971), remains the most influential study of this subject and well worth reading.

"tacit Messianism" would be a more precise characterization. Mark affirms Jesus' messiahship but never explains what he means by it.

In fact, Jesus changes the subject to what, as "the Son of Man" (cf. 2:10, 28), he must endure: great suffering by the hands of fellow Jews, death and vindication by God. In twenty-five words (8:31), Jesus synopsizes Mark's final seventy-five verses. That the Son of Man "must undergo" all these things is a way of expressing Jesus' conformity to God's will. This is no parable; it is said as plainly as Peter rebuffs it (v. 32). Turning to all his disciples (vv. 33–34), Jesus scolds this scold as satanically diverting him from God's intentions: "Get behind me, Satan!" (v. 33; cf. 1:13). Only here in this Gospel does Jesus address an adversary as Satan: ironically, the first of the Twelve whom he called (1:16). Jesus then draws Mark's clearest connection between his own destiny, the cross, and his followers' responsibility to deny themselves, even to the point of death, for the sake of the good news (8:34–37). Honor and shame fueled an engine that propelled ancient society (e.g., Xenophon, *Hiero* 7.3) and to this day drives many cultures. Here Jesus associates shame with embracing the values of "this adulterous and sinful generation" and links honor with fidelity to God (Mark 8:38). Because in 8:31 Jesus switches the conversation from "Messiah" to "Son of Man,"[12] so now must we.

The Son of Man

Except for an aphoristic reference to "people" (lit., "the sons of men") in 3:28, "the Son of Man" appears in Mark fourteen times. Those sayings may be grouped into three categories:

- the *authoritative* Son of Man on earth, as in 2:10, 28;
- the *apocalyptic* Son of Man to come, as in 8:38; 13:26–27; 14:62; and
- the *suffering yet vindicated* Son of Man, as in 8:31; 9:9, 12, 31; 10:33–34, 45; 14:21, 41.

Never does Jesus bluntly assert, "I am the Son of Man" (or, for that matter, "I am the Son of God" or "I am the Christ"). In the Synoptics, Jesus is reticent to identify himself and roundabout when doing so. Mark's different sorts of "Son of Man" sayings appear mutually interpretive: as Son of Man, Jesus exercises veiled authority on earth (2:10a, 28), which will be manifest when he returns from heaven (13:26–27; 14:62). His apocalyptic vindication upon his return comports with his resurrection (8:31; 9:9, 31; 10:34b). Still, Mark weights references to the suffering Son of Man by a ratio of about three to one—a surprising fact, as we shall soon see.

12. For decades and from multiple analytical angles, "the Son of Man" has presented NT scholars a most perplexing problem of interpretation. A good, recent overview of the state of its questions is *The Son of Man Problem: Critical Readings*, ed. Benjamin E. Reynolds (Edinburgh: T&T Clark, 2018).

Mark and the traditions he inherited have drawn from an eclectic array of Jewish sources in fleshing out Jesus as the Son of Man. Like Ezekiel, Jesus acts with prophetic power and suffers others' bereavement (cf. Mark 6:30–44; 8:1–10 with Ezek 4:1–5:17; 12:1–28; 24:15–27). Jesus' authorization by God (1:9–11; 9:2–8; 12:1–12) matches divine conferral of authority on "one like a son of man" in Daniel (7:13–14 RSV). Mark associates the Son of Man with the Messiah (8:29; 14:61), trailing clouds of glory, attended by angels in a heavenly court. So do the Jewish apocalyptic texts *1 Enoch* (46:3–4; 63:11; 69:27; 71:14, 17 [300–100 BCE]) and *4 Ezra* (13:1–4 ["something like the figure of a man"], 12–13 [ca. 100 CE]). Unlike these books, however, the evangelist stresses vindication of the faithful, not punishment of the wicked (Mark 8:38; 13:26–27; 14:62). The Son of Man's redemptive suffering is reminiscent of Isaiah's Servant Songs (Isa 49:6bc//Mark 13:10; Isa 50:6//Mark 10:34; Isa 53:5–6, 10ab//Mark 10:45). The martyrdom of Jesus' disciples, to which reference is immediately made (8:34–37; 10:29–30, 39; see also 13:5–23), squares with persecutions of faithful Jews that preoccupy books like Daniel, *1 Enoch*, and 2 Maccabees. In Mark, the Son of Man's redeeming activity is not limited to Israel (11:17; 13:10), toward which Jewish apocalypticism inclines. What most radically sets apart the Markan Son of Man is the emphasis on his suffering, especially death by crucifixion, and his being raised from death (8:31; 9:31; 10:3–34). There is nothing comparable to this in Jewish apocalyptic literature. Here Mark goes his own way, stamping Son of Man traditions with the indelible impression of the early Christians' passion narrative.

So critical for Mark is Jesus' interpretation of himself as the suffering Son of Man, of discipleship along such a path, and of his disciples' unwillingness or inability to grasp these things that, not once, but three times at this Gospel's heart the evangelist repeats this cycle.

Fig. 17. The Tripartite Cycle of Passion Predictions in Mark			
Specified Location	*Jesus' Prediction of the Son of Man's Self-Sacrifice*	*The Disciples' Misunderstanding*	*Jesus' Teaching about Discipleship as Self-Sacrificial Service*
8:27	8:31	8:32–33	8:34–9:1
9:30	9:31	9:32–34	9:35–37
10:32	10:33–34	10:35–41	10:42–45

This roundelay is framed by the Gospel's only stories of the healing of the blind (8:22–26; 10:46–52). That cannot be accidental. For Mark, blindness has become a metaphor for refusal or incapacity to acknowledge Jesus for who he truly is and what his discipleship demands; vision is a trope for acceptance of both. Again, the paradox: the sightless see; the sighted are blind.

Why does Mark stress the suffering of Jesus and of his followers? The answer may be a combination of reasons historical and theological. Early Christians remembered Jesus' suffering and death "for our sins" (1 Cor 15:3; 2 Cor 4:10–12; Col 1:19–20; 1 Pet 2:21–25; cf. Mark 10:45: "to give his life as a ransom for many"). Mark 13:9–13 implies that discipleship to Jesus has spurred family members to betray one another: "You will be hated by all for my name's sake" (v. 13a). That portrait tallies with a report of Nero's baseless persecution of Christians for the inferno of 64 that engulfed Rome (*Ann.* 15.44), though it falls short of proving Mark's Roman provenance. Lay your ear on a page of this Gospel, and you may hear a wail of lament for the steep price paid for following Jesus. What you won't hear is the yammering of prosperity televangelists who prostitute the Bible with bogus assurances of health and wealth if you'll mail them a check every week.[13]

PARABOLIC HEALINGS

If you are keeping track of Markan paradox, here's another gem. In spite of this Gospel's stringent demands and sheer weirdness, Mark is touched with genius for drawing readers into the story of Jesus and those he encounters. Consider 5:21–43, with two interwoven tales of sufferers at their wits' end. The predicaments they describe are so poignant that, we imagine, they would make a stone weep.

Exemplified in these verses is a literary technique for which Mark has become justly renowned: the sandwiching of one story—the tale of a woman who suffers chronic hemorrhaging (5:24b–34)—inside another: a little girl's teetering on the precipice of death (5:21–24a + 5:35–43). This narrative device, known as intercalation, is exhibited throughout the Second Gospel.

Among these nine intercalations in Mark, 5:21–24a | 5:24b–34 | 5:35–43 is a miniature masterpiece. Each of these stories complements and amplifies the other with mirrored details so subtle that most would register with Mark's listeners only subconsciously, if at all. Observe these points:

♦ Two suppliants, a named synagogue administrator (*archisynagōgos*, v. 22) and an anonymous pauper (v. 26), seek Jesus or are sought by Jesus (vv. 22a, 32) before prostrating themselves before him (vv. 22b, 33b).
♦ Both stories revolve around "daughters": one, actual (v. 23); the other, figurative (v. 34).
♦ Both women are in dire straits. One, twelve years of age, lies at death's door (vv. 23a, 42b); the other is a victim of incessant menstruation for twelve

13. See Jonathan L. Walton, *Watch This! The Ethics and Aesthetics of Black Televangelism* (New York: New York University Press, 2009); Kate Bowler, *Blessed: A History of the American Prosperity Gospel* (Oxford: Oxford University Press, 2013).

Fig. 18. Markan intercalations of passages
(interlaminations or sandwiches)

Framing Unit (The Bread Slices)	Interpolated Unit (The Filling between Them)
2:1–5a + 2:10b–12	2:5b–10a
The healing of the paralytic	Jesus' authority to forgive
3:1–3 + 3:5b–6	3:4–5a
The healing of a man with a withered hand	Jesus' healing on the Sabbath
3:19b–21 + 3:31–35	3:22–30
Jesus' family in opposition	The scribes' controversy over Beelzebul and forgiveness
5:21–24a + 5:35–43	5:24b–34
Jesus' healing of Jairus's daughter	Jesus' healing of the hemorrhaging woman
6:6b–13 + 6:30	6:14–29
The mission of the Twelve	The death of John the Baptist
11:12–14 + 11:20–25	11:15–19
Jesus' cursing of a fig tree	Jesus' assault on temple practice
14:1–2 + 14:10–11	14:3–9
Judas's collusion with the chief priests	A woman's anointing of Jesus
14:53–54 + 14:66–72	14:55–65
Outside: Peter's denial of Jesus	Inside: Jesus' acknowledgment of his messiahship
15:6–15 + 15:21–32	15:16–20
The sentencing and execution of Jesus	The soldiers' mockery of Jesus

years (v. 25). Absent healing, neither will ever experience the joy of childbirth (Ps 113:9).

♦ Their medical cases are hopeless. One "spent all she had" on ineffectual treatments that aggravated her life's seepage (Mark 5:26): "for the blood is the life" (Deut 12:23). The other is dying (Mark 5:23) and will soon be pronounced dead (v. 35a).

♦ Professionals—physicians (v. 26a) or hired mourners (v. 38; cf. Jer 9:17–20)—have proved useless. Spectators react stupidly (Mark 5:31), callously (v. 35), or derisively (v. 40a).

♦ Cryptically (vv. 30, 39), Jesus responds by rejecting those who balk (vv. 32, 36) or ejecting them from the premises (v. 40b).

♦ Perpetual bleeding and death are both ritually defiling, impossible to purify, and socially alienating (Lev 15:19–20; Num 19:11–13). By touch—either the sufferer's (Mark 5:27–28) or the healer's (vv. 23, 41)—the polarity of contamination is reversed.

♦ The Greek verb for their restorations is identical: "made well" (*sōthē*, v. 23/ *sesōken*, v. 34).
♦ In both cases of healing the prerequisite is *pistis*: have "faith" (v. 34a), "believe" (v. 36b), recognizing in Jesus a trustworthy agent of God's curative power (vv. 23, 27–28).
♦ In both cases the greatest challenge to trust is fear (*phobētheisa*, v. 33b//*phobou*, v. 36b).

Random chance would account for a couple of these correspondences. More than a dozen shows deliberate craftsmanship. Mark has twinned these tales with reverberating details. Notice, too, how much longer Mark's version runs than the other Synoptic accounts: 377 Greek words, compared with 292 in Luke 8:40–56 and 139 in Matthew 9:18–26. Commentators who sneer at Mark's verbosity have missed the point: digesting this narrative sandwich takes a lot longer in the Second Gospel—*and time is of the essence.* Unlike Matthew's version, in which Jairus's daughter has just died (9:18), in Mark she is on death's verge, dangling by a thread (5:23). That starts the clock ticking.

Fig. 19. Fourth-century fresco of Christ's healing a woman with an issue of blood, in the Catacombs of Marcellinus and Peter (Rome). Scan from André Grabar, *Die Kunst des frühen Christentums* (Munich: C. H. Beck, 1967).

The storyteller piles on details: some important, others trivial: an obstructive crowd (v. 24b); the woman's case history (vv. 25–26); her deliberation (v. 28) and desperate maneuver (v. 27); Jesus' standstill, interrogation, and search for her (vv. 30–32); the woman's rehearsal of many of these details implied by "the whole truth" (v. 33). All these items in vv. 24–34 take time to recount, devouring precious minutes as a child's life dwindles away. "*While* they were talking"—reminding the reader that the delay in 5:24b–34 needn't have happened—messengers arrive from Jairus's house: "Your daughter's dead. Why are you still bothering the teacher?" The clock's second hand has reached twelve. For a report so heartrending, the language is heartless and witless: Jesus is more than a teacher, as both the reader and Jairus understand, and the synagogue official has hardly been troubling him. The listener's emotions are whipsawed by contesting emergencies. For twelve long years that poor woman's life had bled out of her. When power reciprocally flowed from him (v. 30)—a miracle occurring for both the healer and the healed—Jesus gave this daughter more attention than she wanted (vv. 32–34). But what of Jairus's daughter? After a dozen years, would an hour's delay have mattered to the menstruating woman? For Jairus, it certainly does. For his little girl, it's now too late. Or is it?

When the scene shifts to Jairus's house (5:38), Mark does not hasten things to a conclusion. The second story is unfolded in excruciating detail. Beyond their scorn of Jesus (v. 40a), the very presence of mourners-for-hire explains his expulsion of them: their grief is remunerated, certainly faithless, premature, and as pointless as the woman's medical expenses (v. 26). Jesus' reply to their sobbing is mysterious: "Why your racket and crying? The child isn't dead but only sleeping" (v. 39). That raises a derisory laugh, echoing the skepticism of first the disciples and then those of Jairus's household in 5:31 and 35, which prompts Jesus to bounce the mourners from the death chamber (5:40ab). With the father and mother, Jesus and his associates (v. 37) cross the threshold where the child lies (v. 40c). Jesus has just been defiled by the touch of a woman with a bloody discharge (v. 27); now, in v. 41, he is defiled by touching a presumed corpse. "'*Talitha koumi*' [some MSS], which means, 'Little girl, get up!'" (5:41), is one of several Semitic expressions that Mark translates for a Greek-speaking audience that would not have understood them (see also 7:11, 34; 11:9–10; 14:36; 15:22, 34, 42). Early Christians could have heard in Mark's terms for the child's rising, *egeirō* ("get up," 5:41) and *anistēmi* ("got up," 5:42), the language of resurrection (see 6:14; 12:23–26; 16:6, 9). At Jesus' command the little girl arises and, perhaps to verify her vitality's permanence (cf. 5:34b), walks about (5:42a). That she be given something to eat (5:43b) may reflect the folk wisdom that ghosts cannot eat (cf. Luke 24:29–42). Because mealtimes in the Bible are occasions for social reintegration (2 Kgs 25:27–30; Sir 31:12–32:13), Jesus is doing for the child the same as he did for her elder "sister." Far from being defiled, Jesus has fully restored two of Israel's daughters to their proper homes and communities, from which they had been terribly estranged.

To know Jesus in Mark, the reader needs to penetrate beneath the Galilean prophet, acknowledging that only one so attuned to "the mystery of God's kingdom" (4:11), parabolically cloaked (4:3–34), can deploy its power for the reclamation of God's world from chaos and disease. Jesus is God's eschatological agent, retaking the field of a damaged creation from the forces of its diabolical occupation and restoring the ecology of God's sovereignty on earth (1:32–34; 3:11–12). When Jesus is so viewed, his teaching becomes intelligible, important, and trustworthy. That is why those whose vision of Jesus is constricted or warped by animosity (3:21–23), fear (5:15, 17), or overfamiliarity (6:3) are unable to receive his help. They do not want it. If they did, they would need to own up to their own sickness instead of trying to convince the physician that he's as sick as they are (2:17; 3:22). Those who sincerely (2:5, 11–12; 3:1–5; 5:23)—albeit dementedly (1:23–24; 5:6–7), gutlessly (4:38), or surreptitiously (5:27–28)—seek God's healing from Jesus are never disappointed.

In Mark 5:21–43 and throughout this Gospel, Jesus' mighty works are noteworthy, not so much for their happy endings as for what they disclose about observers' *faith*.[14] Trust (*pistis*) is a human response to calamitous, usually hopeless situations: impregnable obstacles (2:1–12), peril at sea (4:35–41), possession by a demonic (5:1–20), chronic and incurable illness (5:24b–34), sickness that tips over into death (5:21–24a + 35–43). In Mark, Jesus' mighty works do not stimulate belief. The sequence flows in reverse: first comes faith, fostering the conditions under which God's power to restore, mobilized by Jesus, can be realized (5:23; 34a). The opposite of faith is not atheism: it's *fear* (4:40; 5:15–17; 6:50–52; 9:32; 10:32; 16:8). Within the human heart, faith and fear fight it out. Though her situation is hopeless and she's terrified (5:33), the woman bulls her way through the crowd to touch Jesus (5:24b–28). No matter how fatal the news, Jesus encourages Jairus, "Keep trusting" (5:36). Faith in Mark is neither a block of unassailable belief nor an arrow released irrevocably toward its target. Faith waxes and wanes, veering like an oscillating fan from one extreme or another, caught for a time by weak mortals before slipping from their grasp. "I believe; help my unbelief!" cries the anguished father of another sick child (9:24). Not even Jesus himself is spared this internal conflict: "I am deeply grieved, even to death. . . . Abba, Father, . . . remove this cup from me; yet, not what I want, but what you want" (14:34, 36 NRSV). That prayer of Jesus is answered the following day, on the cross toward which he has been inexorably pressing.

---

14. An excellent study of this subject is Christopher D. Marshall, *Faith as a Theme in Mark's Narrative*, SNTSMS 64 (Cambridge: Cambridge University Press, 1989).

Fig. 20. Gethsemane, adjacent to the Roman Catholic Church of All Nations, at the foot of the Mount of Olives in Jerusalem. Photograph by Clifton Black.

A PARABOLIC DEATH

About one-third of Mark's Gospel is dedicated to Jesus' last week in Jerusalem. The evangelist slackens his narrative's pace, stretching time so that every episode in chapters 11–15 carries weight. From Jesus' entrance into the city until his observance of Passover, the evangelist clocks the final days (11:1, 12, 20; 14:1, 12). After Jesus' arrest (14:43–52), trial by the Sanhedrin (14:53–65), and transfer to Roman custody (15:1–5), Mark tolls the terminal hours (15:1, 25, 33a, 33b, 42). The climax comes at Golgotha, "Skull Place" (*kraniou topos*, 15:22), which Jerome's late fourth-century Vulgate translated into Latin as *Calvariae locum* (Calvary Place). Golgotha answers Gethsemane (14:32–42): the Son of Man is delivered into human hands (9:31). The violence smearing his arrest— swords, clubs, a slave's ear butchered (14:47–48)—is wantonly unleashed. As was written of John the Baptist, Jesus' Elijah-like precursor, so it follows for his successor. Both have come, and people did to them whatever they pleased (9:12–13; cf. 1:14, 6:14–29).

The horror of crucifixion is underappreciated by modern readers. In our era its use for capital punishment is rare. (Amnesty International verified its legality in the United Arab Emirates as recently as 1997.)[15] Crucifixion was the impaling of a victim's hands or wrists, genitals, and ankles or feet onto a stake and crossbar. Its raison d'être was public, protracted, humiliating torture. The victim's death had multiple causes: agony, exposure, and asphyxiation when gravity's force prevented the chest cavity's elevation. Crushing the victim's ankles (*crucifragium*, John 19:31b–32) was the coup de grâce. Even after death the barbarism continued: "The vulture hurries from dead cattle and dogs and crosses to bring some of the carrion to her offspring" (*Sat.* 14.77–78). The supreme penalty over incineration, beheading, or a simple noose (*Verres* 2.5.168), crucifixion was decreed by the Roman imperium for punishing seditionists, violent criminals, and revolutionary slaves (*Ass* 3.9.1–2; *Sat.* 6.219–22). Witnesses wrote of it with revulsion (*Rab.* 16; *Dial.* 6; *Ep.* 101). Josephus, who had witnessed many Jews crucified during Titus's siege of Jerusalem in 70, called it "the most wretched of deaths" (*B.J.* 7.203).

Meanwhile, a certain Jew, found innocent by a Roman prefect (Mark 15:14), is hanging between two freedom fighters, also crucified. Mark needn't spell out the grisly details: his audience knows them well. Still, the narrator's restraint is remarkable, especially when compared with the cinematic sadomasochism of Mel Gibson's *The Passion of the Christ* (2004). Mark 15:24 makes a simple statement in the Greek historical present tense: "And they crucify him." Within 15:21–41, that report is embedded in a dissonant, tritonal chord.

The Scriptural Soundtrack

Like a fine film composer, Mark weaves into his narration subliminal themes plucked from the HB, all of which convey scriptural fulfillment (14:49b). Already the evangelist has done this while recounting Jesus' Last Supper with the Twelve and his testimony during his trial by Jerusalem's high council:

"You will all fall away; for it is written, 'I will strike the shepherd, and the sheep will be scattered.'" (Mark 14:27)	"Strike the shepherd, that the sheep may be scattered." (Zech 13:7)
And Jesus said, "I am; and you will see the Son of Man	"I saw in the night visions, and behold, there came one like a son of man. . . ." (Dan 7:13)
seated at the right hand of Power,	The LORD says to my lord: "Sit at my right hand. . . ." (Ps 110:1)
and coming with the clouds of heaven." (Mark 14:62)	". . . with the clouds of heaven." (Dan 7:13)

15. Amnesty International: "UAE: Fear of Imminent Crucifixion and Execution," September 1997, https://www.amnesty.org/en/documents/MDE25/011/1997/en/.

Likewise, during Jesus' crucifixion, Scripture (RSV) resonates for those with ears to hear it:

And they crucified him, and <u>divided</u> his <u>garments</u> <u>among them</u>, <u>casting lots</u> for them. . . . (Mark 15:24)	They <u>divide</u> my <u>garments among them</u>, and for my raiment they <u>cast lots.</u> (Ps 22:18)
And those who passed by derided him, <u>wagging</u> <u>their heads.</u> (Mark 15:29)	All who see me mock at me; . . . they <u>wag their heads.</u> (Ps 22:7) My accusers . . . <u>wag their heads.</u> (Ps 109.25)
Jesus cried with a loud voice, . . . "<u>My God, my God,</u> <u>why hast thou forsaken me?</u>" (Mark 15:34)	<u>My God, my God,</u> <u>why hast thou forsaken me?</u> (Ps 22:1)
And one ran and, filling a sponge full of <u>vinegar</u> . . . <u>gave</u> it to him <u>to drink.</u> (Mark 15:36)	They gave me poison for food, <u>and</u> for my thirst they <u>gave</u> me <u>vinegar to drink.</u> (Ps 69:21)

Unmistakable as they are, these reverberations are not denoted by Mark as fulfillment of scriptural promises (cf. 1:2–3; 7:6), even less as credible proof of Jesus' messiahship and his mission's validity. Instead, they function more allusively, tinting Jesus' death with OT sepia that enables the listener to visualize the ways in which "the Son of Man goes as it is written of him" (14:21). Jesus dies, not by accident, but according to an elliptical plan designed by God and unwittingly executed by human participants—except, of course, Jesus himself, who realizes exactly what he is doing and why.

The Irony of It All

Mark is a master dramatic ironist:[16] never more conspicuously than in his passion narrative, never more pointedly than when recounting Jesus' crucifixion and death. The *reader*, beneficiary of the evangelist's guidance, can perceive with greater clarity what is happening than the story's characters, who act and speak in ways either profoundly correct or sometimes inaccurate without realizing their full significance. By the time we've reached this Gospel's climax, that dramatic irony crashes in intense, relentless waves.

♦ In another intercalation of passages (Mark 14:1–2 and 14:10–11 enclosing 14:3–9), Mark inserts the tale of Jesus' beautiful anointing by an anonymous disciple inside Judas' machinations with his teacher's would-be killers. Jesus'

---

16. "Irony occurs when the elements of the story line provoke the reader to see beneath the surface of the text to a deeper significance." Jerry Camery-Hoggatt, *Irony in Mark's Gospel: Text and Subtext*, SNTSMS 72 (Cambridge: Cambridge University Press, 1992), 1.

interpretation of his anointment as an embalming for his burial (v. 8) coincides with Judas and the chief priests' scheme to expedite Jesus into his grave. Though the reader never learns the name of the woman who did "what she could" (v. 8), Jesus avers that what she has done will be remembered wherever the gospel is preached (v. 9). Thanks to Mark, it has been remembered. Judas also did what he could. For that, neither has he ever been forgotten.

♦ Mark's association of Passover with the religious leaders' scheme (14:2, 12) whispers more irony. Passover is Israel's signal remembrance of its liberation from foreign oppression (m. Pesaḥ 10.1–9). In all the Gospels, this Passover would be remembered for its shotgun wedding of Israel's hierarchy with their Roman overlords, owing to a perceived need to destroy Jesus.

♦ The most outrageous setting for a trusted confidant to knife his patron is at the dinner table: in Eastern culture, the setting where acquaintances become family (cf. Ps 41:9). This is precisely the place for Jesus' betrayal—as good as done according to Jesus' prediction—not only by "one dipping bread in the same dish with me" (14:20), but, in fact, by all of his supper companions (14:27).

♦ Simon Peter, emphatic in his fealty (8:29, 32–33; 9:5; 10:28; 11:21), twice repudiates Jesus' prediction of his threefold defection, to take place before the cock has twice crowed that very night (14:29–31a). Peter's peers join with him in equally strong protestations of their allegiance (14:31b). Jesus holds fast to his forecast, promising his own postmortem fidelity to them in Galilee (14:28; cf. 16:7). Mark twists the ironies past and coming even more tightly: Jesus' mandate that his followers must deny themselves (8:34); their precipitate refutation of their imminent denials of Jesus; his denial of himself by giving up his life out of loyalty to those who will prove traitorous.

♦ At Gethsemane, Jesus asks Peter, James, and John to "to stay awake" (*grēgoreite*, 14:34), just as he had instructed them two days earlier on the Mount of Olives (13:33, 35, 37). Interrupting his agonized prayer, three times Jesus returns to his waiting trio and finds them asleep every time (14:37a, 40a, 41a) when they ought to have been as vigilant as servants in Jesus' parable: expected to stay alert for their master's return (13:37; cf. vv. 33–37). Simon can't keep his eyes open for even an hour (14:37).

♦ At the arrest (14:43–50) "the scriptures [are] fulfilled" (14:49b). Judas's identification of Jesus *with a kiss* is deeply ironic since a rabbi was entitled to receive such affection from a devoted disciple (Prov 27:6). Yet another ironic touch: Jesus is apprehended as a would-be "bandit" (*lēstēs*). Jesus is no revolutionist, but he likened those buying and selling in the temple to brigands (*lēstai*) who take refuge in their lair (Mark 11:17).

♦ A youthful follower fled naked into the night, leaving behind his linen garment (*sindōn*: 14:51–52). Jesus' corpse will be wrapped in a *sindōn*, a linen winding sheet (15:46).

♦ During Jesus' nocturnal trial by the Sanhedrin, portrayed by Mark as a kangaroo court, the high priest's direct question of the defendant cracks open the proceedings in a way the judge cannot understand: "You are the Christ, the Son of the Blessed?" (14:61). In Greek this clause is a *declarative* statement; only the context (14:60) suggests its formulation as a question. Hence, a crucial irony is in effect, though not by intention: the high priest addresses his prisoner using the very titles of reverence toward Jesus and God that early Christians adopted as central in proclaiming the gospel (cf. 1:1, 11; Matt 16:16; John 20:31; Rom 9:5; Eph 1:3). At Caesarea Philippi, Peter's confession of Jesus as the Christ was immediately silenced (Mark 8:29–30). Here at 14:62, Jesus accepts another's oblivious acclamation ("I am," 14:62) in the very moment that it will seal his death warrant (10:33–34). Mark repeats the same ironic technique, with equivalent consequences, in 15:2a: Pilate's address the next morning to Jesus, "[So] you are the king of the Jews."

◆ After the guilty verdict has been returned, Jesus is abused by bullies taunting him to prophesy (14:64–65). Just outside, Jesus' prediction in 14:30 that Peter will deny him is coming to pass. Mark has sandwiched Jesus' interrogation (14:54–65) inside the questions to Peter (14:53 + 14:66–72). Each ironically interprets the other. Jesus stands at the center of his trial (v. 55); Peter, "at a distance" (v. 54), withdraws (v. 68b). Jesus is arraigned before Jerusalem's elite, with murderous intent (vv. 53–55); Peter, confronted by nobodies, is never threatened (vv. 66, 69, 70b). The questions put to Jesus are false (vv. 56–58) and incoherent (vv. 56, 59); the comments to Peter are crisp and accurate (vv. 67, 69, 70). Jesus holds his ground, truthfully acknowledging his identity (vv. 61a, 62); Peter retreats, lying about himself and Jesus (vv. 68, 70a, 71). Jesus is falsely charged with cursing God (v. 64a); Peter curses with prevarication (v. 71). His lies about his discipleship (14:70a) reveal the unintended truth about himself and all of the Twelve: "I neither know nor understand what you are saying" (v. 68; cf. 4:13; 6:52; 8:17, 21). In reply to an accurate identification of him (v. 70b), Peter finally says, "I don't know this man you are talking about" (v. 71): the last words uttered by a disciple in Mark. Peter not only lies about Jesus; he's also denying the truth about himself. By rejecting Jesus, cravenly trying to save his own life, Peter has lost himself—just as Jesus has promised (8:35–37).

◆ Jesus' crucifixion is layered with yet more ironies. Five times "the King of the Jews" is applied to Jesus (15:2, 9, 12, 18, 26), and nobody believes it. In 15:6–15 a convicted murderer, Barabbas (lit., "Son of the Father"), is released, thanks to another "Son" of a different "Father" (1:11; 9:7; 13:32; 14:36 [*Abba*]) who, by imperial concession, has done no evil (15:14). One Simon (of Cyrene) is compelled to carry Jesus' crossbeam (15:21); another Simon (Peter) refused to "take up his cross and follow [Jesus]" (8:34). Two seditionists are crucified, one on Jesus' right and the other on his left (15:27): the status positions for which two of the Twelve had jockeyed (10:35–38). The taunt, "He saved others; he cannot save himself" (15:31), ignorantly inverts Jesus' affirmation of his destiny as Son of Man, "who came not to be served, but to serve, and to give his life as a ransom for many" (10:45). When Jesus cries "Eloi, Eloi" ("My God, my God," 15:34), some mistake his summons as being to Elijah (15:35): Jesus is addressing God; his auditors misunderstand the cry as one to Elijah, whom they may have thought might return to save Jesus.[17] A sponge is soaked with vinegar and put on a reed, extended to the victim in one last unavailing attempt to pump Jesus' miraculous rescue from

17. In later rabbinic texts that likely reflect earlier traditions, Elijah was believed to be the vigilant protector of the innocent in evil times (b. ʾAbodah Zarah 18b; b. Šabbat 33b; b. Baba Meṣiʿa 84a). Matthew 27:46 clarifies Mark's point by substituting "Eli" for "Eloi" in Jesus' cry from the cross.

Fig. 21. Léon Bonnat, *Christ on the Cross* (1874). Housed in the Petit Palais, Paris.

heaven (15:36): an act so misbegotten that it sets the mind reeling. Before crucifixion Jesus refused an analgesic (v. 23). Why would he accept this now? Still the Son of Man goes as it is written of him (14:21, 49b), to the bitterest end. The previous offering was probably a painkiller; this is vinegar (*oxos*), stuck on a stick (*kalamos*) of the sort the soldiers used to club him (15:19). The runner fulfills Scripture by unintentionally mimicking another's lament (Ps 69:21). A faithless generation seeks a sign (Mark 8:11–12)—even one so gruesome as the showstopping rescue of a tortured innocent. The reader *knows* no sign is forthcoming, because in John the Baptist, Elijah already has returned and was decapitated (6:27–28; 9:13). During his ministry few have understood Jesus. At his death their stupidity persists.

♦ After Jesus' death, "the centurion, who stood facing him, saw that he in this way breathed his last and said: 'Truly this man was God's son'" (15:39). For the first and only time in this Gospel, a mortal other than Jesus himself has correctly identified him as God's son. That is supremely ironic. While Gentiles have been well disposed to Jesus (3:8; 5:20; 7:24–31), this one was among Jesus' executioners. Moreover, a Roman legionnaire would betray his imperial fealty by acclaiming anyone other than Caesar Augustus a *divi filius*, a divine son. Still more: Mark clearly states that this soldier has witnessed nothing other than the traumatic death of another crucified Jew (cf. Matt 27:51b–54; Luke 23:39–47). And yet more: there's no way to determine whether the centurion confesses sincere faith or is every bit as sarcastic as the high priest (Mark 14:61), Pilate (15:9), and the rabble's taunt (15:32). Mark's readers know that Jesus' executioner speaks the truth. Does the speaker know that?

Abandonment

More than any other Gospel, Mark's account of Jesus' death stands out for its sheer terror. The whole earth is plunged into darkness (14:33; cf. Amos 8:9). In abject shame the crucified Jesus is completely abandoned: without friends (Mark 14:50; cf. Luke 23:48; John 19:25–27), bereft of any consolation. His family has been absent since 3:19, 31–32; all of the Twelve forsook him in 14:50, 66–72. All the characters at Golgotha have turned against him, sadistically enjoying the spectacle (15:29–32a)—even those crucified with him, who should know better than anyone what he is enduring (v. 32b; cf. Luke 23:39–43). There remain only a few female disciples, but even they witness the proceedings "from a distance" (Mark 15:40–41). The nightmare of crucifixion was a given. To die in this way utterly derelict, *altogether alone*, is a plunge into hell. Worst of all: in 15:34, Jesus stares into God's veiled face and asks why the Almighty "has left him in the lurch" (*enkatelipes*). To an apparently absent God, Jesus hurls back the intense, personal address that the heavenly voice has twice used in addressing the beloved Jesus: "You are *my* son" (1:11), "This is *my* son" (9:7). The dying Jesus, none other than the beloved Son, prays to "*my* God, *my* God," who, like everyone else, has evidently deserted him.

Some commentators reject this godforsaken interpretation. They suggest that Jesus' last words in Mark, replicating the opening of Psalm 22, point one to that psalm's concluding verses, which describe the psalmist's vow of thanksgiving for healing (vv. 25–31). I've never been convinced by that argument. Had the evangelist wished to place on the dying Jesus' lips a promise from the last verse, "The poor will eat and be satisfied" (Ps 22:26a NIV), he could easily have done so. Are some interpreters unnerved by Mark's lacerating cry of dereliction? Certainly this Gospel does not end with the calm equanimity of Socrates (ca. 470–399 BCE), who, "holding the cup of hemlock to his lips, readily and cheerfully quaffed the poison" (*Phaedo* 57, 117); or the philosophy of the Stoic emperor Marcus Aurelius Antoninus: "Then leave [this life] satisfied, for he also who releases you is satisfied" (*Med.* 12.36). Still, Jesus does not die by cursing God (cf. Job 2:9). He dies, himself accursed (Deut 21:22–23; Gal 3:13), praying to the God whose presence now eludes him. Jesus replicates the cry of the epileptic child's father: "I trust; help my lack of trust" (Mark 9:24).

On a cellar's walls in Cologne, where Jews hid from Nazis, these words were inscribed:

I believe in the sun even when it is not shining.
I believe in love even when feeling it not.
I believe in God even when He is silent.[18]

Is there a prayer more faithful than one addressed to the God whose presence is
no longer palpable?

Mark the Molder

A Conversation with Elizabeth Shively

*Elizabeth Evans Shively (PhD, Emory) is Professor of Christian Scriptures at the
George W. Truett Theological Seminary of Baylor University. For eleven years
formerly she taught New Testament at the University of St Andrews (Scotland);
before that, she served on the pastoral staff of Park Street Church in Boston
(1998–2004). Currently she is preparing a monograph on Gospel genre for
Oxford University Press and a commentary on the Greek text of Mark's Gospel
for Wm. B. Eerdmans. Dr. Shively and her husband, Todd, live in Waco, Texas,
and have two adult children, Evan and Jack.*

*CCB: Elizabeth, most of your published scholarship has been devoted to the
Gospel of Mark. What is it about this Gospel that has captured your attention?*

EES: I love Mark because it is uncluttered. It moves quickly to work out who
Jesus is, what he came to do, and what it means to follow him. There's a simplicity to it, but that doesn't mean Mark is simple. In fact, it's pretty thorny. Mark
has knotty parts, knotty people, and knotty sayings that make it challenging
to untangle exactly what he wishes to say about who Jesus is, what he came
to do, and what it means to follow him. I think this mixture of simplicity and
complexity is what keeps me coming back.

*CCB: Of all the Synoptics' portraits of Jesus, Mark's has long struck me as
among the most enigmatic. Do you agree? If someone asked you what Mark
believes about Jesus, what would you say?*

EES: I agree, and I think what Mark believes about Jesus—or at least how he
goes about explaining what he believes about Jesus—is part of what makes this
Gospel mysterious. Mark says what he believes in the very first verse: Jesus is
the Messiah, God's promised redeemer. The rest of the Gospel then unpacks

---

18. Nathan N. Glatzer, ed., *The Schocken Passover Haggadah* (New York: Schocken Books, 1996), xxvii.

who the "Messiah" is and what he does. But Mark's unpackaging is neither straightforward nor anticipated. In my view, Mark paints a portrait of Jesus as God's Spirit-anointed Messiah and Son, who carries out the Servant's mission to extend God's kingly power through his suffering, death, and exaltation. This portrait is unexpected, because suffering and dying don't fit the typical messianic profile. And it isn't straightforward, because Mark renders this portrait through a narrative that mostly shows but only sometimes tells what "Messiah" means.

CCB: As you well know, Mark's portrayal of Jesus' disciples, particularly the Twelve, is stark and most unflattering. Why does Mark come down so hard on Jesus' chosen followers?

EES: Mark's portrayal of the Twelve captures how difficult it was for Jesus' earliest followers to grasp the nature of both Jesus' mission and their own. While that portrayal probably reflects something of the historical disciples, I think it also reflects something of Mark's theological and practical aims. He wants to show what it looks like for people to figure out who this Jesus is and how to follow him. The disciples really want to follow Jesus, but they fail, utterly. Yet this isn't the end of the story. In the same breath with which he predicts that his disciples will abandon and deny him, Jesus promises to go before them to Galilee after God raises him (14:27–28). There, under those circumstances, they will see him. Ultimately the "success" of discipleship doesn't depend on human loyalty, but on God's faithfulness. Anyone trying to follow Jesus in a hostile environment can relate to this portrayal and ultimately find hope.

CCB: Another aspect of Mark that puzzles me and many scholars is its appropriation of the HB. What's your view of this?

EES: Mark's narration is what gives meaningful coherence to his use of Scripture. We can't understand Mark's use of Scripture in isolation. It makes sense only in the context of his story. Mark's statement that the good news of Jesus the Messiah is according to Isaiah the prophet (1:2) provides an overarching framework for the Gospel that facilitates interpretation of the rest of the narrative. I think Mark musters a "plot" from Isaiah 40–66. Isaiah unfolds the announcement of the Lord's coming reign, the suffering and exaltation of the Lord's Servant for Israel's redemption and the Lord's universal reign (Isa 40–55), and then applies the Servant's mission to righteous servants who continue the Servant's mission in the face of opposition after he is gone (Isa 54, 56–66). Mark incorporates other Scriptures—like Daniel 7; Psalms 22, 68, 110; and Zechariah 14—that both cohere with and elaborate this Isaianic plot as he interprets and applies it to God's activity, to Jesus, and to his followers' mission.

Mark uses Hebrew Scriptures to persuade his earliest audiences—and audiences of every age—to *confess* that this suffering Messiah is the one through whom God establishes his reign, and then to *continue* Jesus' mission as a community of servant-followers in the face of hostility and suffering until he returns.

CCB: A lot of other things in Mark, and only in Mark, stump me. For instance, Jesus conveys to outsiders everything in parables, with the express intention of preventing their repentance (4:12). That flatly contradicts his earlier mandate that listeners should repent and believe in the gospel (1:15). Moreover, "those about him with the Twelve" have been given the mystery of God's kingdom (4:11), but the insiders seem as confused as "those outside" this group. What sense do you make of all this?

EES: This is one of Mark's fattest knots, and I'm still trying to untie it. Here are some thoughts. Jesus' mandate to repent and believe in the gospel in light of God's coming kingdom is programmatic for the whole narrative. If we take seriously this initial call to repent, then forgiveness is one of the key benefits of God's kingdom (thus, 2:10, 17). The problem is that many don't understand or receive Jesus and his message. For instance, Jesus' kin and certain scribes refuse to see and hear Jesus' mission to bring God's kingdom. As a result, they find themselves without forgiveness and outside the house where Jesus forms a new "family" that does God's will (3:22–35). This new family is the same group that surrounds Jesus to ask for understanding when he tells parables. Jesus says that they receive parables, like everyone else, but they also receive the mystery of God's kingdom (4:11, 33–34). By contrast, those outside—like the scribes and kin who reject him—receive *everything* in parables, so that they may neither perceive nor understand nor be forgiven. In my view, Jesus uses Isaiah 6:9–10 to explain a problem that has already begun to play out in Mark's story and will continue to develop. The mystery of the kingdom has to do with its unanticipated nature, which pivots on the unanticipated nature of the Messiah: his suffering and death. In spite of Jesus' special teaching, insiders won't be able to grasp it until after he is raised from the dead (8:27–10:45).

CCB: As my readers will soon encounter, Mark's ending baffles us. Our best Greek texts end at 16:8 with the women, informed of Jesus' resurrection and commissioned to proclaim it, fleeing the empty tomb in fearful silence. Do you think Mark wrote a longer ending that never survived, or did Mark intend to end his Gospel with such an abrupt surprise?

EES: While I can't prove it, I think it most likely that 16:8 is the intended ending. Perhaps someone objects and says that Mark partakes of a genre, like ancient biography or novel, that invites suitable closure. I reply that generic rules were made to be broken. Ancient writers could depart from generic rules to make rhetorical points. In fact, abrupt or "open" endings were not uncommon in Jewish, Greco-Roman, and even New Testament literature: thus, the book of Jonah; Homer's *Iliad* and *Odyssey*; Vergil's *Aeneid*; and Luke's Acts of the Apostles. The probability that Mark broke the rules at the end for a rhetorical purpose increases when we consider the Gospel's literary and sociohistorical contexts. Mark has created a portrait of disciples called to imitate Jesus in a suffering–dying–rising pattern but are unable to do so because of their imperception, faithlessness, and fear. The ending at 16:8 fits this pattern. Moreover, we only need to read Paul's Letters to see that a crucified Messiah *was* a stumbling block to belief in the gospel (1 Cor 1:23). This social context suggests that Mark's portrait of the disciples' struggle reflects the experience of early Christ-followers. And so Mark's ending, like the Gospel as a whole, aims to shape the real-life thinking and actions of early Christians. Jesus' disciples, probably not unlike many in Mark's earliest audiences, increasingly struggle [in the narrative] to grasp the logic of suffering, dying, and rising that informs Jesus' own submission to God's will as the Lord's Servant—the Isaianic plotline to which I've referred. Rhetorically, then, the unresolved ending achieves a couple of things. First, by announcing God's resurrection of Jesus, it confirms that this Messiah who suffered and died is now vindicated and exalted. Second, it invites an informed audience to embrace Jesus' suffering–dying–rising as servants who join with the disciples in Galilee to look for the risen Christ and expect his return as the Son of Man while they continue his missional activity (Mark 13).

CCB: Your earliest monograph considers Apocalyptic Imagination in the Gospel of Mark.[19] *What do you mean by that? If twenty-first-century readers allow Mark to shape their imaginations apocalyptically, how might that reconfigure the way they view everything else?*

EES: At the root of Mark's apocalyptic imagination is Mark's narrative imagination. What I mean is that narrative provides Mark with a way of creating a world that presents an alternative to the one considered real and a mode of discourse counter to what is currently on offer. Mark's apocalyptic imagination is generated by weaving apocalyptic language and themes throughout the narrative to reveal a spatial setting and time frame that can't be seen with the naked eye. Conflict between God's kingdom and Satan's kingdom is the setting for Jesus' mission and that of his followers (1:12–13; 3:22–35). History is

---

19. Subtitled *The Literary and Theological Role of Mark 3:22–30*, BZNW 189 (New York: Walter de Gruyter, 2012).

moving toward the goal of Jesus' return as the Son of Man to judge those who are ashamed of him and to vindicate those who endure to proclaim the gospel (8:34–9:1; 13:1–37). By shaping this spatial-temporal world, Mark gives audiences of all times the eyes to see what human vision would otherwise miss regarding the experience of rejection, suffering, domination, and worldly power. The suffering and death of the Messiah and the persecution of his followers look like failure to human eyes; an apocalyptic imagination reinterprets these experiences as countercultural success and even divine necessity. As it did in the first century, Mark's apocalyptic imagination provides a positive lens through which today's Christ-followers maintain their identity as servants who continue to proclaim the gospel in a hostile environment. This is crucial, because our culture relentlessly measures success in terms other than self-sacrificial service. Mark's apocalyptic imagination also reminds us that evil is real and pervades our world. It gives us eyes to see that we possess the spirit of the risen Christ (13:9–13), so that we may—and should—courageously name and resist evil, even if it results in ostracism or suffering. It also gives us eyes to see that we can—and should—persevere because God has determined evil's end.

CCB: Whether the reader be Christian or not, is Mark still worth reading?

EES: Yes! There is a humanity to Mark's Gospel that is unique and sometimes downright uncomfortable when compared to the other Gospels. This contributes to the knottiness I mentioned at the beginning of our conversation. But the knottiness of Jesus' and his disciples' humanity challenges me every time I work through Mark. I'm forced to look at knotty actions like prayer and prayerlessness, faithfulness and betrayal, understanding and imperception, and knotty emotions like anger, love, regret, anguish, and fear. Working through a story like Mark's has a way of confronting me with my own humanity: the sort of human I ought to be as I seek to follow Jesus. In *Signposts in a Strange Land,* Walker Percy writes, "Bad books always lie. They lie most of all about the human condition, so that one never recognizes oneself, the deepest part of oneself, in a bad book."[20] Mark is a good book. Because of this, its narrative can perform a normative function in the church and society, not only by holding up a mirror to the reality of human frailty, but also by communicating the surety of God's faithfulness, and the grace, forgiveness, and love of Jesus.

CCB: Thank you, Professor Shively, for writing such good and learned books about a good and truthful book.

---

20. Walker Percy, *Signposts in a Strange Land,* ed. Patrick Samway (New York: Farrar, Straus & Giroux, 2000), 364.

A Parabolic Finish

"They said nothing to nobody—they were afraid, you see."

That's a fairly literal, inelegant English rendering of our best Greek manuscripts of Mark 16:8. Could the evangelist have ended his Gospel like this?

Various manuscripts, later and of inferior quality in Greek, add endings to Mark. The best known, appearing in the KJV, includes 16:9–20, which contains vocabulary that deviates from the rest of the Gospel and appears to be a pastiche of elements drawn from the others (see Matt 28:16–20; Luke 24:13–35; John 20:1–18; cf. Acts 28:3–6). Clearly later copyists of Mark were unsettled by its abrupt conclusion at 16:8 and tried to give it an ending in greater conformity with the other Gospels' conclusions.[21] Most scholars concur: there's no question that our earliest texts of this Gospel end at 16:8. Did the author continue beyond 16:8 with an ending that was lost? Did he intend something beyond 16:8 but was prevented from writing it? Neither alternative is impossible, but both are speculative: they lack any biblical or traditional basis for verification. Is it preposterous that Mark deliberately ended his Gospel at 16:8?

Visiting the tomb at dawn after the Sabbath (16:1–2) is the same female trio who beheld Jesus' crucifixion and death at a distance (15:40). Two witnessed his burial (15:47). Long after the Twelve had vamoosed (14:50, 72), these are among many women who followed and ministered to Jesus (15:41). Though well intentioned, their mission is superfluous: an unnamed female benefactor has already anointed their teacher's body for burial (14:3–9). Mark 16:3–4 refers to the stone-stopper used to seal the tomb (15:46). These women "look up" (16:4). Elsewhere in this Gospel "looking up" describes Jesus' regard of heaven before performing mighty works (6:41; 7:34) and restoration of sight after two blind men have encountered him (8:24; 10:51–52). The verb "behold" connotes wondrous apprehension (3:11; 5:15, 38; 12:41). The stone's removal from the tomb's mouth is expressed with a verb conjugated in the passive mood: "The stone had been rolled away." Its unseen mover must have been God, "for this was a very big rock" (16:4).

The stage is set for a revelation, but Mark's description (16:5) is more restrained than that of the other Gospels (cf. Matt 28:2–4; Luke 24:4; John 20:4). "Sitting on the right side" was favored in antiquity, especially if seated beside the right hand of power (1 Kgs 2:19; Ps 110:1; Mark 10:37–40; 12:36; 14:62). Other than Jesus at his transfiguration (9:3), the young man inside the tomb is the only character in this Gospel who wears white, the color of apocalyptic glorification (Dan 7:9; 12:3; Matt 13:43; Rev 7:9, 13). Mark forgoes supernatural pyrotechnics, but the vision at the tomb is enough to leave the women flabbergasted.

---

21. For a far more detailed analysis of all the endings that were later added to this Gospel, see C. Clifton Black, *Mark*, ANTC (Nashville: Abingdon Press, 2011), 345–60.

The young man's declaration (Mark 16:6) is fourfold: (1) "Don't be alarmed." (2) "You are looking for Jesus, the Nazarene." Time and again in Mark (11:18; 12:12; 14:1, 55), those searching for [*zēteite*] Jesus have been up to no good. While intending nothing ill, these women, like others (3:21, 32; 8:11–13), have mistaken what they found because of what they were seeking: a dead man instead of a living Messiah. (3) Because of God's direct intervention, states the young man, "the one crucified has been raised": one of the NT's primary claims (Acts 4:10; Rom 4:24; 1 Cor 15:3–4; 2 Tim 2:8). (4) The women are then entrusted with a message for Jesus' disciples, among whom Peter is singled out (cf. Mark 14:66–72). The risen Jesus has preceded them to Galilee, where he awaits. Again, as throughout Mark (6:48; 10:32), Jesus is in the lead, and others hurry to catch up. The return to Galilee indicates a fresh start, where Mark's narrative of Jesus' ministry begins (1:14). Jesus will appear to his disciples: alongside the resurrection itself, this is the other basic Easter confession (John 21:14; Acts 2:32; 1 Cor 15:5–8). This announcement is "just as he said" (to the Twelve at their Last Supper: Mark 14:28). At the empty tomb two promises of fidelity are validated: God's fidelity to Jesus, and Jesus' loyalty to his disciples.

By now we might expect this evangelist to spin a final, ironic twist for us. That's just what we get: the women flee the tomb, bewildered and terrified (16:8). Those who had followed Jesus longer than all others fall short from fear, as his disciples have repeatedly done. Now is the time to speak in faith (cf. 8:29–30), yet the proclaimers are muted by fear. The end.

Mark's Gospel is not simply a tale about a wonder-working Jewish teacher who ends up nailed to a Roman cross. It is a peculiar proclamation of the hidden explosion of God's kingdom into this world with Jesus, a strange messianic vanguard, and a befuddled band of followers who try to ride the kingdom's rocket yet keep falling off. Jesus doesn't merely tell parables; as God's crucified and risen Messiah, Jesus *is* a parable of the kingdom he preaches. To proclaim that proclaimer, Mark has tailored his Gospel into a parable itself: an announcement of good news that teases and offends, perplexes and provokes, in the same way that Jesus does by action and deed. "What new teaching is this?" (1:27a). "Who, then, is this?" (4:41b). Why does he teach to confuse (4:11–12)? By what authority does he do such things (11:28)? What kind of kingdom is planted as the smallest seed and grows into the biggest rutabaga (4:31–32)? What kind of disciples utterly fail to understand their teacher (6:52), nod off when they should stay awake (14:32–42), babble when they should shut up and listen (8:32–33; 9:6–7), and go mute when they ought to speak up (16:7–8)? What kind of Christ dies crucified (15:32, 39)? What kind of victor is vindicated from death, yet no one is expressly reunited with him afterward (16:8)?

Mark's Gospel ends with a mysterious confirmation that God and Jesus have kept faith and have done just what they promised (16:6–7; cf. 8:31; 9:31; 10:33–34;

14:28). For this Gospel to have ended on another's triumphant flourish—indeed, for it to have ended any way other than it does—would have sabotaged everything this evangelist has said about God's kingdom, its Messiah, and his subjects. Mark is a book about God's shattering of human expectations. Mark *as* a book shatters everything its readers thought they understood—even the conventions of how a Gospel should end. "The good news must be preached to all nations" (13:10): if Jesus commanded that, then that shall surely happen. When it does, it is likely to occur as much *in spite of* his disciples as because of them.

Back to Galilee, back to the beginning, are sent the women and Peter and the disciples and this evangelist's readers. When the latter return, they may notice with opened eyes how this parabolic Gospel opened: "*a beginning* of the good news of Jesus Christ" (1:1). The reader starts afresh, reads through to the end, then repeats over and again an unending process by which disciples of God's kingdom are formed. Mark's greatest intercalation is the Second Gospel itself and as a whole: the sandwiching of Jesus' summons to God's kingdom into the reader's own life.

That is the Mark of genius.

THE CONVERSATION CONTINUES

Proclaiming the Synoptics Faithfully

A Conversation with William Willimon

Bishop William H. Willimon (STD, Emory) served as a pastor in local churches for three decades before his election to the episcopacy of the United Methodist Church in 2004 (retired, 2012). He is a former Dean of the Chapel at Duke University and currently Professor of the Practice of Christian Ministry at Duke Divinity School. He has written more than threescore books on a wide range of subjects in biblical interpretation and theology, which have sold over a million copies; Willimon is regarded as one of the best-known, most influential preachers in the United States.

CCB: Will, how do you prepare yourself to interpret from the pulpit a passage from any of the Gospels?

WHW: First, I read the passage, preferably reading it aloud because I'm reading on the way to a sermon. I read with the conviction that I'm working with a fellow preacher: it seems to me that Mark's job in assembling a Gospel is close to mine in a sermon. As I read, I try to record first impressions. I've learned to value first impressions. A Gospel passage is a piece of literature, and literature always has some immediate impact. I don't want that impact to be blunted by further study. In my first reading I look for what is weird, troublesome, or surprising in the text because I'll probably want to work that in as I preach from the text. Then I go to the commentaries in the same way I might sit down with a wise friend who has given her life to studying Scripture and ask, "What interests you about this passage? Show me something I may have missed."

CCB: I want to pick up on your analogy of Mark's job alongside your own. It seems to me that Christian preachers have a challenging responsibility that's similar to that of the evangelists themselves: not merely to convey the church's remembrance of Jesus, but also to bring that tradition to life among their listeners. Do you agree? How does one fulfill the responsibility of an interpretation that lives and energizes?

WHW: Right. The evangelists were better than amateur historians, biographers, or even primitive poets: they were preachers. They were attempting, using an astonishing array of literary forms, to lure people into encountering and then following Jesus. Now, sometimes they are sly about that, luring us in with "Let me tell you a story about some Jews long ago," so that we are jumped by the truth of the gospel in the present moment. (Luke comes to mind.) In other Gospels (John, maybe?) they delight in constructing a strange narrative world in which Jesus plops down into our quotidian, mundane world in such a way that forces us to take note and maybe even to stumble after him.

I wish I were even half as bold, resourceful, and creative in my preaching as Matthew, Mark, Luke, and John are in their gospeling.

CCB: Among the Synoptics, do you have a favorite Gospel from which to preach—one whose theological attitude naturally resonates with your own? Do you find one or another of the Synoptics more difficult to interpret? As a preacher, which presents for you the harder test: the Gospel from which you feel more distant, or the one in which you feel so much at home?

WHW: That's like asking me to pick a favorite grandchild! I manage to love them all, but differently. One of the fun things about preaching from the Revised Common Lectionary[22] is that I get to have a different voice, a different slant on the gospel, in each year. In Year A, Matthew's year, I have a wonderful time with Jesus in slamming doors, bringing down the gavel, and separating sheep from goats. However, I'm already looking forward to Advent and Year B, so Mark and I can rattle their tame, little, liberal world with eschatological, apocalyptic drama. When in seminary I complained about not liking John ("Will Jesus ever shut up?" I asked), a fellow student advised, "Drop some acid, and it will make more sense."

CCB: Ah, the 60s. Both of us managed to survive them—twice. Often preachers are confronted with particular scriptural passages that just make them shudder. Are there any such passages in Matthew, Mark, or Luke that trip your worry-wire or make your hackles rise? How do you deal with this?

WHW: I assume that a major intent of the gospel is to make us shudder. I'm also trying to overcome my modern, Western arrogance that tempts me to believe I'm more righteous than Mark or Matthew. I was all ready to go with David Bentley Hart's takedown of hell,[23] but then the lectionary stuck me with Luke 16:19–21, where Jesus sends somebody like me who drives a car like mine to hell, and, well, I shudder.

22. A three-year schedule of biblical passages used by Roman Catholic and Protestant Christians in worship.

23. *That All Shall Be Saved: Heaven, Hell, and Universal Salvation* (New Haven, CT: Yale University Press, 2019).

CCB: I drive the same car. White-knuckled. A specific problem that all preach-ers face is the Gospels' presentation of Judaism, even though Jesus and his earliest disciples were all Jewish. Historically, the church has not handled this matter with conspicuous sensitivity and, as a result, has acted atrociously. Do you carry that burden with you into the pulpit?

WHW: I've long been interested in how Christian anti-Judaism is a hard habit to break. It occurs when we Christians insidiously insert ourselves into a family argument between Jew and Jew over who is a real Jew now that another Jew, Jesus, has disrupted God's family and, as you say, cruelty happens. We Gen-tiles must constantly remind ourselves that we are the Johnny-come-latelies and that our only hope is that the God who made and kept promises to Israel will graciously include us in those promises.

CCB: Befitting human frailty, all of us suffer weaknesses and blind spots in our perceptions and their interpretations. In your time you've heard a lot of crummy preaching on the Gospels. What bad habits do you wish preachers would break? When you sit in a pew, what really burns your bacon?

WHW: Among my pet peeves are these:
   1. Reducing the wonderful, weird, challenging Gospels to mere common sense and good advice. Any preacher who opens a sermon with "Here are three biblical principles for a happy marriage" is on the way to a decidedly non-gospel sermon.
   2. Turning Jesus' gracious good news into petty, moralistic scolding. Most Methodists come to church expecting to receive a "to-do list." "This week church wants you to work on your sexism, your racism, your classism. Come back next Sunday, and I'll give you another list." Sermons like that make me grateful that our Lord is nonviolent.
   3. Transforming theological texts about God into anthropological musings about us.

CCB: Have you learned to recognize mistakes to which you yourself are prone, from which others might learn in assessing their own errors of judgment?

WHW: I'm a Methodist, so moralizing is an ever-present temptation, the reduc-tion of the gospel into something we are to think, feel, or do rather than a wondrous appreciation for what God has done and is doing in Christ. I'm also tempted to try to get the gospel to talk about what I'm interested in (sex, poli-tics, self-salvation, etc.) rather than what God is interested in.

CCB: You have stood in thousands of pulpits across fifty years of preaching. How much and in what ways have Christian congregations changed during that time, changes that have required you to grow as a preacher of the gospel, preaching from the Gospels?

WHW: I wonder if my listeners have become ever more arrogant in thinking that they already have all they need to make judgments about the gospel because they are thinking, loving, caring, reasonable Americans. They also are under the widespread delusion that they know what they are talking about when they use the word "God." The conviction that God is a Jew from Nazareth who lived briefly, died violently, and rose unexpectedly is scandalous in every generation and is a truth that's undiscoverable except through confrontations with the reading and preaching of Scripture.

CCB: For two millennia, Christians have preached the Gospels in weather fair and foul, amid unimaginable cultural changes, technological and otherwise. In the 2020s and the foreseeable future, how radically do you expect preaching to change? Do you think the modes of preaching will remain basically unchanged?

WHW: I really have no idea because the work of the Holy Spirit is unpredictable. I am sure that, some way or another, God in Jesus Christ, in the power of the Holy Spirit, *will* have the last word.

CCB: At day's end, after you have finished preaching a sermon from one of the Gospels, what do you hope you have accomplished?

WHW: I hope somebody will say, "Yep, that's the truth about who God is and what God is up to. How can I hitch on to that?"

CCB: Is there anything we haven't discussed that you want to put on the table?

WHW: If you have a clue why God called someone like me to preach the words of people like Matthew, Mark, Luke, and John, let me know. I'm still baffled, humbled, and intimidated by my vocation. The Bible is so much more interesting than I am.

CCB: It's a lot more interesting than any of us. I can no more explain your vocation than I can my own, but I know we are in good company. Sarah (Gen 18:9– 15), Moses (Exod 3:1–12), Amos (7:14–15), Isaiah (6:1–8), Paul (1 Cor 15:9–11), and a host of others claimed to feel much the same.

WHW: Right. To be called by God to interpret the Gospels and to preach is to be awkwardly thrust into the "great company of preachers," being joined to a motley crew. It's a heck of a way for Jesus to assemble a new people, to form his bodily, visible presence here on earth, but preaching from the Gospels seems to be uniquely his way. What a joy to have fellow preachers like Mark egging me on!

CCB: You yourself have egged us on. Thank you, Bishop Willimon.

3

Jesus according to Matthew

Torah Incarnate

Mark's depiction of Jesus is dyed to its deepest fibers in mystery. Adapting that Gospel around 80–100, Matthew does not resolve all of his predecessor's conundrums. How could he? Why should he? Both evangelists are convinced that Jesus is God's uniquely beloved Son (Matt 3:17//Mark 1:11); as such in both Gospels, Jesus flouts commonplace expectations right and left. We shall witness the same in Luke. Jesus does this, not as an egotistical gadfly, but because he is privy to divine revelation beyond human ken and can relay that to selected others.

> At that time Jesus declared, "I praise you, Father, Lord of heaven and of earth, that you have hidden these things from the wise and insightful, and you have revealed them to infants. Indeed, Father, so it has been your great delight. All things have been handed over to me by my Father; and no one recognizes the Son except the Father, nor does anyone recognize the Father except the Son and to whomever the Son may choose to reveal [*apokalypsai*] it." (Matt 11:25–27//Luke 10:21–22 [Q])

Anyone hopeful that Matthew will dispel all of Mark's obscurities will be disgruntled.

That said, much of the fog in which Mark is enshrouded evaporates in Matthew. This evangelist throws sunshine to brighten and clarify his predecessor's narrative. Here's how.

1. Matthew *expands* Mark's story. The NT's first Gospel is about 35 percent longer than its second. The most obvious dilations occur at the beginning and end. Matthew opens with Jesus' genealogy and a detailed account of events surrounding his birth, both of which Mark lacks. At his Gospel's conclusion, Matthew rounds off the story with what many would regard as a proper finale: unabashed joy at the empty tomb (Matt 28:8) plus three more episodes, two involving the risen Jesus (28:9–10, 16–20).

Fig. 22. Matthew's Gospel Outlined and Summarized	
1:1–2:23	Prologue: The Messiah's birth anticipates his passion
Contents:	Jesus' genealogy (1:1–17), birth and infancy (1:18–2:23)
3:1–7:29	First major section: Inauguration of the announcement of the kingdom
Contents:	Prelude to Jesus' ministry (3:1–4:17), followed by the calling of the first disciples (4:18–22), transitional summary of Jesus' ministry (4:23–35), and Jesus' Sermon on the Mount: **Matthew's first major discourse: 5:1–7:29**
8:1–11:1	Second major section: The kingdom activated: The Galilean mission of Jesus and the Twelve
Contents:	The mighty works of Jesus (8:1–9:34), with a summary transition (9:35–37) to the calling of the Twelve (10:1–4) and their missionary discharge: **the second major discourse: 10:5–11:1**
11:2–16:12	Third major section: Jesus and Israel in confrontation
Contents:	A series of disputes over Jesus' authority (11:2–12:50), Jesus' parabolic rejoinder—**the third major discourse: 13:1–52**—a climactic rejection (13:53–58), an intensifying differentiation of Israel and the community around Jesus (14:1–16:12)
16:13–20:34	Fourth major section: Jesus' ministry to his disciples
Contents:	Prefaced by Peter's confession (16:13–20), Jesus' extended instruction on authentic discipleship (16:24–17:21, 24–27) and disciplined life in the Christian community—**the fourth major discourse: 18:1–35**—accented by predictions of the passion (16:21–23; 17:22–23; 20:17–19) and capped by Jesus' journey to Jerusalem (19:1–20:34)
21:1–25:46	Fifth major section: Jesus and his community in Jerusalem
Contents:	A penultimate clash between Jesus and the Jewish authorities (21:1–23:39), followed by his eschatological address to the disciples: **the fifth major discourse: 24:1–25:46**
26:1–28:20	Sixth major section: The passion and post-resurrection narratives
Contents:	The suffering and execution of Jesus (26:1–27:66), followed by his resurrection (28:1–15) and Great Commission to his disciples (28:16–20)

2. Matthew *restructures* Mark's framework. Examine figure 22 (above), and you'll see what I mean. Immediately one notices that this Gospel comprises five thematic sections, each punctuated by an equal number of discourses by Jesus ranging in length from thirty-eight to just over one hundred verses. In two of these lectures, sizeable chunks (Matt 13:3–13, 18–23, 31–32; 24:2–9, 13–24, 29–36, 42) are drawn from the only two uninterrupted addresses of Jesus in Mark (4:3–12, 13–20, 30–32; 13:5–10, 14–32, 35). The rest of these Matthean speeches are constructed of sayings shared with Luke (Q) or unique to Matthew (M). The fact that there are *five* such disquisitions tips off one of this Gospel's primary interests: Jesus' alignment with Israel's history, figures, and events. We hear five speeches

in Matthew alongside five books in the Hebraic Pentateuch[1] (Genesis, Exodus, Leviticus, Numbers, and Deuteronomy). The correspondence is irresistible—all the more since Jesus delivers his first and most famous Sermon from a mountain (Matt 5:1–2).[2] So, too, did Moses receive the law, the pattern for Israel's conduct, from a mountain (Exod 24:12–13; Deut 9:9).

3. Even as he elaborates on Mark, Matthew *abbreviates* a lot of Markan material. A good example is Mark 5:1–43, two of whose stories are separated in Matthew 8:28–34 (the healing of the demon-possessed men) and 9:18–26 (the interwoven healings of a ruler's daughter and a chronic menstruant). What Mark narrates in forty-three verses, Matthew dispatches in sixteen. Comparing these versions, one finds that Matthew has stripped out most of Mark's vibrant or poignant details (the terrifying, piteous conditions of the demoniac and the suffering woman: Mark 5:3–6, 7b–9, 26, 29–33), accelerating the reader to what, for Matthew, is the primary point: Jesus is the consummate healer (9:22b).

4. Matthew makes minor *changes* in Mark's wording for maximum impact, often to magnify Jesus' superlative stature. If Jesus is the wonder-worker par excellence, then Mark's comment that, back home, he "could do no mighty work there" (6:5) is unsettling. Matthew tweaks the predicate to assure his readers that the faithlessness of Jesus' audience in no way inhibited his ability: "And he *did* not do many mighty works there" (13:58). If Jesus is the peerless teacher, then Mark's suggestion that the parables are intended to blind and deafen (4:12) won't do. And so Matthew alters Jesus' rationale for speaking in parables: "*because* seeing they do not see, and hearing they do not hear, nor do they understand" (13:13–15; cf. Isa 6:9–10). The hardness of the human heart is less firmly predestined, as in Mark; rather, it is a preexisting disposition that parabolic instruction may overcome. "Blessed are your eyes, for they see, and your ears, for they hear" (Matt 13:14); Jesus' acclamation of the Twelve is entirely absent from Mark. In that Gospel his closest disciples never get what he's driving at: "I neither know nor understand what you mean," says Peter to the high priest's maidservant (Mark 14:68)—a lie about his association with "the Nazarene" that reveals a deeper truth about Peter's diminished capacities. While Matthew preserves the memory of Peter's collapse under questioning (26:69–75), he also commends the disciples in a manner missing in Mark. "'Have you understood all this?' They said to [Jesus], 'Yes'" (Matt 13:51). In that affirmation there's no suggestion of irony. To the contrary, the wisdom embodied in Jesus (11:19; 12:42; 13:54) has been revealed to infants (11:25).

1. An alternative designation for the HB's Torah, derived from the Greek *pentateuchos*: *penta* (five) + *teuchos* (implement, book, container holding scrolls).
2. The parallel lecture in Luke 6:17–49 is delivered "on a level place" (v. 17), reflective of that evangelist's preoccupation with the common man and woman.

What to Look for in Matthew

1. *A well-organized structure:* Matthew's narrative is bracketed and buttressed by five orderly blocks of teaching.

2. *Biblical billboards:* Repeatedly the narrator steps in and emphasizes Jesus' fulfillment of Hebrew Scripture's deepest intent, making overt connections between some aspect of the story of Jesus with events or declarations in the HB. "All this took place to fulfill what the Lord had spoken by the prophet" (Matt 1:22, with more such affirmations to follow).

3. Matthew has the most consistently exalted presentation of Jesus among all the Synoptics. Jesus fills to the full every expectation of Israel and virtually every representation of the Lord God imaginable: the servant of the Lord (12:17–21; cf. Isa 42:1–4); divine wisdom (11:19, 28–30); faithful Israel (4:1–11); the new Moses (5:1–7:29); the apocalyptic Son of Man (24:37, 39, 44; 25:31; 26:64), with profound human authority (9:6; 11:19), who suffers (17:22–23; 20:18–19); the Son of David (1:1, 20; 9:27; 12:23; 15:22; 20:30; 21:5, 19; 22:42); the Lord (7:21–22); the Son of God worthy of worship in his mortal life (2:11; 3:17; 14:33); Emmanuel, or God-with-Us (1:23; cf. 18:20; 28:20).

4. *A positive portrayal of fallible yet teachable disciples* (Matt 8:26; 13:51; 14:31; 16:8; 17:20) who have been called out—*ekklēsia*[3]—by Jesus (16:18; 18:17) to follow his lead in demonstrating what a faithful Israel looks like.

5. The gift and demand of a higher righteousness—*dikaiosynē*—that reflects God's genuine character, through action. Simply knowing who Jesus is and believing what he teaches is insufficient. "Not everyone who says to me, 'Lord, Lord,' shall enter the kingdom of heaven, but the one who *does* the will of my Father who is in heaven" (Matt 7:21). Orthopraxy, right conduct, is every bit as important as orthodoxy, right belief.

BEGINNINGS: A FAMILY TREE,
A MOST UNCOMMON BIRTH

We come now to an actual fact, or a factual act: the best orientation to Matthew is close study of its first two chapters. In a single stroke they achieve two objectives: (1) an overture to the rest of this Gospel's symphony and (2) a reprise of Israel's past. Using techniques both blatant and delicate, the evangelist is saying, "You'll

---

3. Usually translated into English as "church," this Greek term corresponds with the Hebrew *qāhāl* (e.g., Deut 5:22; 2 Chr 24:6; Joel 2:16) the particular people from among the nations whom the Lord God called into congregational covenant: Israel. See also Deut 28:10; 2 Chr 7:14; Isa 42:6; 62:12; Rom 9:25.

understand Jesus when you realize that he recapitulates the whole of Israel's history. Grasp that, and the gospel falls into place as neatly as can be."

Matthew 1:1–17 opens the proceedings with a record of the "genealogy" (Gk. *genesis*: Get it?) of "Jesus Christ, the Son of David, the son of Abraham" (1:1). These claims are turbocharged: from this Gospel's first verse, the reader knows that Jesus is God's anointed (Messiah, or Christ), descended from Israel's most revered earthly sovereign (2 Sam 7:8–17) and the nation's progenitor (Gen 15–17). For readers in the United States, it's like saying that a president's lineage may be traced straight back to George Washington by way of Abraham Lincoln. Like Mark (1:1), Matthew evinces no need to prove these claims about Jesus. They are, instead, basic presuppositions for everything that follows.

Can you imagine a snoozier beginning for a Gospel than Matthew's option: a genealogy (Heb. *tōlĕdōt*)? In the KJV (1611), these are the "begats": "Abraham begat Isaac; and Isaac begat Jacob; and Jacob begat Judas and his brethren" (Matt 1:2). Well, "Wake Up Little Susie."[4] Matthew has adopted a venerable genre from the HB that creates a viaduct from one narrative to another (cf. Gen 5:1–32; 11:10–32). The bridge the evangelist builds is from Israel's patriarchal history to the story of Jesus. Matthew's genealogy consists of three sets of fourteen generations (1:17). Why fourteen? Here's a possibility. Every consonant in the Hebrew alphabet was assigned a numerical value. While Matthew is written in Greek, the sum of the letters D[a]V[i]D in Hebrew is fourteen: D (4) + V (6) + D (4). Did Matthew expect Greek-speaking readers to catch the symbolism? Beats me. *But*—Matthew goes out of his way to acclaim Jesus as "Son of David" at points where Mark does not (Matt 1:1//Mark 1:1; Matt 12:23//Mark 3:20; Matt 15:22//Mark 7:26; Matt 21:9, 15//Mark 11:10; Matt 22:42b//Mark 12:35). Clearly this evangelist is legitimating Jesus by connecting him to the Davidic line (see also Matt 1:20; 9:27; 20:30).

Wholly unexpected in Matthew's genealogy of Jesus is the appearance of four women: Tamar (1:3), Rahab and Ruth (v. 5), "the wife of Uriah" (Bathsheba: v. 6). In biblical tradition, Semitic descent is traced through fathers, not mothers. Is there a common denominator among these four females? At least three—Tamar (Gen 38:1–6), Rahab (Josh 2:1–2), and Ruth (Ruth 1:1–4)—were not Israelites: they were as Gentile as the Babylonians into whose captivity Israel would be exiled (597–539 BCE; Matt 1:11–12). Irregular sexual relations are attached to all four. Mistaken for a cult prostitute of the goddess Ishtar, Tamar the Canaanite was bedded by Judah, her father-in-law, who ended up declaring her "more righteous than I" (Gen 38:15–19, 24–26). Rahab, a harlot in Jericho, sheltered Joshua's reconnoitering spies (Josh 2, 6; cf. Heb 11:31; Jas 2:25). The quick wit and compassionate fidelity of Ruth, a Moabite woman, won the love of Boaz, a

---

4. Written by Felice and Bordleaux Bryant; recorded by the Everly Brothers in 1957; triumphantly reprised in 1981 by Simon and Garfunkel, *The Concert in Central Park* (Warner Bros. Records, 1982).

Fig. 23. *The Tree of Jesse* (Anonymous). *Speculum Humanae Salvationis*, Kremsmünster Abbey Library, Austria.

wealthy Israelite; by their marriage she became David's great-grandmother (Ruth 1–4; N.B. 4:13–22). Subsequently that king forced himself upon beautiful Bathsheba (the wife of a Hittite; see 2 Sam 12:9), then orchestrated a suicide mission for her husband, Uriah (2 Sam 11:2–27). Another woman—Mary, conspicuously named in the genealogy in relation to Joseph, her husband (Matt 1:16)—will be blamelessly but sexually imperiled (1:18–19). Embedded in Israel's history, with room for Gentiles, the story of Jesus will again verify God's propensity for writing straight even on crooked lines.

The events surrounding Jesus' birth (1:18–2:23) highlight Matthew's intent to marry Jesus with Israel's past in so many ways, with a palette so vibrant that one would have to be totally ignorant of Hebrew history to mistake their importance. Modern readers, particularly those who have grown up with Christmas pageants, may zero in on the virginal conception, a claim accented as early as the second-century Apostles' Creed ("Jesus Christ, conceived by the Holy Spirit, born of the Virgin Mary"). It may surprise them to learn that many illustrious figures of antiquity were said to have been conceived without a human father: Perseus (*Metam.* 4), Alexander the Great (*Lives* 2.2–5), Augustus (*Aug.*), even Moses (*Mos.*).[5] Had Matthew (and Luke) *not* asserted such of Jesus, it would have been surprising (as it may be for readers of Mark's Gospel and Paul's Letters, neither of which refer to the virginal conception). That's *not* to say that Jesus' divine origin is superfluous for Matthew: through God's initiative, Mary's miraculous conception surpasses the pregnancies of infertile Sarah (Gen 17:15–18:15); Manoah's wife, mother of Samson (Judg 13:2–25); and Hannah (1 Sam 1:1–2:10). It *is* to say that Jesus' sonship to God is more than a matter of biological anomaly (Matt 3:13–17; 4:1–11), and a lot more is rumbling around Matthew's first two chapters than the single issue of Jesus' spiritual conception. After 1:23, the evangelist never mentions it again.

As Matthew tells it, the story of Jesus' birth and infancy is, from hem to throat, Israelite déjà vu, revisiting critical figures and moments in that nation's life. The same Spirit that rustled the waters of primordial chaos (Gen 1:2) has returned to create extraordinary activity in Mary's womb (Matt 1:18, 20). She is "engaged"—contractually betrothed by their families—to Joseph, whose dreams are preternatural, like the Joseph of Genesis (Matt 1:20; cf. his namesake in Gen 37:5–11; 42:9). "Behold" (cf. Gen 17:4, 20; 18:2, 27, 31): an angel of God quells fear and assures deliverance, as with visitations in the OT like those to Moses in the wilderness (Matt 1:20; cf. Exod 23:20; 32:34). Like Abram (Gen 17:5) and Jacob (32:28), the child born to Mary and Joseph will receive a name of prodigious significance: "Jesus"—a variant of Joshua—"for he will save [Heb. *yāša*] his people from their sins" (Matt 1:21, 25). Like other "righteous" (Gk. *dikaios*) men and women before

---

5. See David R. Cartlidge and David L. Dungan, eds., *Documents for the Study of the Gospels* (Minneapolis: Fortress Press, 2015), 129–36.

him (Gen 6:9 [Noah]; 38:26 [Tamar]; Isa 53:11 [an unnamed servant]), Joseph acts with integrity toward Mary, whose premarital pregnancy would have been societally humiliating for him and, for her, potentially fatal, punishable by stoning (Matt 1:19; cf. Deut 22:13–21). He does "as the angel of the Lord commanded him" (Matt 1:24), exemplifying the obedience to God's voice or covenant, expected of Israel (Exod 19:5; Deut 13:18; Josh 24:24; Ezek 11:20; Zech 6:15).

The old story continues to unspool afresh. Herod the Great (ca. 38–4 BCE), a client ruler under Roman patronage, receives an embassy of "wise men" (Gk. *magoi*), Gentile court priests who wish to prostrate themselves before "the king of the Jews" (Matt 2:2; cf. 14:33; 28:9, 17). (To them Herod might have replied: "And just whom, gentlemen, do you think you're addressing?") The telltale eastern star they have observed harks back to another Gentile diviner in the Torah, Balaam, whose oracle in the days of Moses promised that "a star shall come forth out of Jacob, a comet arise from Israel" (Num 24:17 NEB). (These astrologers seem to know Hebrew Scripture better than the titular Jewish king!) Recognizing a political threat, Herod convenes his brain trust—"all the chief priests and scribes," the very same sacerdotal aristocrats and scholars who will eventually conspire in Jesus' execution (Matt 16:21; 20:18; 21:15; 27:41)—to ascertain his rival's whereabouts (2:4–5). They quote to him Micah 5:2, which, without precise reference to "the Messiah," has promised that from backwater Bethlehem shall come forth Israel's shepherd-king, David (1 Sam 17:12). Pretending that he, too, wishes to worship the newborn, Herod steers the magi toward the small town; the eastern star guides them to the proper house (Matt 2:7–9). There they revere the child, offering gifts (2:11), exactly as "the kings" of all nations should before God's appointed sovereign (Ps 72:1, 10–11: the likely origination of "We Three Kings," whose number and monarchy Matthew never specifies). Their presents are impractical—diapers would have been useful—but are fit for royalty: gold, frankincense (Ps 72:15; Isa 60:56), and myrrh (1 Kgs 10:25; Ps 45:8).

At this point the earliest and, alongside Jesus' death, most harrowing violence in Matthew explodes. The principal adversaries in this conflict are divine angels and earthly potentates, the former always a step ahead of the latter. Warned in dreams (as angels are wont to employ: Gen 28:12; 31:11), the magi bypass Herod (Matt 2:12), and Joseph takes the child and his mother to Egypt for safekeeping (2:13–15). Furious at having been duped, Herod slays all of Bethlehem's male infants two years old or younger (2:16). After Herod's own death, his son Archelaus, Judea's Roman governor (4 BCE–6 CE), is a sufficient threat that Joseph, again warned in a dream, settles in the nondescript Galilean village of Nazareth (2:19–23; cf. John 1:46), which, in Luke, is Mary and Joseph's homeplace (1:26; 2:4, 39, 51). Tersely narrated, this episode rides many scriptural waves from the HB, all cascading over one another: an earlier Joseph's refuge in Egypt (Gen 37:28), Pharaoh's massacre of Israelite male infants (Exod 1:8–22), Israel's

Fig. 24. Stained-glass window in St Andrew's Cathedral, Sydney, by John Hard-man & Co. (Birmingham, U.K.). From left to right the four panels depict the Magi's discovery of the star, their entrance to Jerusalem, their audience before Herod, and their adoration of the Christ child. Photograph courtesy of Amandajm.

escape from Egypt at Passover (Exod 12:1–51)—another liberation from political enslavement—as well as five of Matthew's famous "formula quotations": passages of Jewish Scripture that, for Matthew, anticipate moments in the life of Jesus. Beyond his infancy narrative, Matthew draws the reader's attention to many such biblical correlations throughout this Gospel.

Matthew's interpretive method stymies modern readers, who find it clumsy, tendentious, or outrageous. In 2:23 "He will be called a Nazorean" seems a pun on "Nazarene," someone from Nazareth. No known passage in the HB corresponds with Matthew's wording here; the suggested parallels that commentators have made with Judges 13 and Isaiah 11 are guesses. Isaiah 7 presents a more troublesome snag. Nothing in the prophet's vision of a young woman's naming her child "Immanuel" obviously extends beyond the Syro-Ephraimite war of 735–732 BCE. Nothing is expressly *messianic* in the sign of the mother soon-to-be, which the Lord gives King Ahaz (vv. 10–17). In Hebrew she is described as an *'almâ*: a woman of child-bearing age. Her designation as a "virgin" (*parthenos*) in Isaiah 7 enters the text only at the time of the Septuagint (early 2nd c. BCE–early 1st c. CE), the Greek synagogue Bible of Hellenistic Jews like Matthew—thus

---

Fig. 25. Formula Quotations in the Matthean Infancy Narrative

All this took place to fulfill what the Lord had spoken by the prophet:	"Therefore the Lord himself will give you a sign.
"Behold, a virgin [Gk. *parthenos*] shall conceive and bear a son, and his name shall be called Emmanuel, Which means, 'God with us.'" (Matt 1:22–23)	Behold, a young woman [Heb: *'almâ*] is with child and shall bear a son, and shall name him Immanuel." (Isa 7:14)
"For so it is written by the prophet 'And you, Bethlehem, in the land of Judah, Are by no means least among the rulers of Judah; For from you shall come a ruler who is to shepherd my people Israel.'" (Matt 2:5b–6)	"But you, O Bethlehem of Ephrathah, who are one of the little clans of Judah, from you shall come forth for me one who is to rule in Israel. . . ." (Mic 5:2)
This was to fulfill what had been spoken by the Lord through the prophet,	Thus says the LORD: "Israel is my firstborn Son" (Exod 4:22). "When Israel was a child I loved him,
"Out of Egypt I have called my son." (Matt 2:15b)	and out of Egypt I called my son." (Hos 11:1)
Thus was fulfilled what had been spoken through the prophet Jeremiah:	Thus says the LORD:
"A voice was heard in Ramah wailing and loud lamentation, Rachel weeping for her children; she refused to be consoled because they are no more." (Matt 2:17–18)	A voice is heard in Ramah, lamentation and bitter weeping. Rachel is weeping for her children; she refuses to be comforted for her children because they are no more. (Jer 31:15)
So that what had been spoken through the prophets might be fulfilled, "for the boy shall be a Nazirite [consecrated] to God from birth."	It is he [as Nazarite, *nazîr*] who shall begin to deliver Israel. . . . (Judg 13:5)
"He will be called a Nazorean." (Matt 2:23b)	A shoot will come out of Jesse, and a branch (Heb. *nētzer*) shall grow out of his roots. (Isa 11:1)

rendering the analogy with Mary even more inexact. When, in 1952, the RSV published its translation of Isaiah 7:14 with the words "a young woman," correcting "virgin" in the KJV of the same verse, irate Christians flung hundreds of copies of the RSV into bonfires. Asked what he thought of the hue and cry, Harvard's Henry Joel Cadbury, a member of the RSV team, deemed it a sign of progress: "I can remember a time when they burned, not just translations, but the translators."

Fig. 26. More Matthean Formula Quotations

Matthew	Hebrew Scripture	Fulfillment
3:3	Isa 40:3	"The voice . . . crying in the wilderness: Prepare the way of the Lord."
4:14–16	Isa 9:1–2	Jesus "withdrew to [Naphtali] in Galilee."
8:17	Isa 53:4	"He took our infirmities and bore our illnesses."
12:17–21	Isa 42:1–4	"Here is my servant. . . . And in his name the Gentiles will hope."
13:14–15	Isa 6:9–10	"You will indeed listen, but never understand, . . . [though] I would heal them."
13:35	Ps 78:2	"I will . . . speak in parables; I will proclaim what has been hidden."
21:4–5	Isa 62:11; Zech 9:9	"Tell the daughter of Zion, Look your king is coming to you. . . .'"
26:56	[unspecified text]	"But all this has taken place, so that the scriptures might be fulfilled."
27:9–10	Zech 11:12–13;	"And they took the thirty pieces of silver, . . . and they gave them
	Jer 18:1–3; 32:6–15	for the potter's field. . . .'"

We need to remember that Matthew operates with the interpretive conventions of his day, which are far more like the Dead Sea Scrolls' pesharim (biblical commentary of "presaged reality")[6] than twenty-first-century historical criticism. Even when discerning contemporary meaning in ancient texts, Matthew knew that God's son, called out of Egypt in Hosea 11:1, was in the first instance Israel, because that's precisely what the writer of Hosea 11 indicates. But Matthew does not stop at this first level of interpretation. Understanding that may draw us more closely to how the evangelist understands scriptural fulfillment: for Matthew, the prophets spoke of more than they were aware, because Jesus *fills to the full* what Scripture is driving at. If one begins at Matthew's starting point—Jesus, son of David, son of Abraham, is God's true Messiah—one finds, not that Jewish Scripture explains Jesus, but just the opposite. It is Jesus who throws light on Scripture, helping the reader to understand the Bible with an intense vibrancy that would otherwise be missed. For that reason Matthew can construe as scriptural fulfillment an event in Jesus' life—the night of his arrest—without quoting any text at all, simply stating that the Scriptures have said that events must happen in this way (26:54, 56). (Other NT writers do the same: Mark 14:49; John 17:12; Paul,

6. See Krister Stendahl, *The School of St. Matthew and Its Use of the Old Testament*, 2nd ed. (Philadelphia: Fortress Press, 1968); W. D. Davies, *The Setting of the Sermon on the Mount* (Cambridge: Cambridge University Press, 1966).

in 1 Cor 15:3–4.) Already, in this evangelist's opening chapters, Jesus recapitulates the story of Israel: its calling and exile, champions and antagonists, justice and rancor, murder and deliverance, repetition with variations, the challenge of obedience amid recurring perils. Unlike Israel in the wilderness, who time and again succumbed to disobedience (Exod 32:1–35; Lev 10:1–20; Num 11:1–16:35), Jesus was repeatedly tempted to swerve away from the Lord God's purpose but never gave himself over to "the devil" (or Satan, Matt 4:1–11). And because Jesus is "God with us" (1:23), the Gospel that unfolds from this point is the continuing story of God's dedication to and expectation of Israel and the nations.

A Horde of Herods

Two Herods play small but significant roles in the Synoptics. The first, Herod the Great (late 70s–4 BCE), is mentioned in connection with the births of Jesus (Matt 2:1–19) and John the Baptist (Luke 1:5). The other, Herod Antipas (ca. 20 BCE–40 CE), was responsible for John's arrest and death (Matt 14:1–12//Mark 6:14–28//Luke 9:7–9) and, according to Luke (23:6–12), questioned and ridiculed Jesus on the day of his death. This second Herod was son of the first. Both were members of a dynasty that ruled Jewish Palestine for about two hundred years (100 BCE–100 CE). That family served at the pleasure of whatever Caesar sat, at the moment, on the imperial throne. The machinations of the Herod family, among themselves and in cahoots with the Roman Empire, were

Fig. 27. Portrait of Herod the Great. From *The holy court, in five tomes,* by Nicolas Caussin (1650). Digital image provided courtesy of Pitts Theology Library, Candler School of Theology, Emory University.

relentless, complicated, and bloody. Our best evidence about them comes from Josephus (esp. *B.J.* 1–2; *A.J.* 14–20). These ripsnorting reads make Scorsese's *GoodFellas* (1990) look like Disney's *Little Mermaid* (1989).

Like his father Antipater II (d. 43 BCE), Herod the Great, an Idumean (of Edom), wasn't a member of the Jewish royal family, the Hasmoneans. During the reign of the Hasmonean John Hyrcanus I (134–104 BCE), Antipater's family converted to Judaism (*A.J.* 14.7–18). In 40 BCE Herod wangled an appointment by the Roman Senate as "king of the Jews" living in the territories of Galilee (northwest Israel), Judea (southwest), Perea (or Peraea, southeast, east of the Jordan River), and Iturea (northeast of Israel). Like most politicians, Herod was obsessed with securing his governance, made trickier by divisions among his Jewish subjects. After a wobbly start, during which he executed both his Hasmonean (second) wife Mariamne and her grandfather Hyrcanus II (every family has its squabbles), the first fourteen years of Herod's reign (27–14 BCE) were relatively calm and prosperous. Herod had a knack for throwing his weight behind Roman strongmen—Pompey (106–48 BCE), Julius Caesar (100–44), Cassius (ca. 85–42), Mark Antony (83–30), Caesar Augustus (63 BCE–14 CE)—and consolidating total power over every influential institution in his realm: the Sanhedrin (Jewish supreme court), the high priesthood, and the military (with garrisons dispersed throughout, to quell rebellions).

Following Caesar's lead, he reveled in grandiose building projects. He was a pushover for palaces (at least fifteen) but didn't skimp on city walls, harbors, colonnades, marketplaces, theaters, baths, sewage systems, fountains, the modestly named Herodium (a combined fortress/palace/tomb estate), even entire cities (Sebaste and Caesarea Maritima). His pièce de résistance was a rebuilt temple in Jerusalem, double the size of Solomon's original (1 Kgs 6–8; 2 Chr 2–4), which Babylonian troops had destroyed centuries earlier (ca. 587 BCE). Herod wore his Judaism lightly, but resuscitating Israel's ritual heart was sure to endear him to Jews ever suspicious of his half-breed background. The strategy worked. Said one rabbi, "Whoever has not beheld Herod's [temple] has never in his life seen anything beautiful" (b. Bava Batra 4a). Its description by Josephus (*B.J.* 5.136–219) staggers the imagination, as does its scope: thirty-five acres, more than forty-six American football fields. But the good times never last. The last decade of Herod's reign (13–4 BCE) collapsed under the weight of intrafamily conspiracy, aggravated by external revolts. It's hard to keep a firm grip on things while unruly children jockey for your throne and your dead wife's sons hold a grudge against you for killing her. Spurred by peevish relatives, the sons attempted patricide and wound up executed, like their mother. By the time he was ready to cash in his own chips, Herod was running out of heirs apparent. Fortunately, along the way he had remarried and fathered other sons

Fig. 28. *Christ before Herod* (Antipas), from *The Small Passion*, by Albrecht Dürer (ca. 1509). Housed in the Metropolitan Museum of Art, New York.

by two wives, among three of whom (Archelaus, Philip, and Antipas) Augustus divided Herod's kingdom after his death in 4 BCE.

Antipas was sovereign over Perea and Galilee. Perea, a hardscrabble territory, is associated with John the Baptist; Galilee, a richer area, with Jesus (Luke 3:1). Although Antipas followed his father's footsteps with building projects (*A.J.* 18.27), much of his reign was hamstrung by yet more family intrigue. After a long marriage to Phasaelis, daughter of a neighboring king in Nabatea, Antipas fell for Herodias, who, awkwardly, was the wife of one half-brother and the daughter of another half-brother (*A.J.* 18.109). Condemning Antipas for incest is the reason Mark gives for John the Baptist's arrest and execution (6:17–29). Josephus explains the slaying differently: Antipas's concern about John's potential as a rabble-rouser (*A.J.* 18.116–19). Matthew 14:3–5 splits the difference, suggesting both motives. Luke 13:31–33 says Antipas had murderous intent toward Jesus, which may account for the anecdote, recounted only by Luke (23:1–12), of Antipas's interrogation of Jesus by referral from Pilate, Judea's imperial prefect. It's ironic: the innocent Jesus, played as a pawn between sparring Roman and Jewish officials, ends up mending the rift between Herod and Pilate and making allies of them (23:12).

Fig. 29. Herod Agrippa I   Fig. 30. Herod Agrippa II

We must draw to a close this heartwarming saga with Agrippa II (ca. 28–92), Great Herod's great-grandson, who visits the pages of Acts (25:13–26:32) and was governing when the Synoptic evangelists were writing. After the death of his father, Agrippa I (11 BCE–44 CE), Agrippa II was in line for the throne but considered too young to sit in it. About six years later he was ready to roll. Agrippa and his sister Bernice/Berenice (28–post 81) did their best to bend Jewish will to imperial demands, even to the point of commissioning forces to fight beside Roman legions against the Jewish revolt of 66–73. That war's climax was the destruction of Great Herod's majestic temple before its completion. After the rebellion had been quelled, Agrippa and Bernice received appreciative goodies from the Romans. Bernice enjoyed a steamy affair with Titus Vespasian, one of the Flavian dynasty of emperors (69–96), but he dismissed her because the Roman populace didn't approve of their contemplated marriage. It may have had something to do with her family.

THE HEART OF MATTHEW:
JESUS' SERMON ON THE MOUNT

If I had to point someone to the core of Matthew's message, it would be 5:1–7:28: the first of Jesus' five great blocks of teaching in this Gospel. Most of Matthew's remainder develops what these three chapters summarize.

The first thing to observe in this celebrated exposition of Israel's Torah is that it opens with no rule of any kind: nary an ought, a must, nor a should. It opens with Jesus' announcement of *blessing*, or beatitude, upon nine recipients:

some predictable (the merciful, the pure in heart, the peacemakers: 5:7–9), others unlikely (the poor in spirit, the mourning, the meek, those famished for justice, the condemned and persecuted: 5:3–6, 10–11). Responsibility to the God revealed by Jesus begins with a joyous response to that God's gracious, unmerited, astonishing generosity of blessing. Before obedience to the command comes a realization of divine favor.

This insight that God's blessing comes first, capitalized by Matthew, did not originate with Jesus. It is built into the preambles of all the Hebraic covenants between the Lord God and Israel, most famously the Decalogue (or Ten Commandments): "I am the LORD your God, who brought you out of the land of Egypt, out of the house of bondage" (Exod 20:2). For Matthew, it is crucial that the creation and maintenance of discipleship to Jesus is God's *gift* to the church, even as the original gift of Torah was God's gift to Israel. If that be forgotten, then both Christians and Jews risk tumbling into the trap of a moralistic attempt at self-salvation, in which no divine intervention whatever is necessary. Not so: God's favor precedes and enables human obedience. Detach Matthew's admonitions from their theological and christological context, and the business of discipleship becomes a vapidly sentimental travesty. Matthew allows no slack to ease the tension so that we might relax. As E. Stanley Jones warned, "We are inoculating the world with a mild form of Christianity, so that it is now all but immune against the real thing."[7]

As the Sermon unfolds, time is telescoped: Israel's past, present, and future converge.

♦ *The past*: Torah, the Lord God's incomparable gift to his chosen people, retains its eternal validity. "For truly I tell you, until heaven and earth pass away, not one letter, not one stroke of a letter, will pass from the law until all is accomplished" (Matt 5:18 NRSV). Make no mistake: though it unnerves some Christians to read it, Matthew is insistent on a faithful legalism, every bit as much as an observant Jew would follow. But the legalism Matthew calls for here defies its colloquial connotation of petty exactitude, which Jesus exhibits no reluctance to attack (Matt 12:9–13; 19:1–9; 22:23–33; 23:1–39). Matthew's legalism is based on the assumption that the law and teaching *of God*, the Torah, is the compass that points creatures true north, to conduct consistent with their Creator's will.

♦ *The present*: Taken altogether, Jesus' identity, teaching, and life constitute the indispensable prism through which the intention of God's Torah should be understood, interpreted, and enacted. This belief radiates most boldly in Jesus' signature corrections in Matthew 5:21–43, whose repetitive form— "You have heard that it was said, . . . but I say to you"—have prompted scholars to refer to them as "the Matthean antitheses." In these verses' six representative cases, Matthew presents Jesus as the decisively authoritative arbiter of the law, the Chief Justice nonpareil. In three instances Jesus radi-

---

7. E. Stanley Jones, *The Christ of the Indian Road* (New York: Abingdon Press, 1925), 119.

calizes the Torah's demands. Whereas Israel's ancestors forbade murder (Exod 20:13), Jesus forbids anger, insults, and grudges against others (Matt 5:21–26). The Decalogue prohibited adultery (Exod 20:14); Jesus protects vulnerable women from what is nowadays called "the male gaze":[8] the eye or hand that would dehumanize a woman into a sexual object for gratifying rapacious appetite (Matt 5:27–28). The command to love the neighbor while permitting hatred of the enemy (Lev 19:18, 34) is utterly reformulated: "But I say to you, Love your enemies and pray for those who persecute you" (Matt 5:43–44), because God does the same for us (vv. 45–48). In three other cases Jesus' redefinition of Torah's requirements seems so radical as to effectively abrogate them. Deuteronomy 24:1–4 granted the husband, but not the wife, the right of divorce; Jesus proscribes divorce altogether (save in the case of *porneia*, either sexual immorality or an illicit marriage), which protects the woman who would be left destitute unless she were able to remarry (Matt 5:31–32). Whereas the ancients prohibited "false oaths," which invalidate trustworthy testimony (Lev 19:12), Jesus bans any oath whatsoever (Matt 5:33–34), perhaps for the same reason as did Philo: "By the mere fact of swearing at all, the swearer shows that there is some suspicion of his not being trustworthy" (*Decal.* 84). Instead of seeking proportionate compensation for damages (Exod 21:33–34), the injured party should not retaliate whatsoever in response to insult, litigation, forced service, damages, or requests for a loan (Matt 5:38–39). In all these cases, Matthew is making two primary points: (1) the law's abiding validity rests on its interpretation *by Jesus* (see also 12:1–14; 15:1–20; 19:3–12, 16–22), who (2) perfectly points to the character of the God who underwrites Torah. That God does not operate by shrunken human standards of tit for tat. God is *teleios*—faultlessly honorable, "mak[ing] his sun rise on the evil and on the good, and send[ing] rain on the just and on the unjust" (5:44). God acts in unwavering accordance with his own wholehearted integrity. So has his Messiah (3:13–17). And the same is expected of followers of that Lord (5:45).

♦ It may seem odd to us that Matthew would think of Jesus, a figure of some sixty years earlier, as situated in the *present*. For the evangelist, that is precisely true. Jesus was not a prophet from history's dust and ashes. Jesus *is* the church's living Lord, present wherever two or three of his disciples are gathered (18:20), abiding with and continuing to lead them, to the close of the age (28:20). Such a belief remains hard for modern Christians to wrap their minds around if they've convinced themselves that the main reason for God's raising of Jesus from death was to book them on a one-way passage to heaven. Not so for Matthew. By his resurrection, Matthew insists, Christ continues to direct the church of the present in his teachings of the kingdom until the day of reckoning arrives (Matt 25:31–46). In Matthew 5–7 Jesus did not instruct others on a hill far away, once upon a time. He is teaching *still*. And obedience to him is justified, since never was anything like this seen or heard in Israel (9:23; cf. 7:28–29). "Behold, something greater than Solomon is here" (12:42).

8. See John Berger, *Ways of Seeing* (New York: Viking Press, 1972); Laura Mulvey, "Visual Pleasure and Narrative Cinema," in Laura Mulvey's *Visual and Other Pleasures*, 2nd ed. (New York: Palgrave Macmillan, 2009), 14–30.

◆ Thus, the present opens up to *the future*, into the ongoing life of Jesus' disciples. By freely following the one who embodies and articulates God's deepest intent in the law, Jesus' followers are also expected to fulfill Torah by pious mercy (6:1–4, 16–18), cogent prayer (6:5–13), unmitigated forgiveness (6:14–15) and forbearance of judgment (7:1–5), unqualified trust in God (6:16–34; 7:7–12), self-discipline (7:13–14), and wise discernment (7:15–20, 24–27). In short, they are expected to do the will of the Father in heaven (7:21). All these topics are restated and elaborated in the rest of this Gospel:

- reverent mercy (9:10–13; 10:40–42; 14:13–21; 15:32–39; 18:10–14; 19:13–15);
- forgiveness (9:1–8; 18:15–36);
- prayer (9:35–38; 14:23; 19:13; 24:20; 26:36–41);
- discernment (10:16, 34–39; 12:33–50; 13:18–23, 24–30, 36–43; 16:1–4, 17–22; 17:24–27);
- humble self-discipline (13:36–43; 16:24–28; 18:1–4);
- confident trust (4:1–11; 8:5–13, 23–27; 9:14–31; 10:17–33; 13:44–46; 15:21–28; 17:20; 19:25–29); and
- the incomparable importance of doing God's will (3:13–17; 12:46–50).

Notice that all of this Sermon's directives are realized *in community* (5:1–2; 7:28–29). The same is true for the entirety of Jesus' teaching in this Gospel. No less than Mark or Luke, Matthew refutes a corrupted Christian narcissism: "Just me and Jesus," which inevitably devolves into "Just me. Forget about Jesus." This evangelist expects his readers to confront and junk their religious hypocrisy (6:1–6, 14–24; 7:1–20), then open themselves to the fullness of a trusting, obedient discipleship, embodied in Jesus and lived out in the church. The point is not to collect merit badges. Stated only in Matthew (5:16), the point could not be clearer: "Let your light so shine before others, so that they may see your good works *and give glory to your Father in heaven*" (emphasis added). The community of Jesus' followers does *not* act with the self-serving aggrandizement in which societies—including churches, at their amnesiac worst—typically operate: lying, hating, holding grudges, backbiting, showboating, worshiping wealth, worrying, degrading human beings into things. None of these is in God's nature. None is humanity's destination, to which God's Messiah leads. None expresses how we want others to treat us. Therefore, those who remember how to follow Jesus refuse to treat others so (7:12).

As long as "the kingdom of heaven" is misidentified with the sweet by-and-by or a political clique of the pinched like-minded, the church's business can be consigned to the ash heap of empty relics. Matthew will have none of it. In Jesus, God's sovereignty is exercised now (4:23) and forever (28:20), intent on restoring relationship between God and humanity, thus also among humans. Jesus infuses society's bowls of vanilla ice cream with jalapeños, and there's no quenching the burn for us or its potential offensiveness to others. Whether Flannery O'Connor or someone else said it, the point is thoroughly Matthean: "You shall know the truth, and the truth shall make you odd."

THE DISCIPLES IN MATTHEW: SINKING YET UPRIGHT

Clearly Matthew is as interested in Jesus' followers as in Jesus himself. All of this Gospel's five great discourses (5:1–7:29; 10:5–11:1; 13:1–52; 18:1–35; 24:1–25:46) are addressed to them, although a larger audience is listening in (7:28–29; 13:2). Jesus' disciples constantly accompany him, except when sent by their master in mission (10:1–11:1) and when deserting him after his arrest (26:56–27:10). Matthew 14:22–33 captures, not only this evangelist's depiction of the Twelve, but also his adaptation of miracle stories found in Mark.

The tale begins true to Markan form. After assisting their teacher in feeding a multitude with sparse resources (Matt 14:13–21//Mark 6:30–44), Jesus dispatches his followers in a boat while remaining in solitude on a mountain to pray (Matt 14:22//Mark 6:45–47). A squall erupts on the sea, distressing the disciples. Aware of these developments, Jesus walks on the waves to the tempest-tossed ship, reassuring those who by now are the more frightened because they think Jesus is a ghost (Matt 14:24–27//Mark 8:48–50). In Mark, predictably, the Twelve are utterly unnerved and baffled after Jesus boards the boat and the gale abates (6:51–52).

Matthew's version of this tale ends quite differently, in a manner compatible with this evangelist's view of the Twelve. A sequel, absent from Mark, is appended. After Jesus identifies himself, reassuring them that they have nothing to fear (Matt 14:27), Peter (Rocky), the Twelve's usual spokesman (15:15; 16:16, 22; 17:4; 18:21; 19:27), answers, "Lord, if it is you, command me to come to you on the water" (14:28). Jesus summons him: "Come." And so Peter does: stepping out of the boat, walking on the waves toward his teacher (v. 29). With Jesus' support, Peter can follow his teacher, penetrating seemingly insuperable tumult. When Rocky loses focus, distracted by the typhoon, he is frightened, starts sinking like a stone, and pleads to his Lord for rescue (v. 30). Immediately Jesus catches him and asks, "You of little faith, why did you doubt?" (v. 31). As in Mark, faith's adversary is fear that stirs up doubt (21:21; 28:17). The climax: both enter the boat, and all the passengers worship Jesus as God's true Son (14:32–33)—just as the Magi had done at Jesus' birth (2:11) and as the women will revere the risen Christ (28:9).

Obviously this is a miracle tale. Just as obviously, Matthew isn't fascinated by Jesus' or Peter's ability to hydroplane without visible means of support. The

Fig. 31. Floor mosaic in the sixth-century basilica at Horvat Beit Loya (Khirbet Beit Lei) in Israel. Photograph courtesy of Bukvoed.

miracle is a springboard into a magnificently refashioned lesson about disciple-ship.[9] Following Jesus is no pleasure cruise: disciples' lives are truly endangered (5:11, 44; 10:23; 23:34). Unlike Mark, whose ending dangles with the disciples' bewilderment and hardened hearts (6:51b–52), Matthew attests that Jesus' earliest devotees *did* have faith in him: Peter is ready to screw his nerve up to the sticking place if it truly *is* his Lord who will support him. The problem is twofold: the peril is terrifying, and Peter's trust—real though it is—needs a booster shot: "O ye of *little* faith" (Matt 6:30; 8:26; 16:8; 17:20 RSV). His Lord is there to save him (cf. 1:21). Calm is restored. Jesus' disciples worship him with the same devotion

9. A classic study of this passage is by Günther Bornkamm, "The Stilling of the Storm in Mat-thew," in Bornkamm, Gerhard Barth, and Heinz-Joachim Held, *Tradition and Interpretation in Matthew*, trans. Percy Scott, NTL (Philadelphia: Westminster Press, 1963), 52–57.

that they would after Easter. No wonder that one of the earliest images for the infant church was the little boat whose mast was the cross.

WHO WERE IN MATTHEW'S CONGREGATION? A MULTICULTURAL MYSTERY

The ethnic composition of the church was as much a hot-button issue in the first century as in the twenty-first. Its earliest manifestation lay in how Gentiles were to be accommodated in a religious movement that originated in Judaism (Acts 10:1–11:18; Rom 9:1–11:36; 1 Pet 2:9–10). For Jews and probably many Jewish Christians, this was no triviality: the point of covenant-observance was dissociation from *gôyîm*[10] (Lev 26:45; 2 Kgs 17:15; 2 Chr 32:17).

If most scholars are correct in dating Matthew around 80–100, then that very Jewish Gospel emerged at a critical moment in Christianity's relationship with Judaism. The era between two disastrous Jewish revolts against Rome—the first, 66–73; the second, 132–35—has lately been characterized as "the parting of the ways."[11] After these catastrophes, climaxed by the destruction of Israel's cultic center, the Jerusalem temple, in 70, Judaism began a process of retrenchment around the Torah, led by the Pharisees' descendants, the rabbis. At the same time Christianity, begun as a Jewish sect, was making major missionary inroads among Gentiles who had never adhered to Torah but joined with a Jewish Christian minority in their dedication to Jesus as Lord over Israel and all the world's nations. Statements in the Hellenistic Jewish Gospel of John, probably composed between 90 and 110, suggest that some Jewish disciples of Jesus were apparently subjected to expulsion from their native synagogues, or worse (John 9:22; 12:42; 16:2). Matthew's Gospel implies that its readers were also coming to terms with both its parent Judaism and the gospel's unexpected reach among Gentiles.

It's hard to pin down the ethnic composition of Matthew's readership. Four main scholarly hypotheses have been ventured, which may be graphically displayed along a continuum of possibilities:

Matthew as an utterly	*Matthew in intramural*	*Matthew in extramural*	*Matthew as an utterly*
Jewish composition	*debate with Judaism*	*debate with Judaism*	*Gentile composition*

Fig. 32. The Ethnic and Religious Spectrum of Matthew's Audience

---

10. A Jewish name for non-Jewish people (Heb. *gôy*, "people" or "nation").

11. James D. G. Dunn, *The Partings of the Ways between Christianity and Judaism and Their Significance for the Character of Christianity* (Philadelphia: Trinity Press International, 1991); James D. G. Dunn, ed., *Jews and Christians: The Parting of the Ways A.D. 70 to 135* (Grand Rapids: Wm. B. Eerdmans Publishing Co., 1992).

The first proposal best approximates traditional attestations about Matthew, as remembered by Papias (*Hist. eccl.* 3.39.14–16): that the Gospel was composed in Hebrew or Aramaic by a disciple of Jesus for a community of Palestinian Jewish Christians.[12] The strength of this view lies in Matthew's meticulous Jewishness. It also squares with Jesus' exclusive mandate for the Twelve's missionary scope, without counterpart in either Mark (6:7–13) or Luke (9:1–6): "Go nowhere among the Gentiles, and enter no town of the Samaritans, but go instead to the lost sheep of the house of Israel" (Matt 10:6). Repeatedly Jesus slurs Gentiles' inappropriate conduct (5:47; 6:7, 32; 10:18; 20:19, 25). On the other hand it's hard to reconcile the hard-nosed restriction of Matthew 10:6 with all the Gentile figures that pop up in this Gospel's infancy narrative (1:3, 5, 6; 2:1, 9–12) and with Jesus' own relaxation of Gentile limits in Matthew 15:21–28. "When Jesus heard [a Roman centurion's humble plea], he marveled, and said to those who followed him, 'Truly, I say to you, not even in Israel have I found such faith'" (8:10 RSV).

The second and third possibilities are identical in one major respect: both recognize in Matthew the evidence for scorching controversies between Jesus and his fellow Jews (9:10–11, 34; 11:6–24; 12:2–14, 24–42; 15:1–20; 16:1–12; 23:1–39). These debates continued five to seven decades after Jesus between members of the Matthean community and their Jewish coreligionists. What's unclear is whether Jesus' followers in Matthew's day were still wrangling with their confrères, Jews who rejected Jesus as the Messiah, *inside* a common synagogue, "within its walls," but had not yet broken off from the majority Jewish community; *or* whether an *extramural* split among those who followed Jesus and those who did not had already occurred. In the latter scenario one would assume two groups, both dedicated to Jewish tradition, each defining itself against the other regarding Jesus' significance: Matthew's synagogue in argument with "a synagogue across the street," so to speak. Supporters of an intramural divide[13] point to texts like Matthew 23:2–3: "The scribes and the Pharisees sit on Moses' seat; so do and hold whatever they teach you—but don't act as they do, for they don't walk their talk." Those who believe that Matthew is the product of a schismatic Jewish congregation that has broken off from another Jewish community[14] note that the evangelist tends to refer to "their [i.e., others'] synagogue[s]" (4:23; 9:35; 10:17; 12:9; 13:54). Only in Matthew's version of the parable of the wicked tenants does Jesus conclude, "Therefore, I tell you, the kingdom of God will be taken away from you, and given to a nation [Gk. *ethnei*] that yields the

12. Adolf Schlatter, *Die Kirche des Matthäus* (Gütersloh: Bertelsmann, 1929); Anthony J. Saldarini, *Matthew's Christian-Jewish Community* (Chicago: University of Chicago Press, 1994). See his discussion of Matthew's putative provenance in chap. 1.

13. G. D. Kilpatrick, *The Origins of the Gospel according to St. Matthew* (Oxford: Oxford University Press, 1946), 101–23; Davies, *Setting of the Sermon on the Mount*, 191–315.

14. Stendahl, *School of St. Matthew*, 13–35; David Hill, *The Gospel of Matthew*, NCB (Grand Rapids: Wm. B. Eerdmans Publishing Co., 1981), 48–52.

proper fruit" (21:43 NEB). It is an open question whether Matthew believes that "nation" to be Gentile (cf. 24:14; Gen 17:4–6; Ps 78:55; Isa 2:4) or a more faithful Israel (cf. Amos 9:9; Zeph 2:9), meaning those in the Jewish community who follow Jesus.

The fourth possibility is the first's mirror image: although the Gospel presupposes an indigenous Judaism, the break from its ancestral religion is complete.[15] Continued argument with other Jews has become impossible, irrelevant, or nonexistent; the risen Jesus has commissioned his disciples to "Go therefore and make disciples of all the nations," the *goyîm* (Matt 28:19), and the Jewish Christian community sets its focus exclusively on Gentiles. The difficulties with this reading are at least two. First, as Hebrew Scripture suggests, "the nations" can sometimes *include* Israel. Second, it's hard to imagine a Gospel so drenched in Judaism as this to have irrevocably turned the corner, abandoning Israel altogether.

The fact that all the puzzle pieces do not fit snugly supports the likelihood that Matthew was written for a congregation *in transition*: born and nurtured in Judaism, yet expanding its vision to embrace Gentiles who respond faithfully to Jesus. That is precisely the picture that emerges in other NT writings, especially in Acts and Paul's Letters. Whether Matthew's community has severed itself as a synagogue across the street from Jews who deny Jesus as the Messiah is neither demonstrable nor paramount for this Gospel's interpretation. By the second century the separation of Christianity from Judaism had become sharpened. In the late first century it was ill-defined. That would account for this Gospel's blurred image of Jewish-Gentile relations.

IS MATTHEW'S GOSPEL ANTI-SEMITIC?

To begin with, that question's customary formulation is both imprecise and anachronistic. "Semite" is a racial designation that covers other peoples besides Jews, such as Arabs, Arameans, and Assyrians. *Antisemitismus* first appeared in German print in 1879, evidently as workaround jargon for *Judenhass*, "Jewish hatred."[16] Therefore, what scholars and everyday readers are really asking is "Does Matthew hate the Jews?"

Blunt as it is, that question has agonized Jews, Christians, and others who have read this Gospel. What shall we make of the vitriol that Jesus spews against his Jewish contemporaries in Matthew 23? To cite some of the fieriest fusillades:

15. Wolfgang Trilling, *Das wahre Israel: Studien zu Theologies des Matthaüs-Evangeliums*, 3rd ed., SANT 10 (Munich: Kösel, 1964), 124–52; Sjef van Tilborg, *The Jewish Leaders in Matthew* (Leiden: Brill, 1972).
16. Alex Beim, *The Jewish Question: Biography of a World Problem*, trans. Harry Zohn (Rutherford, NJ: Fairleigh Dickinson University Press, 1990), 595; Deborah Lipstadt, *Antisemitism: Here and Now* (New York: Schocken Books, 2019), 22–25.

> But woe to you, scribes and Pharisees, hypocrites! For you lock people out
> of the kingdom of heaven. . . . For you cross sea and land to make a single
> convert, and you make the new convert twice as much a child of hell as
> yourselves. (vv. 13, 15)

> For you are like whitewashed tombs, which on the outside look beautiful,
> but inside they are full of the bones of the dead and of all kinds of filth.
> (v. 27b)

> You snakes, you brood of vipers! How can you escape being sentenced to
> hell? (v. 33 NRSV)

No wonder modern Jews shudder to read Jerusalem's invocation of the curse
on itself for Jesus' crucifixion: "His blood be on us and on our children!" (only in
Matt 27:25; cf. 2 Sam 1:16; Jer 26:15). Sensitive Christian pastors will not touch
verses like these. Some NT scholars have washed their hands of Matthew, as Pilate
did of Jesus' execution (Matt 27:24), and have diagnosed this Gospel as incurably
anti-Jewish.

Nothing is to be gained by turning a blind eye to such passages. Mischief is
invited by ignoring them or reading them outside the contexts in which they were
written. There's no getting around it: this side of the Shoah, which eventuated
in the extermination of six million Jews by a self-styled Christian nation during
World War II, Matthew 23 is an ugly read. The Holocaust was intended as "The
Final Solution" to centuries of Jewish massacres in all parts of the world, a persecution that persists to the present day.[17] Calling down woes upon scribes and
Pharisees as hypocrites, like whitewashed tombs—outwardly beautiful, but filled
inside with decadent bones (Matt 23:27)—seems like so much gasoline poured
on an unquenchable fire. How shall one respond? NT scholars are of different
minds. Here are some considerations that seem to me apropos and important.
They depend on clear thinking, an expansive scriptural perspective, a lively historical imagination, and genuine Christian kindness.

1. Let's be clear that the invectives in Matthew 23 are not, strictly speaking,
anti-Semitic—though they have certainly and deplorably been deployed for racist
ends. Rather, they are harsh criticisms of particular Jewish leaders by another Jew:
Jesus. His denunciations might be considered anti-Jewish, but even that classifica-
tion misses the mark. If Matthew were truly an anti-Jewish book, it could not be
so inextricably embedded in Jewish Scripture and tradition: "Do not think that
I have come to abolish the law or the prophets; I have come not to abolish but
to fulfill" (Matt 5:17). In this Gospel the nullification of Judaism is no option for

---

17. The mordant observation by Israel Zangwill (1864–1928) is justified: "The Jews are a frightened people. Nineteen centuries of Christian love have broken their nerves" (*The War for the World*
[New York: Macmillan Co., 1917], 416).

Jesus' disciples. Far from it: they are charged to observe its commandments with a rigor that eludes the most pious Jews of Jesus' day (5:19–20).

2. Jesus' reprimands of fellow Jews in Matthew need to be read "trimanually," three-handedly. On one hand, if he leveled "woes" against his coreligionists, then he did nothing other than what prophets within Israel had done across that nation's stormy history.

> Woe to those who call evil good
> and good evil,
> who put darkness for light
> and light for darkness,
> who put bitter for sweet
> and sweet for bitter!
> (Isa 5:20 RSV)

> I have seen your abominations,
> your adulteries and neighings,
> your lewd harlotries,
> on the hills in the field.
> Woe to you, O Jerusalem!
> How long will it be before you are made clean?
> (Jer 13:27 RSV)

> After all your wickedness—
> woe, woe to you!
> says the Lord GOD.
> (Ezek 16:23 RSV, adapted)

On the second hand, none of these prophets, including Jesus, despised their ancestral faith. They censured their people's shortcomings with grief. "Jerusalem, Jerusalem . . . ! How often have I desired to gather your children together as a hen gathers her brood under her wings, and you were not willing!" (Matt 23:37 // Luke 13:34; cf. Jer 3:19; Ezek 18:30). On the third hand, sometimes Matthew's Jesus is anachronistically speaking for the evangelist himself, as a synagogue suffers painful divorce over the importance of Jesus in understanding Judaism's identity and responsibilities. Recall, from our comments in chapter 1, the *M*A*S*H* analogy: the interpretive overlay of one historical crisis upon an earlier trauma, occurring decades previously. Speaking for a minority movement within Judaism, Matthew has ratcheted up the insults—"hypocrites" (23:13, 15, 23, 25, 27, 29), "blind guides" (vv. 16, 24), "blind fools" (v. 17), "snakes" and "brood of vipers" (23:33–34)—against his fellow Jews, some fifty to seventy years later.

3. Matthew's slander needs to be viewed in the light of verbal abuse that characterized the rhetoric of the evangelists' day. Here I bow with appreciation before Luke Timothy Johnson's seminal study of polemic among adherents of religions

and philosophical schools in the ancient world.[18] A disciple of Epicurus, Colotes assailed Plutarch's philosophical champions as "buffoons, charlatans, assassins, prostitutes, [and] nincompoops." Plutarch gave as bad as he got: Epicureans were irreligious quacks, their communities populated with whores (*Mor.* 1086E, 1100C, 1124C–1129B). Gentiles attacked Jews as seditious, atheistic, and misanthropic (*Ap.* 2.6, 14); Josephus and even mild-mannered Philo retaliated that Gentiles were "frivolous and utterly senseless specimens of humanity" (*Ap.* 1.25). Alexandrians, in particular, were promiscuous, shameless, frenzied, and "more brutal and savage than fierce wild beasts" (*Embassy* 18.120, 131–32). Among the Jews at Qumran, not only Gentiles but also Jews who did not measure up to Essene piety were numbered among "the lot of Satan" and worthy of eternal damnation:

> May [the LORD] deliver you up to torture at the hands of all the wreakers of revenge! May you be cursed without mercy because of the darkness of your deeds! May you be damned in the shadowy place of everlasting fire! May God not heed you when you call upon him, nor pardon you by blotting out your sin! May he raise his angry face toward you for vengeance! May there be no peace for you in the mouths of those who hold fast to the fathers! (1QS 2.4–10)

Compared with that withering blast, Jesus' scolding of scribes and Pharisees in Matthew 23 seems tepid. Johnson also reminds us that, if the NT's authors as a whole rake anyone over the coals, it's especially Gentiles (Matt 6:7, 32; Rom 1:18–32; 1 Cor 6:9–10; Eph 2:11–12; 1 Thess 4:5, 13; Titus 1:12; 1 Pet 1:14, 18; 4:3–4) and errant disciples of Jesus (2 Cor 11:1–6, 14–21; 2 Tim 2:14–3:9; 2 Pet 2:1–22; Jude 5–19; 1 John 2:18–25; 2 John 7; Rev 2:13–29).

4. From this soul-stirring tour of scurrilousness, we may draw some commonsense conclusions. *First*, those with whom we are closest are often the targets of our worst character assassination. If you don't believe it, listen to how members of opposing political parties within the United States fulminate at each other.[19] Whether the family is religious, national, or residential, the nastiest fights and harshest words erupt among those within the same home. *Second*, Matthew cannot be held responsible for how his rhetoric, written in a particular place and time, has been hijacked, centuries after he wrote and under circumstances beyond his control, to endorse an

---

18. "The New Testament's Anti-Jewish Slander and the Conventions of Ancient Polemic," *JBL* 108 (1989): 414–41; rpt., idem, *Contested Issues in Christian Origins and the New Testament: Collected Essays*, NovTSup 146 (Leiden and Boston: Brill, 2013), 515–40.

19. Coincidental with one drafting of this chapter was the publication of Eli J. Finkel, Christopher A. Bail, Mina Cikara, et al., "Political Sectarianism in America," *Science* 370 (October 30, 2020): 533–36. Drawing upon political science, psychology, sociology, economics, management, and computational social science, Finkel and fourteen other investigators surveyed dozens of other research studies, published across five decades, concluding that "the current state of political sectarianism" in the U.S.A. is a "poisonous cocktail" of othering, aversion, and moralization that produces extreme prejudice, cognitive distortion, and dysfunctional government.

anti-Judaism or anti-Semitism that was the farthest thing from his mind. *Third*, when reading passages like Matthew 23, let's remember—especially if we are Gentiles—that we've stepped into the middle of an old Jewish family's bickering that in no way sanctions religious bigotry in our day. *Fourth*, kindness requires that we humans recognize ourselves as kindred at both our best and worst. Jesus' followers take their cue from the Most High God, who "is kind to the ungrateful and the wicked. Be merciful, just as your Father is merciful" (Luke 6:35–36). *To conclude*, Matthew, as Jewish as any Gospel could be, offers no warrant whatsoever for Christians' abuse of Jews or of anyone else. Sad to say, twenty centuries later, some Christians have been duped into believing that Judaism must be condemned as false in order for their own religion to be proved true. Of all the Gospels, Matthew precisely demonstrates the reverse. Shear Israel's heritage away from the good news of Jesus the Messiah, son of David and of Abraham, and you rip the heart out of Christianity.

"Taking the High Road"

A Conversation with Alan Culpepper

R. Alan Culpepper (PhD, Duke) is Professor of New Testament, founding Dean Emeritus of the McAfee School of Theology, Mercer University (1995–), and Extraordinary Professor at University of the Free State, Bloemfontein, South Africa (2014–). He has also served as Distinguished Visiting Professor at Candler School of Theology, Emory University (2019). One of this generation's most highly respected scholars on the Gospel of John, his publications span the entire NT. At last count he has written or edited at least nineteen books, including major commentaries on Luke (1996), Mark (2007), and Matthew (2021), the last for the New Testament Library of Westminster John Knox Press.

CCB: Alan, across your career, you have written major commentaries on all four of the NT's Gospels. In your opinion what interpretive challenges does Matthew in particular present?

RAC: Matthew is very Jewish. In fact, I think it comes from a first-century Jewish community of Jesus-followers who were in debate with the Pharisees. Shifting from reading the Gospel as a Christian text to seeing it as a Jewish text—before the so-called parting of the ways between those religions—is especially challenging because ingrained assumptions are hard to shake.

CCB: Matthew's presentation of Jesus seems to me very complicated. Do you agree? If you had to sum up what this evangelist believes about Jesus, what would you say?

RAC: It is complicated. Multiple things seem important for Matthew. Jesus was the Davidic Messiah who fulfilled the law, which he interpreted in a radical way. Jesus was also a new Moses: not in the sense that he brought a new law, but he was the *fulfillment* of the law. At Jesus' birth, therefore, the Jewish king kills Jewish children, and the family needs to flee to Egypt. Their return fulfills the pattern of Israel's exodus from pharaoh's bondage: "Out of Egypt have I called my son" (Hos 11:1). Jesus is also the Danielic Son of Man (Dan 7:13), a title that had acquired messianic significance by the first century. So Matthew understands and interprets Jesus through the frames or filters of the Jewish Scriptures.

CCB: As I have mentioned elsewhere in this chapter, Matthew has a peculiar way of reading Hebrew Scripture. It's not the kind of biblical interpretation that many readers nowadays would adopt or consider defensible. In dealing with this, what should we bear in mind?

RAC: Matthew was written for Jewish readers who read the Scriptures in their first-century Jewish context, approached interpretation in ways that are foreign to us, held assumptions we can grasp only indirectly, and argued with other Jews about Jewish messianism in a historical setting now largely lost to us.

CCB: One standard dictionary defines "ethics" as "the branch of knowledge that deals with moral principles governing a person's conduct." Matthew is clearly interested in the responsibilities of Jesus' disciples. Does this Gospel intend to offer a study of ethics?

RAC: Foundational for any grammar of ethics is the structural interrelation of *what* ought to be done and *why* this ought to be done. When one pursues Matthew's rationale for ethical behavior—the "why?"—three warrants keep recurring: Christology, Scripture, and eschatology.

In word and deed, Jesus shows how Scripture should be interpreted, with an emphasis on purity of heart, love, justice, and mercy. In Matthew 22:34–40 a Pharisaic legal expert asks, "Which commandment *in the law* is the greatest?"—focusing on Torah and giving no thought to there being a second command. Jesus' response adds three statements not found in Mark (12:28–31): (1) Complete love of the Lord God "is the greatest and *first* commandment" (Deut 6:5); (2) "A *second* is like it: you shall love your neighbor as yourself" (Lev 19:18); and (3) "On these *two* commandments hang all the law and the prophets" (Matt 22:40). The effects of Matthew's changes of Mark are to affirm the law's continuing authority, to emphasize serving God out of love, to expand the basis for one's ethic to include the prophets, and to make the command to love one's neighbor an expression of one's love for God—which becomes the norm by which one determines what is of greatest importance.

In Matthew, Jesus reiterates the priority of mercy even above Sabbath observance (9:13; 12:7; cf. Hos 6:6). By showing mercy, a measure of one's love for one's neighbor, one demonstrates love for God. Adopting the attitude of apocalyptic Judaism, Jesus' promises of rewards for the righteous and punishment for the wicked at the last judgment inextricably link ethics and eschatology.

CCB: For many readers a thorny problem is Matthew's depiction of Jesus' fellow Jews as a "brood of vipers," "hypocrites," "blind fools," even "children of hell" (23:13, 15, 17, 33). Some scholars believe that Matthew is downright dangerously "anti-Semitic." How do you respond to such concerns?

RAC: Matthew is hardly anti-Semitic. Such a charge completely misunderstands Matthew and the context in which it was written. The Matthean Jesus is thoroughly Jewish: he is the Messiah of Israel, and he announces the coming of the kingdom of heaven, which will bring blessings to the faithful who follow him by keeping the law of Moses. To a remarkable degree, Matthew shares the worldview of the sectarians at Qumran. Like them, he perceives the corruption of Jewish leadership in Jerusalem. The Essenes assumed that "the spirits of truth and of injustice feud in the heart of man, and they walk in wisdom or in folly" (1QS 4.23–24). Accordingly, humanity is divided between the children of light and the children of darkness (1QS 1.9–10) until "the last day," when God will obliterate injustice forever (1QS 3:17, 19). Albeit sectarian, all this is as Jewish as can be, even though Matthew lacks the Essenes' determinism and explanation of moral differences between people as due to each person's allotted share of good and evil inclinations.

Matthew's debate is not with Judaism but with the Pharisees. In his view the Pharisees, alongside the scribes and the chief priests, have led the people of Israel into lawlessness, with the result that Jerusalem will be or has been destroyed. Foreseeing this judgment, Jesus calls the covenant people to repentance and a greater righteousness based on the "weightier matters" of the law (23:23), and he lays down his life as an atonement for the righteous, who bear the "fruits of repentance" (3:8). Joseph's dream before Jesus was born captures Jesus' messianic identity and mission in one sentence: "He will save his people [Israel!] from their sins" (1:21). The question is not whether Matthew was anti-Semitic, but how Gentiles might also be saved.

CCB: It's safe to say, I think, that the author of Matthew's Gospel had no idea that we would still be reading it nineteen centuries later. At what points, do you think, is Matthew susceptible to a misunderstanding over which the evangelist had no control?

RAC: I see Matthew as arising out of a specific situation and being written primarily for its community or allied communities. The genealogy and the following birth narrative recap the history of Israel, repeatedly reference Israel's Scriptures, and announce their fulfillment in Jesus. In other words, for those steeped in the Scriptures, Matthew writes "the rest of the story," perhaps even intending it to be accepted as an addendum to the Law and the Prophets.

Beyond the challenges of reading any ancient text written in a foreign language, which presupposes an ancient worldview with angels, demons, miracles, and stars that move and social customs foreign to us (such as relations among patrons, clients, brokers; purity codes; and conventions of honor and shame), Matthew is set within an intra-Jewish debate with the Pharisees of his day. Matthew also edits Mark, one might even say correcting and replacing it, and rejects Paul's law-free mission to Gentiles, while advocating Peter (16:18) as the leader of the mission to "all nations" (24:14; 28:19). The most common misunderstandings, therefore, arise from reading Matthew as a Christian gospel that supersedes God's covenant with Israel, based on the spurious assumption that God has rejected Israel because the Jews rejected Jesus.

CCB: Very early and throughout history, Matthew's Gospel has been the most popular and most influential in the church. What do you think is the reason for its impact?

RAC: You're right. The dissemination and influence of Matthew can be seen in allusions to it from the early decades of the second century, in the fragments of Papias of Hierapolis (ca. 60–163). Matthew's popularity in the second century is evident in the number of papyrus copies that have survived, even though most are incomplete, single leaves. The earliest papyrus text containing substantial portions of Matthew and the other Gospels is $\mathfrak{P}^{45}$ (ca. 200). Ten copies of Matthew from the second and third centuries give us 142 of the Gospel's 1,070 verses. It is likely that Matthew was read liturgically, because, among all the Gospels, it has the most stable and fixed text. And we can readily understand why that would be the case. Only Matthew contains the account of the star and the magi, followed by the flight to Egypt (2:1–2, 13–14); the Sermon on the Mount (5–7), with the traditional form of the Beatitudes and the Lord's Prayer (5:3–12; 6:9–13); many of the parables, including the parables of the weeds (13:24–30), the hidden treasure and the pearl and the fish net (13:44–50), the wise and foolish maidens (25:1–13), and the sheep and the goats (25:31–46); Peter's walking on the water (14:28–32) and the conferring of the keys to the kingdom to Peter (16:17–19); and the Great Commission (28:18–20). Matthew's style is more polished than Mark's; it often groups material topically and in triads for easy memorization. It's no wonder, then, that it has been called "the church's Gospel."

CCB: Whether the reader be Christian or not, why is Matthew still worth reading? What does this Gospel help us to understand about Jesus and his followers that is distinctive and important?

RAC: A colleague once remarked, "Even if I knew there were no God, I would still follow Jesus." For instruction in righteousness, purity of heart, forgiveness and mercy, and a call to a high standard of morality along with a scathing attack on hypocrisy, the Gospel of Matthew is incomparable. It should rightly be read and pondered today by anyone who is serious about taking the high road, living wisely and rightly, acting generously and mercifully, doing good, and blessing others. Start with Jesus' teachings in Matthew, especially the Sermon on the Mount (Matt 5–7), the parables in chapter 13, and the teaching material in Matthew 18–22 and 25. Read a paragraph or two a day, chew on it, and see if you don't keep coming back to it.

CCB: Indubitably you have given us much to masticate, Professor Culpepper. We are grateful to you.

A CAUTIONARY CONCLUSION: MERCY AND JUSTICE

> Blessed are the merciful,
>   for they will receive mercy. (Matt 5:7)
> Then I will declare to them,
>   "I never knew you;
>   go away from me, you evildoers." (Matt 7:23)

However much we might wish it otherwise, God's righteousness sustains justice and mercy in tension. God's mercy is uncomfortably just; God's justice is disturbingly merciful. The best evidence for these contentious contentions lies in two parables, found only in Matthew, in 20:1–16 and 25:31–46. Read them. See if they do not make you quiver with anger, shiver in fear, or both.

The vineyard, always commonplace in Galilean and Judean agriculture, is an old metaphor for Israel, especially its wayward tendencies (Isa 5:1–7; Jer 2:1; Ezek 19:10–14; Hos 10:1). In the parable of the vineyard's laborers (Matt 20:1–16), the vineyard belongs to a single landowner; early one morning he begins hiring hands to cultivate his property. All parties agree on a fair wage: a denarius for a day's work (vv. 1–2), which would have been enough to feed a peasant family for a single day. As the day unfolds—nine in the morning, noon, three in the afternoon—the landowner returns to the marketplace, hires other day laborers, promising everyone fair compensation (vv. 3–5). Even at five o'clock, an hour before quitting time, the landowner hires and sends more workers into his vineyard (vv. 6–7). Before sunset the landowner, "the lord of the vineyard" (v. 8), instructs his manager to summon all and pay them their wages, beginning with the last hired, then proceeding to the first and earliest. Surprise: *everyone receives a full day's wage* (vv. 9–10), irrespective of how many hours they worked. The workers since dawn grumble over the incommensurability of effort and compensation (vv. 11–12). The parable's last words belong entirely to the landlord: "Buddy," he says to a protester, "I haven't cheated you. Didn't we agree on the payoff? Take what's yours and scram. It's my choice to pay the last laborer just as much as I've paid you. Can't I dispose of my belongings as I please? Or do you begrudge my generosity?" (vv. 13–15). Most of this parable's listeners *do* begrudge such compassion, unsoftened by their memory of the last of Jesus' antitheses in the Sermon on the Mount (5:43–48). The message here is that disciples should comport themselves with the integrity by which God acts: as a heavenly Father whose goodness in no way depends on human achievement or failure, sending sunshine and rainfall impartially on the just and the unjust alike. None of the laborers in this parable *earns* what he deserves. All receive, in equal measure, a righteously merciful *gift*. Matthew insists that the gospel's obedience cannot be severed from God's overriding grace. Neither can human standards of equity ever do justice to God's goodness. If we can't understand that, then we've gotten the point: God's graciousness is incomprehensible.

Matthew's tableau of the ultimate eschatological judgment (25:31–46) draws on an old type scene that his audience would have recognized: a climactic division between the upright, "who will stand with great boldness . . . and live forever" (Wis 5:1–2, 15), and the sinful, "thrown into the fiery abyss" (*1 Enoch* 90:20a, 26–27), "with the humiliation of destruction" (1QS 4.6b–14).

There, however, the similarity with Matthew 25 ends. Those vindicated in traditional Jewish apocalypticism are on the side of the angels. The righteous know who they are. The books to whom they are addressed alleviate their present affliction and consolidate their confidence. In the Wisdom of Solomon (ca. 50 BCE), the ungodly confess their reprehensible idiocy in two dozen eloquent metaphors: "Fools that we were!" (5:4). In line with traditional apocalypticism, only the sinful are surprised by their fates. In Matthew, *all* are shocked by their outcomes—sheep no less than goats. *Nobody* knew exactly what she was doing or to whom she was doing it. The conduct on which all are judged is what later rabbis called *gĕmîlût hăsādîm*, "the giving of loving-kindness": feeding the hungry, giving drink to the thirsty, hospitality to strangers, clothing the naked, visiting the sick

Fig. 33. A Byzantine mosaic of Christ's separation of sheep from goats (early 6th c.), housed in the Metropolitan Museum of Art, New York. Provided by the Johnston Fund, 1924.

and imprisoned (25:35–39, 42–43; cf. Isa 58:7; Sir 7:35; m. Pirkei 'Abot [Sayings of the Fathers] 1.2; b. Sukkot 49b). None of this constitutes Ethics 922: Advanced Problems in Moral Reasoning. Equally revealing is the sheep and goats' identical question (Matt 25:37–39, 44): "Lord, when was it that we saw you?" The implication is obvious: had they known it was Jesus in need, they would have been on their best behavior. They never knew it. No one recognized their Lord in "the least of these." The "consummate integrity" (*teleios*) demanded of Jesus' disciples is precisely such uncalculating mercy, without expectation of reward (5:43–48). The goats bumble into eternal punishment; the sheep, into eternal life (25:46). Matthew projects no Technicolor slides of either hell or heaven. His stress lies on hordes of bewildered livestock, who've been put on notice regarding the responsibilities of discipleship in the heavenly kingdom ushered in by Jesus Christ.

THE CONVERSATION CONTINUES

Elevating God's Pure Love to a Level beyond Words

A Conversation with Markus Rathey on Bach's *Matthew Passion*

*Markus Rathey (PhD, Westfälische Wilhelms-Universität, Münster) is the Rob-
ert S. Tangeman Professor in the Practice of Music History at the Institute of
Sacred Music at Yale University, where he also serves on the faculty of its Divinity
School. He has authored or edited seven books, including* Johann Sebastian
Bach's Christmas Oratorio: Music, Theology, Culture,[20]—*the first study of that
composition in English, and an introduction to* Bach's Major Vocal Works: Music,
Drama, Liturgy,[21]—*which has fast become a standard work on Bach's sacred
vocal music. Praised for "bringing musicology to the public" (Academia, 2017),
his commentaries on Bach and the relationship of music and religion have been
heard on BBC Radio and read in* The Economist and The Wall Street Journal.
*Professor Rathey is past president of the American Bach Society (2016–20) and
of the Forum on Music and Christian Scholarship (2009–11).*

*CCB: Markus, what religious or theological winds were blowing in Bach's place
and time (Germany, 1685–1750)? Where among them should he be positioned?*

MR: Bach lived in an interesting time. While Germany's Lutheran churches were
deeply rooted in Luther's teachings, a new form of devotion developed, which
revived a medieval mysticism emphasizing the deeply personal love between
the believer and God or Christ. Reflected in theologians like Philipp Jacob
Spener (1635–1705) and August Hermann Francke (1663–1727), this movement
came to be called Pietism. One of its centers was in Halle, not far from Leipzig,
where Bach spent the last twenty-seven years of his life. While in Mühlhausen
(1707–08) Bach had come in contact with Pietist preachers and must have been
familiar with Pietism.

*CCB: Martin Luther (1483–1546), whose Bible in the German vernacular Bach
used, believed that Christ's passion should be engaged in the believer's life. Is
there evidence that Bach believed similarly?*

MR: Bach grew up in a Lutheran environment and, for all we know, remained a
devoted Lutheran all his life. He owned several sets of Luther's printed works.

---

20. New York: Oxford University Press, 2016.
21. New Haven: Yale University Press, 2016.

We can be sure that he was quite familiar with Luther's theology. In the official positions he held at such churches as Leipzig's Thomaskirche and Nikolaikirche, he remained in the realm of Lutheran orthodoxy. While his cantata texts and *Passion* librettos have a very personal tone, there is no indication that Bach was a Pietist. Pieces like the *Matthew Passion* remained very much in line with what orthodox Lutherans would have read, sung, and preached during this time.

We know little of Bach's own devotional beliefs. We *do* know that the passion of Christ played a major role in the devotional life of his contemporaries. People read passion meditations. New hymns about Christ's passion were written. Printed passion sermons found a receptive audience. Notably, in 1722 the widow of a Leipzig jeweler, Maria Rosina Koppy (1682–1722), endowed the celebration, for all eternity, of a special vespers service on Good Friday at Nicholas Church.

The texts for Bach's *Passion*s demonstrate this major role of Christ's passion in the devotional life of Bach's time. In the *Matthew Passion* a chorale addresses Christ as "Most beloved Jesus" (*Herzliebster Jesu*, no. 3); in an aria, the soprano promises, "I will give my heart to you" (*Ich will dir mein Herze schenken*, no. 13). These texts were written not by Bach but by his librettist, Christian Friedrich Henrici, known as Picander (1700–1764); however, Bach decided to set them to music, and we have no reason to assume that he disagreed with their sentiments. In fact, his musical settings underscore the emotional message of these texts.

CCB: Speaking for myself, some of the Matthew Passion*'s most moving moments are those arias and recitatives whose librettos Picander wrote. What were he and Bach trying to achieve by them?*

MR: The musical passion settings of the seventeenth and eighteenth centuries grew out of the medieval chanting of the passion story during Good Friday vespers. Over time, passion liturgies added other material, such as hymns and poetic reflections. When composers started to incorporate operatic forms, such as recitatives and arias, into their music, these reflections expanded even more. Such interpolations function as small "sermons" on the preceding text. When Jesus and his disciples come to Gethsemane, he asks them to wait for him while he is praying and admits that his "soul is distressed to the point of death" (Matt 26:38). After the biblical text, Picander inserts a short recitative for the tenor (no. 19), which reflects on what this means for the believer: *O Schmerz! Hier zittert das gequälte Herz; wie sinkt es hin, wie bleicht sein Angesicht!* ("O agony! Here the afflicted heart trembles; how it sinks to the ground; how his face pales!") We can imagine a spectator watching this scene from afar, reflecting on Jesus' suffering. Just as a good sermon tries to explain what a biblical text means for the believer, the interpolations in Picander's libretto evoke what the passion text means for the listener.

CCB: I gather that musicologists disagree over Bach's motives in the sacred works he produced: whether he was religiously devout, professionally ambitious, or both. What do you think?

MR: The pendulum is swinging back and forth on this question. Soon after Bach's music was rediscovered in the nineteenth century, he was labeled the paradigmatic Lutheran composer: his music was viewed as reflective of his Lutheran devotion. A backlash occurred in the mid-twentieth century as scholars learned more about Bach's everyday employment and came to appreciate his secular works. I think we need to take Bach seriously as a human being and not glorify him to a point where he becomes an idea, not a man of flesh and blood. Bach had professional obligations that he had to fulfill, yet it was up to him how he did it. His job in 1727 was to compose a setting of the passion, but no job description would have asked for a magnificent work like the *Matthew Passion*. We should be cautious when juxtaposing professional obligation and personal dedication. They are not mutually exclusive. It would be fallacious to argue that a tenured theology professor wasn't a devout believer only because his university paid him. The same applies to Bach. He was employed as a church musician in Leipzig, and there were certain things he had to do. That doesn't mean his heart and soul weren't in it as well.

CCB: Describe for us, if you would, the structure of the Matthew Passion *and its integration into the Good Friday vesper service at Leipzig's Thomas Church.*

MR: This is an interesting question because it helps me to highlight how different our way of listening to Bach is from his own time. When we listen to Bach's *Matthew Passion*, we usually do so either in a concert hall or in a church that serves as a performance space. Bach's music is the only item on the program, and we come to hear the magnificent music. In Bach's time it was only part of a long Good Friday service. Bach's *Matthew Passion* consists of two parts; in a concert today we usually take a break between them, during which the performers and audience can stretch their legs. In 1727, when the *Passion* was first performed, its two halves were separated by a sermon of about an hour in length! The sermons preached during Bach's *Passion* performances have not survived, but we can assume that they also interpreted Christ's passion. So Bach's listeners would have heard his musical interpretation interrupted by a homiletical interpretation. The service would also have included other liturgical elements:[22]

22. See Rathey, *Bach's Major Vocal Works*, 78, 108–11.

Hymn: *Da Jesus an dem Kreuze stund* ("When Jesus stood at the cross")

Passion (Part 1)

Hymn: *Herr Jesu Christ, dich zu uns wend* ("Lord Jesus Christ, turn yourself toward us")

Sermon

Passion (Part 2)

Motet: *Ecce, quomodo moritur justus* ("Behold, how the righteous dies," Jacob Handl [1550–91])

Collect Prayer

Biblical verse: "The punishment is upon him" (Isa 53:5)

Hymn: *Nun danket alle Gott* ("Now thank we all our God")

My point is that Bach's listeners would have heard the *Matthew Passion* more as an expanded reading of the Gospel's text than as a concert piece.

CCB: For what was Bach reaching in his presentation of Jesus or the "Daughters of Zion," whom Matthew mentions only in passing (21:5) but who function for Bach as a Greek chorus?

MR: The main purpose of Bach's setting of Picander's text is to intensify the listener's emotional response. Take the opening chorus: Picander's presentation of a dialogue between the "Daughters of Zion" and "the Believers." The latter are urged to prepare for the bridegroom's arrival and to welcome him as the Lamb that is led to be slaughtered (cf. Matt 25:1–12; Rev 5:12; 19:7–9). Bach sets the text, not as a conversation between individuals, but rather as a grand dialogue between two *choirs* and two *orchestras*; and he crowns the whole setting with a chorale melody (a German version of the *Agnus Dei* [Lamb of God]), sung by a *third* group of singers. From the very outset we hear the story as something emotionally overwhelming.

Bach pays a lot of attention to the setting of Christ's words. Bach usually sets the Gospel text in the *Matthew Passion* as sparsely accompanied ("secco") recitatives in declamatory fashion. The words of Jesus, however, are always accompanied by the strings, creating the impression of a halo around his words. Sonically, Bach is differentiating the words of Jesus from the rest of the dialogue—with one exception. The question, *"Eli, Eli, lama sabachthani?"* ("My God, my God, why have you forsaken me?" [Matt 27:46]), is *not* accompanied. We hear Jesus' words of abandonment. The musical halo has vanished for a few measures.

I've mentioned the emotional passion devotion in Bach's time. While the soprano aria, *Ich will dir mein Herze schenken* (no. 13), declares the believer's love, the music goes a step further, setting it in a love song of longing. The text invites the Savior to sink into the believer's heart: "Sink into it, my Salvation" (*Senke dich, mein Heil, hinein*). Bach's setting is a beautiful, optimistic aria in G major. Two oboi d'amore (mezzo-soprano oboes) engage in little dialogues, moving in harmonious, parallel motion—just as we would expect of a secular love duet in an eighteenth-century opera. The soprano follows the two instruments' lead and sings her text with an ascending motive, breaking out in a joyful sigh on the noun *Herze* (heart), and descending on the verb *senke* (sink). Bach's music truly stages the emotions evoked by the text.

CCB: We have no eyewitness account of the premiere of either the Matthew Passion *(1727) or its predecessor, the* John Passion *(1724). If the congregants of Thomaskirche realized they were hearing one of the most wondrous talents in musical history, nothing was said of it. Over a century later a performance of the* Matthew Passion *in Königsberg was dismissed in 1843 as "out-of-date rubbish." What are we hearing today that Bach's earliest audiences could not?*

MR: For a lot of modern listeners, Bach's works are among the most magnificent pieces of music, and it seems inconceivable that his contemporaries did not react to it as we do. But we have to keep in mind that Bach's *Passion*s, like his other oratorios and cantatas, were pieces for the church's liturgy. I am sure that members of Bach's congregation appreciated the music, but liturgical music would not have been reviewed in local newspapers of the early eighteenth century. That isn't so different from today: concerts are reviewed but not pieces played in churches. Some in Bach's time might also have been put off by the dimensions of the pieces: if you went to church to hear a passion sermon and maybe sing some hymns, a large-scale passion setting might have been more than you had wanted.

For that commentator in 1843, Bach's music was indeed out-of-date. Music had moved on. Audiences had learned to appreciate Beethoven, who had died in 1827, and Wagner composed *Der fliegende Holländer* (*The Flying Dutchman*) only eleven years after that criticism was made. A deeper appreciation for "Early Music" was still developing at this time. Audiences' ears had to get attuned to the sounds of a bygone era of music history.

CCB: In both of his Passion*s, Bach's portrayal of Jesus' antagonists has been faulted for its anti-Judaism. Yet in 1829 Felix Mendelssohn (1809–47), who remained proud of his Jewish heritage after conversion to Christianity, almost single-handedly rescued the* Matthew Passion *from obscurity. More recently,*

Leonard Bernstein (1918–90) extolled it as "that glorious work that started me off on my own private passion for Bach." How does one account for this seeming contradiction?

MR: If a Jewish listener takes offense with the perspective on Judaism represented in Bach's *Passions*, I take that seriously.[23] Both the *John* and *Matthew Passions* were written as liturgical music for the Lutheran church, which had traditionally held a negative view of Judaism. But we should read the texts for these two *Passions* carefully. The anti-Jewish tendencies, especially in the *John Passion*, are already part of the biblical text. The reflective interpolations in the arias and recitatives do not emphasize this aspect. Instead, the librettos highlight the responsibility of the individual believer. Early in the *Matthew Passion* we have Christ's last Passover, during which he announces that one of his twelve disciples will betray him. A chorale (no. 10) draws contemporary congregations into this scene by inserting a hymn stanza, commonly the voice of the community of believers: *Ich bin's, ich sollte büssen, . . . Das hat verdienet meine Seel* ("I am the one, I should atone; . . . My soul has merited that"). While the disciples in the narrative are pondering the question of who the betrayer might be (nos. 9d and 9e; Matt 26:22), the Christian congregation confesses its own responsibility for Christ's suffering and death. Thus Bach's librettist makes sure not to blame the Jews for Jesus' death. Christ dies for the sins of believers.

CCB: Based on his sacred works, how would you rate Bach as a theologian and biblical interpreter?

MR: Bach was a dedicated Lutheran with a keen interest in theology and an impressive knowledge of it. We see that from the theological library he left to his family after his death. He had a deep understanding of the Bible and of the theological climate of his time. But first and foremost, he was a magnificent composer who was able to translate the texts at his disposal into music. We see this in the settings of biblical texts as well as in compositions based on eighteenth-century poetry, such as Picander's *Passion* libretto. When Picander writes a text about love, Bach composes a love aria that emotionally takes the idea of God's love to a new level.

CCB: Markus, what haven't we discussed that you think important for us to consider?

MR: One thing I would like to highlight is the end of the *Matthew Passion*. As in its very first movement, Bach composes a piece for two choirs, the Daughters of

23. For further consideration of this subject, see Michael Marissen, *Lutheranism, Anti-Judaism, and Bach's St. John Passion* (New York: Oxford University Press, 1998).

Zion and the Believers. But, instead of a dialogue, the two choirs now sing the same text, a cradle song for the dead Jesus: *Wir setzen uns mit Tränen nieder und rufen dir im Grabe zu: Ruhe sanfte, sanfte ruh!* ("With tears we sit down and call to you in the grave: You rest in peace, in peace rest!"). Bach composes this farewell song as a calm lullaby: in slowly rocking triple meter, with flowing musical lines in the instruments and the voices, and a simple, songlike texture in the vocal setting. The music is calm: not because the listener knows that Easter Sunday is just two days away, but rather, that Jesus' death was necessary for the forgiveness of sins (Matt 26:28). Jesus has died because of his pure love for humankind—as the very first movement of the *Matthew Passion* had announced.

CCB: Our readers might do well to rip from this book my third chapter and instead go and listen to Bach's Matthew Passion. *For sharing with us your insights, Professor Rathey, please accept my sincere thanks.*

4

Jesus according to Luke

Joyous Boundary Breaker

In my history of our *Antiquities*, [A] most excellent Epaphroditus, I have, I believe, made sufficiently clear to any who may peruse that work [B] the extraordinary antiquity of our Jewish race, the purity of the original ancestry, and the manner in which it established itself in the country that today we inhabit. [C] That history embraces a period of five thousand years and was written by me in Greek, on the basis of our sacred books. [D] Since, however, I observe that a considerable number of persons, swayed by the malicious slanders of certain individuals, discredit the statements in our history concerning our antiquity and adduce as proof of the comparative modernity of our race the fact that it has not been thought worthy of mention by the best-known historians, [E] I consider it my duty to devote a brief treatise to all these points, [F] in order at once to convict our critics of malevolence and deliberate falsehood, to correct the ignorance of others, and to instruct all who desire to know the truth concerning the antiquity of our race.

The Jewish historian Josephus introduces his defense of Judaism in *Against Apion* (1.1.1–3) with these words.[1] Note these half-dozen items: [A] its complimentary address to a named recipient, [B] a concise statement of its subject, [C] the author's assertion of his qualifications for writing, [D] acknowledging predecessors, and [E] a comment about his procedure coupled with [F] a clear statement of purpose. Compare that preface with Luke's introduction to his Gospel (1:1–4):

> [D] [1:1]Inasmuch as many have undertaken to compose an orderly account of [B] the events that have been fulfilled among us, [C] [2]just as they were handed on to us by those who from the beginning were eyewitnesses and

---

1. We met Josephus (ca. 37–ca. 100) in this book's introduction, and he's made return appearances since then. I know you remember him. By this time we've gotten to know each other rather well. You're a smart cookie.

Fig. 34. Luke's Gospel Outlined and Summarized

1:1–4	Preface: The evangelist's statement of intention
1:5–2:52	Prologue: The Messiah's birth looks backward and forward
Contents:	The birth and childhood of John the Baptizer (1:5–80) and Jesus (2:1–52) are paralleled.
3:1–4:13	First major section: The prelude to Jesus' public ministry
Contents:	John's ministry (3:1–20) sets the stage for Jesus' baptism (3:21–22), genealogy (3:23–38), and temptation (4:1–13).
4:14–9:50	Second major section: Jesus' ministry in Galilee
Contents:	A complex interweaving of

- controversial instruction (4:14–30, 42–44; 5:17–26; 5:29–6:11; 7:36–50),
- the Sermon on the Plain (6:20–49) and other teachings (7:16–35; 8:4–21),
- mighty works (4:31–41; 5:1–9, 12–16, 26; 6:17–19; 7:1–17; 8:22–56; 9:10–17; 9:28–43a), and
- calling of disciples (5:10b–11, 27–28; 6:12–16; 8:1–3; 9:1–9, 18–27, 43b–50).

9:51–19:27	Third major section: Jesus' journey to Jerusalem
Contents:	The "exodus" of Jesus (9:31) as the framework for sayings and parables drawn primarily from Q and L. Near the end of Luke's central "travelogue" (9:51–18:14), Luke picks up more material from Mark and Matthew (18:15–19:27).
19:28–21:38	Fourth major section: Jesus' ministry in Jerusalem
Contents:	Jesus' teaching in the temple (19:28–48; 21:37–38) brackets continued controversies (20:1–21:4) and the eschatological discourse (21:5–36).
22:1–23:56a	Fifth major section: The passion narrative
Contents:	The plot and the supper discourse (22:1–38); anguish at Olivet (22:39–46); Jesus' arrest (22:47–53), arraignment (22:54–23:25), crucifixion, and burial (23:26–56a).
23:56b–24:53	Sixth major section: The post-resurrection narrative
Contents:	Jesus' exaltation, commissioning of his witnesses, and ascension to the Father.

ministers of the word, [3]I, too, decided, after scrupulously investigating everything from the very first, [E] to write an orderly account for you, [A] most excellent Theophilus, [F] [4]in order that you may know the veracity concerning the things of which you have been instructed.

The elements are shuffled, but all are present: [A] a flattering address to a named recipient (v. 3b), [B] a succinct allusion to the subject (v. 1b), [C] the author's qualifications for writing (v. 2) that [D] recognizes his precursors (v. 1a), and [E] an emphasis on orderly organization (v. 3a) [F] tailored to the achievement of a specific purpose (v. 4).

Josephus presents himself as a competent historian of a religious movement, previously described by others: he endeavors to provide his reader a reliable account. In his Gospel's preface, Luke does the same. This evangelist presents himself as a historian. At strategic points he anchors his history in recognizable places, alongside personages well known to his readers. Yet Luke's is a history shaped by specific religious convictions: God's intervention in human history, beginning in Israel and culminating in Jesus. Josephus is preoccupied with Judaism's venerable antiquity: he insists on that characteristic at least five times in his preface. While Luke shares that concern, he is especially interested in the decisive appearance of Jesus within the history of God's salvation[2] among Israel and the nations (1:65, 77; 2:30–32; 3:6).

Weaving his traditional sources—Mark, Q, and L—Luke has indeed fashioned an orderly account.

What to Look For in Luke

1. *A carefully wrought narrative, composed in an elegant, versatile style.* Among all the Synoptics, Luke is unique in extending the narrative of God's activity through Jesus into the ministry of his witnesses. Alongside his Gospel, Luke creates a second volume, the Acts of the Apostles[3] (see Acts 1:1–5). In both books Luke is a master of Greek diction, adjusting his style to shifts in subject, which can be captured only partially, if at all, in English translation.

2. *A historically sensitive, broadminded positioning of Jesus in Judaism and in the world at large.* Luke is the only Gospel that begins and ends in "the City of the Great King" (Ps 48:2), Jerusalem (Luke 2:22–45; 24:52), and its religious center, the temple (1:5–22; 2:27–49; 24:53). The risen Lord mandates "that repentance and forgiveness of sins should be preached in his name to all nations, beginning from Jerusalem" (24:47). This motif is restated at the beginning of Acts: after forty days the risen Jesus assures his emissaries, "You shall

---

2. Known in German as *Heilsgeschichte*. The classic investigation is by Oscar Cullmann, *Salvation in History*, trans. Sidney G. Sowers (New York: Harper & Row, 1967). More recently, see Brendan Byrne, *The Hospitality of the Gospel: A Reading of Luke's Gospel* (Collegeville, MN: Liturgical Press, 2000), 9–16.

3. Because this second volume develops Luke's thought, sometimes in this chapter I shall refer you to it. Among the evangelists, Luke most consistently denotes the Twelve as "apostles" ("envoys" or "emissaries": 6:13; 9:10; 11:49; 17:5; 22:14; 24:10). That term appears only once in Matthew (10:2) and once in Mark (6:30).

be my witnesses in Jerusalem and in all Judea and Samaria and to the end of the earth" (1:8b).

3. *Coordination of Jesus' life and ministry with God's Holy Spirit*, the engine that drives events surrounding Jesus' birth (1:15, 35, 41, 67; 2:25–27) and, at Pentecost, a spiritual birth of the church (Acts 2:1–21). In every phase—with the prophets, Jesus, the fledgling church—the Spirit activates God's will on the historical stage.

4. *Traveling:* After ministering in Galilee, in chapter 9, Jesus "sets his face to go to Jerusalem" (Luke 9:51), where "his exodus" will be accomplished (9:31). For the Gospel's next ten chapters (until 19:27), Jesus is on the move. Out of 154 occurrences in the NT, the Greek verb *poreuesthai*—"to go," "move along"— occurs 51 times in Luke. (The same verb recurs 38 times in Acts.) Jesus' journeys in Luke anticipate his emissaries' mission in Acts (1:8b).

5. *A ministry that restores society's marginalized: women, Samaritans, Gentiles, the poor, and pariahs.* This theme recurs in Mark and Matthew, but Luke enlarges it. Unlike Matthew's version, Luke's infancy narrative places *two* mothers at center stage (1:24–63). Only Luke presents the parable of "the good Samaritan" (10:30–37): an oxymoronic exemplar for Jesus' pious Jewish listeners. No other Gospel—and aside from the Epistle of James, no other NT book— says more about money, its expenditure and temptations, and relationships between rich and poor as does Luke (e.g., 6:20–25; 12:13–21; 16:19–31; cf. Jas 1:9–11; 2:5–7, 14–16; 5:1–6).

BEGINNINGS: FROM ISRAEL TO JOHN, FROM JOHN TO JESUS

To appreciate this evangelist's adroit coordination of the five points just highlighted, Luke 1:5–2:52 is a model segment. This Gospel does not begin with Jesus' genealogy (cf. Matt 1:1–17); that will be held back until 3:23–38 and presented in reverse sequence with some differences in patrimony.[4] Instead, and altogether unlike Matthew, Luke begins by narrating not one but two infancy stories: the first, that of John the Baptist; the second, that of Jesus. Owing to the interaction of their mothers, who are kinswomen (1:36), the parallel lines converge in an account that could not be more orderly.

---

4. Unlike Matthew's tracing of Jesus' lineage no farther than Abraham, father of the Jewish people (1:1–2), Luke reaches all the way back to "Adam, the son of God" (3:38), thus making a more universal identification.

Fig. 35. A Tale of Two Nativities

John the Baptist		Jesus of Nazareth	
1:5–7	The parents are introduced.	1:26–27	The parents are introduced.
1:8–11	An angel appears to his father.	1:28	An angel appears to his mother.
1:12	The father is terrified (*etarachthē*).	1:29	The mother is terrified (*dietarachthē*).
1:13–17	The angel says:	1:30–33	The angel says:
	"Do not be afraid." (v. 13a)		"Do not be afraid." (v. 30)
	"Will bear a son" (v. 13b),		"Will bear a son," (v. 31a)
	"and you shall call his name John." (v. 13c)		"and you shall call his name Jesus." (v. 31b)
	A hymn follows. (vv. 14–17)		A hymn follows (vv. 32–33)
1:18	The father asks a dubious question.	1:34	The mother asks a dubious question.
1:19–23	The angel replies.	1:35–37	The angel replies.
1:24–25	The mother declares what God has done.	1:38	The mother declares what God has done.
1:57	The time comes: the mother gives birth.	2:1–7	The time comes: the mother gives birth.
1:58	Kinfolk rejoice.	2:8–20	Shepherds rejoice.
1:65–66	News is "laid up in the heart" (*en tē kardia*).	2:19	News is "kept in the heart" (*en tē kardia*).
1:59–64	The infant circumcised on eighth day.	2:21	The infant circumcised on eighth day.
1:69–79	A prophetic hymn: God's act → John's function	2:22–38	A prophetic hymn: God's act → Jesus' function
1:80	The child grew and became strong.	2:39–40	The child grew and became strong.

These congruities are not stylish for style's sake. For Luke, they reveal a theological purpose: God's salvation in history unfolds in a perceptible pattern.[5] What better way to express that belief than in parallel narratives with doubled design?

Style follows substance. Take, for example, the opening and closing of Mary's song of praise (the Magnificat)[6] in Luke 1:46b–47 and 1:54a–55b. Not only are these glorious expressions of praise and remembrance of the Lord God's salvation of Israel; they also exquisitely paraphrase God's mighty acts of deliverance in ages long past.

---

5. See Charles H. Talbert, *Literary Patterns, Theological Themes, and The Genre of Luke-Acts* (Missoula, MT: Scholars Press, 1974).

6. Four oratorios in Luke's infancy narratives have been traditionally dubbed with Latin titles, referring to their first words in the Vulgate, the late fourth-century Latin translation by Jerome (ca. 342–420): the Magnificat (1:46–52), Benedictus (1:67–79), Gloria in Excelsis (2:14), Nunc Dimittis (2:29–32).

Fig. 36. Prelude and Coda
The Magnificat as Reorchestration of Israel's Songs of Praise

My soul proclaims the greatness of the Lord. (Luke 1:46b)	Then my soul will find gladness in the LORD; it will take pleasure in his salvation. (Ps 35:9)
And my spirit has found gladness in his salvation. (1:47)	My heart is strengthened in the LORD; My horn is exalted in my God. I delight in your salvation. (1 Sam 2:1–2)
	I shall find gladness in the LORD; I shall rejoice in God my Savior. (Hab 3:18)
He had helped his servant Israel. (Luke 1:54a) In remembrance of his mercy (1:54b) As he spoke to our ancestors (1:55a)	You, O Israel, my servant Jacob, whom I chose, Seed of Abraham whom I loved, Whom I have helped from the ends of the earth. (Isa 41:8–9)
To Abraham and his posterity forever (1:55b)	He has remembered his mercy to Jacob, And his goodness to the house of Israel. (Ps 8:3)

These coincidences haven't been cherry-picked. Whoever knows the HB can spot its tiles in the mosaic of *virtually every verse*[7] of Mary's song in Luke 1:46–55. Matthew bellows Scripture; Luke whispers it. For both, God's advent in Jesus is no novelty. Both honor the gospel's august antiquity: its embeddedness in ancient Israel.

Also exemplified in this Gospel's opening chapters is Luke's situation of Jesus on the theater of the Roman Empire. Zechariah's vision in the temple occurs in "the days of Herod, king of Judea" and Caesar's client sovereign (1:5). Jesus' birth is coordinated with Augustus's reign (2:1) and Quirinus's governance of Syria (2:2). John's adult ministry and, soon thereafter, that of Jesus are synchronized with "the fifteenth year of the reign of Tiberius Caesar, Pontius Pilate being governor of Judea, and Herod [Antipas] being tetrarch of Galilee," and four other Roman and Jewish authorities (3:1–2a). By implication Luke contrasts the *Pax Christus*, the peace of Christ (1:79; 2:11, 14), with the *Pax Romana*, the peace of Rome. To this topic we shall presently return.

At every point in Luke's infancy narrative, God's Spirit is the prime mover. Matthew presents Mary's pregnancy as the result of divine intervention (1:18, 20). So does Luke, who accents the Holy Spirit's activity in the births of *both* John *and* Jesus. While in utero, John "will be filled with the Holy Spirit" (1:15). Upon receiving her kinswoman Mary, Elizabeth is "filled with the Holy Spirit" as her fetus jumps for joy in her womb (1:41). Gabriel has promised the virgin engaged

---

7. See Raymond E. Brown, *The Birth of the Messiah: A Commentary on the Infancy Narratives in the Gospels of Matthew and Luke*, new updated ed. (New York: Doubleday & Co., 1993), 358–59.

to Joseph, "The Holy Spirit shall come upon you, and the power of the Most High will overshadow you; hence the holy child to be born shall be called the Son of God" (1:35). The Holy Spirit fills both the priest Zechariah, Elizabeth's husband (1:1, 67), and Simeon, a devout Jerusalemite (2:25, 27), until they explode with canticles of praise: respectively, the Benedictus (1:67–79) and the Nunc Dimittis (2:29–32). The latter hymn clarifies that God's salvation knows no boundaries: it "has been prepared in full view of all the nations, a light for revelation to the Gentiles, and glory to your people Israel" (2:31–32).

As Luke-Acts in its entirety dramatizes a gospel on the move, so too does the evangelist's prologue. Notice all the scurrying about. John is prophesied as Jesus' itinerant precursor (1:17): "the prophet of the Most High," who "will proceed before the Lord to prepare his way" (1:76). After Gabriel's annunciation (1:32–35), Mary hurries to Elizabeth (1:39–40). Joseph and Mary journey to Bethlehem, where she gives birth (2:3–7). Prompted by an angelic phalanx singing the Gloria in Excelsis (2:8–14), shepherds hasten to Bethlehem, see the newborn for themselves, then scamper away, "making known the saying told to them about this child" (2:17). All these evangelistic travels are warm-ups for Jesus' own journey in 9:51–19:27 and his followers' far-flung preaching, teaching, and healings recounted in Luke's book of Acts.

Finally, Luke 1–2 announces a theme repeated throughout his Gospel: the sheer *joy*[8] of Jesus' coming for those on the outs (1:14, 44; 2:10; cf. 6:22–23; 10:17; 15:6–10; 19:37; 24:52). Shepherds, not foreign dignitaries, are first on the scene to welcome the newborn Messiah (2:20; cf. Matt 2:1–12). Meanwhile Joseph says nothing, and Zechariah is struck speechless for forty-two verses (Luke 1:22–63); but women, virginal and post-menopausal (1:18b, 27, 34), step into the spotlight to sing arias of bliss that dignify those of low estate (1:48), pull down sovereigns from their thrones while uplifting the humiliated (1:52), fill the hungry with delights and dismiss the rich with empty hands (1:53). Pie in the sky? "With God, nothing will be impossible" (1:37). So these verses spill over with relentless waves of happiness. Young and old, women and men, mortals and angels, bless and praise and give thanks to God (1:47, 64, 68; 2:13–14, 20, 28, 38).

And yet, even as elderly Simeon blesses the parents, he warns Mary:

> Behold, this child is set for the fall and rise of many in Israel,
> and for a sign that is contradicted—
> and a sword will pierce through your own soul as well—
> thus the reckonings out of many hearts may be revealed.
>   (2:34–35)

Luke's readers haven't long to witness that prediction's fulfillment, in all its vile rage (4:16–30).

---

8. In *Christian Character in the Gospel of Luke* (London: Epworth, 1989), 55–70, Brian E. Beck aptly expresses this reaction as "a sense of God."

Fig. 37. A fresco inside the Franciscan Chapel of the Shepherd's Field, built in 1953 southeast of Bethlehem in Palestine's West Bank. According to Roman Catholic tradition, on this site the shepherds received angelic announcement of the birth of "a Savior, who is Christ the Lord" (Luke 2:11). By permission of Custody of the Holy Land. © Enrique Bermejo/CTS.

Synoptic Women

A Conversation with Marianne Blickenstaff

Marianne Blickenstaff (PhD, Vanderbilt) is the author of While the Bridegroom Is with Them *(2005)[9] and with Amy-Jill Levine has coedited seven* Feminist Companions to NT *books.[10] Having taught at Vanderbilt University Divinity School and Belmont University, she has served as lead editor and project manager for Abingdon Press and acquisitions editor at Westminster John Knox Press. Currently she is managing editor of* Interpretation: A Journal of Bible and Theology *and teaches at Purdue University.*

CCB: Marianne, for many years you have studied, in depth, the NT's presentation of women, particularly in the Gospels. Have you found that experience rewarding or frustrating? Or both?

MB: It has been rewarding to see just how integral women actually were to Jesus' mission: they were, in fact, disciples too, even if they are not counted among the Twelve. Most artwork shows Jesus with twelve male disciples, but the Synoptics are full of women like Mary, Martha, Mary Magdalene, and others who also followed him. As we see in Luke 8:1–3, women traveled with Jesus and provided for him, and we find women at the cross and as the first witnesses to the resurrection. A frustration is that some churches still regard women as secondary players.

CCB: We'll return to that point momentarily. Compared with stories involving women in the HB, how sympathetically or derogatorily are women depicted in the Gospels overall?

MB: I think that women are portrayed both sympathetically and derogatorily in both the HB and the NT. The very first woman, Eve (Gen 3:1–24; 4:1), often is blamed for allowing sin into the world in part because of NT interpretations of the story such as 1 Timothy 2:13–14. On the other hand, in the HB, Sarah, Rebekah, Tamar, the midwives Shiphrah and Puah along with Moses' mother, Rahab, Deborah, Jael, Ruth, Bathsheba, and others are remembered for their strong roles in advancing Israel's story (Gen 21:1–7; 25; 37; 38; Exod 1:15–20; Josh 2:1–6:25; Judg 4:4–5:31; 4:17–5:24; Ruth; 2 Sam 11–12; 1 Kgs 1–2). Tamar, Rahab, and Ruth are ancestresses of King David and are listed, along with the

---

9. Subtitled *Marriage, Family, Gender, and Violence in the Gospel of Matthew*, JSNTSup 292 (New York: T&T Clark, 2005).

10. *Matthew* (2001), *Mark* (2004), *Luke* (2002), *John* (2003), *Acts of the Apostles* (2005), *Paul* (2004), and *The Deutero-Pauline Epistles* (2003), all published by T&T Clark International (New York).

"wife of Uriah" (Bathsheba), in Jesus' genealogy (Matt 1:1–17). Beyond the Gospels, Paul names several women church leaders in his letters: Chloe (1 Cor 1:11); Priscilla, who has a house church (1 Cor 16:19); Euodia and Syntyche (Phil 4:2); Apphia (Philem 2); and several women leaders in Romans 16, with the role of "deacon" (Phoebe, v. 1), "co-worker" (Prisca, v. 3), "workers" (Mary, v. 6; Persis, Tryphaena, and Tryphosa, v. 12); and most significantly, "apostle" (Junia, v. 6). Even a more patriarchal letter, 2 Timothy, attributed to Paul (but probably later), honors the strong role of two women named Lois and Eunice, who taught the Scriptures to Paul's co-worker Timothy (Rom 16:21) and brought him up in the faith (2 Tim 1:5; 3:14–15; cf. 1 Cor 4:17).

CCB: Given what we know of the unquestioned patriarchal norms that governed the culture of their composition, is there anything in the Gospels that surprises you as unexpected?

MB: Mary Magdalene is the primary witness to the resurrection in all four Gospel accounts. For this reason, she is called the *apostola apostolorum* ("apostle to the apostles"), the one who tells the other apostles about it, in Matthew 28:8–10 and Luke 24:1–12 (along with other women) and John 20:11–18. In Mark 16:1–8 Mary and other women flee the empty tomb, terrified, but in the longer and later ending of that Gospel (16:9–11), Mary reappears as witness and messenger of the risen Jesus. That the most significant event in the NT was first testified to by a woman, or women, is significant. The Gospel writers did not try to hide this tradition; they honored it.

CCB: Let's break things down a bit. Do you detect notable differences in the way each of the Synoptic Gospels portrays women? Or is the picture about the same across all three?

MB: Women appear as faithful disciples to Jesus in all three Synoptics. Mary the mother of Jesus has a more important role in the Gospel of Luke (1:26–56), but we must use caution with the portrayal of women in Luke.

CCB: I'm glad you brought that up. Some scholars have argued that Luke is sneaky and places female disciples of Jesus in a double bind.[11] What is the best evidence for that reading? Do you agree with it?

---

11. An influential investigation in this vein is Turid Karlsen Seim's *The Double Message: Patterns of Gender in Luke-Acts* (Nashville: Abingdon Press, 1994). Her thesis is that Luke pays positive attention to women as Jesus' disciples yet reasserts conventional female functions in antiquity and deprives women of leadership positions in the first-century church.

MC: Even though Luke seems very sympathetic to women, the Gospel of Luke still portrays them in traditionally feminine roles, such as baking, sweeping a house, and serving, which seems to undermine their role as equals.

CCB: On the other hand, it's interesting that Jesus sometimes describes God in typically maternal ways: nurturing the birds of the air and clothing the lilies of the field (Luke 12:22–28//Matt 6:25–30). Do Jesus' female disciples in the Synoptics come off any better than their male counterparts?

MB: The Gospels often portray the male disciples as misunderstanding who Jesus is or wanting places of honor by his side. Peter's famous fumble was to proclaim him the Christ but then immediately question Jesus' claim that he must suffer and die (Mark 8:29–33). The male disciples all ran away when Jesus was arrested. In the Synoptics, only women are mentioned as being present at the crucifixion (Matt 27:55–56//Mark 15:40–41//Luke 23:49), which was just as much a risk for them as it was for men: women could be crucified, too. Afterward, women are the first to witness the empty tomb and go to tell others (Matt 28:8//Mark 16:7//Luke 24:8–9). Taken as a whole, the women who follow Jesus perform more faithfully than the men.

CCB: Then there's the infamous story of the Syrophoenician woman in Mark 7:24–30//Matt 15:21–28 (omitted in Luke). When she begs for her daughter's healing, Jesus seems to respond as a real jerk. Why is that? Why would early Christians remember and retell such a story?

MB: Jesus calls the woman and her people "dogs" that should not be given the bread meant for the children of Israel. Many Christians find this to be a very harsh presentation of Jesus, which sits uncomfortably with them. But I think the story was remembered and told because it shows the gutsiness of this woman's faith: even though as a Gentile she technically was not part of Israel's promise, she managed to get Jesus to see that she *could* be part of it. It's like Abraham and Moses arguing with God for the fate of the people, and God's changing God's mind (Gen 18:22–33; Exod 32:7–14; Num 11:1–30). Here we have the beginning of the Gentile mission in the Synoptics, which apparently began with this one brave woman's faithful persistence.

CCB: Even though many women have emerged as important spiritual and theological leaders across the centuries, it's no secret that the church has not treated women equitably. Do you think the Gospels are to blame for their second-class citizenship? Or does the problem lie more heavily in the way churches have read the Gospels?

MB: I think the problem lies in the way the church has read the Pastoral Epistles (1 Tim 5:11–16) and some of the Catholic Epistles (1 Pet 3:1–6), which come later than the Gospels and portray women's roles in compliance with conservative social norms rather than the radically sectarian ways of the Gospels. In turn, these conservative roles are read back into the Gospels. In Greco-Roman society women were second-class citizens; while they may have had leadership roles in the earliest Jesus movement and in Paul's churches, they began to lose ground when the church became more institutionalized and conformed to Greco-Roman society's expectations.

CCB: Do you think the Gospels are healthy or hazardous for the women who read them? What reminders or cautions would you suggest to women—to everyone—as they read this literature?

MB: Any interpretation can be hazardous if it subjugates a person to others. Everyone needs to learn critical thinking skills and bring a healthy dose of skepticism to their Bible studies so that they can see many nuances to the portrayal of women—and men—in the Gospels.

CCB: Attention to the nuances is important, I think. Herodias knows how to manipulate her bloviating husband into murdering a righteous man (Matt 14:3–12//Mark 6:14–29). But the Syrophoenician woman demonstrates some faithful pushback against her Lord, who salutes it.

MB: I've enjoyed this conversation!

CCB: So have I! Thank you, Dr. Blickenstaff.

WELCOME HOME—LET'S KILL HIM

Both Mark (6:1–6a) and Matthew (13:53–58) narrate Jesus' cold reception upon returning to teach in his homeland, in Nazareth. In 4:16–30 Luke carefully adapts this account in two crucial ways: (1) he moves it up to the beginning of Jesus' ministry and (2) more than doubles its length. Luke 4:16–30 is Jesus' inaugural address in this Gospel, as the Sermon on the Mount functions in Matthew. Because it amplifies all the themes we have witnessed in Luke's infancy narratives, this passage invites comparable scrutiny. It's a commentary on the remainder of Jesus' ministry in the Third Gospel. Read it carefully, and pay attention to at least these half-dozen components.

Fig. 38. Remains of the Migdal Synagogue, dated ca. 50 BCE–100 CE. Discovered in 2009, this is the earliest of seven known Galilean synagogues from this era. Covering thirteen hundred square feet, it is located on the northwest shore of the Sea of Galilee, on the ancient site of Magdala, associated with Mary Magdalene. In the center is the Magdala Stone, which bears the earliest known images of the temple menorah yet found in a synagogue. Photograph by Clifton Black.

1. *Jesus preaches a contentious gospel, grounded in Jewish Scripture and pious observance.* Returning home to Nazareth, Jesus is accustomed to attending synagogue on the Sabbath and bases his preaching on Scripture (4:16–20a). He is as devoutly Jewish as those figures portrayed before and after his birth: Zechariah and Elizabeth (1:6), "the whole throng of the people" gathered to pray (1:10), Mary and Joseph who continually follow the law (1:30; 2:22–24, 27, 39), righteous Simeon (2:25) and Anna (2:37b). Throughout Luke, much of Jesus' ministry occurs on the Sabbath (4:31; 6:1–9; 13:10–17; 14:1–5) and in a synagogue (4:33–38; 6:6; 7:5; 8:41; 13:10, 14). Sometimes his ministry is received with enthusiasm (4:31, 36–37); at other times, it is fiercely rejected (6:6–11; 13:10, 14). So Simeon had warned Mary that her child was "destined for the rise and fall of many in Israel—a controversial sign" (2:34). Jesus' mission will fracture families (12:49–53). As early as 4:16–30, it incites a riot.

2. *"The Spirit of the Lord is upon me"* (4:18a). For Luke's understanding of the "Savior, who is Christ the Lord" (2:11), Jesus' quotation of Isaiah 61:1 in Luke

4:18a could not be more consequential. While present in Mark (1:8, 10, 12; et al.) and Matthew (1:18, 20; 3:11, 16; et al.), the Holy Spirit is front and center in Luke (and Acts). The same Spirit that authorized Elijah (Luke 1:17) and testifies to God through Scripture (4:18) creates Jesus' very existence (1:35), then empowers his preaching and healing (3:16–22; 4:14, 18). An outpouring of the Spirit fills righteous Jews (1:15, 41, 67; 2:27; 4:1) and, in Acts, will do the same among God-fearing Gentiles (e.g., 2:1–11; 8:14–17; 10:44–48). Combating unclean or malicious spirits (Luke 4:31–37; 8:26–33; 9:37–43a; 13:10–17), the Holy Spirit may be resisted, but never without baleful result (12:10; Acts 19:13–18). For Luke, the Spirit's communion with receptive human spirits is intimate yet universalizing: the Spirit reveals God's will (2:26), strengthens (1:80), consoles (2:25), generates joy (10:21), leads (4:1), and teaches (12:12). The Spirit can be neither wangled nor bartered, as a greedy magician attempts to do in the book of Acts (Acts 8:9–24). For the repentant, the Spirit is God's pure gift (Luke 11:13); after Jesus' heavenly exaltation (Acts 2:33; 5:31), the Spirit will serve as Jesus' proxy (16:7), guarding the church of God obtained by his own blood (20:28).

3. *"Good news to the poor"* (Luke 4:18b) is a Lukan hallmark, often expressed in passages without parallel in the other Synoptics. Unique to Luke are Mary's declaration about God in the Magnificat: "The hungry he has filled with good things, and the rich he has sent away empty-handed" (1:53); a blessing of the indigent paired with woes invoked on the rich (6:20, 24; cf. Matt 5:3); a puzzling characterization of Pharisees as "money lovers" (16:14); three mandates to invite the poor to banquets (14:12–13, 21); and three parables about the heartless avaricious who receive their comeuppance (12:13–21; 16:1–9, 19–31). Luke addresses a society in which, at best, 70 percent scrape by day to day and, at worst, are hobbled in grinding poverty. As for the wealthy, "Every one to whom much is given, of him will much be demanded" (12:48b). Among the Synoptics only Luke identifies women who *financially supported* Jesus and the Twelve (8:1–3). Beyond sensitivity to economic inequities and the virtue of unreciprocated hospitality, Luke believes that God and wealth compete for human adoration (16:13). To this, too, we shall return.

4. *Release for captives, the blind, and the oppressed* (Luke 4:18c) paraphrases Isaiah 61:1, epitomizing Jesus' ministry in Luke. Filled with the Spirit, Zechariah foretells "salvation from our enemies, and from the hand of all who hate us" (1:71). In one episode after another, Jesus fulfills this prophecy: casting out demons (4:31–41; 9:37–43; 11:14), welcoming society's outcasts (7:36–50; 19:1–10), protecting the hungry (9:10–17) and vulnerable (17:1–4; 18:15–30), and curing the sick (5:12–32; 6:6–19; 7:1–23; 8:22–56; 13:10–17; 14:1–6; 18:35–43; 22:49–51). Jesus' prodigious authority to heal is conferred on the Twelve (9:1–6), on seventy others (10:1–12, 17–20), and eventually on his envoys in Acts (2:37–41; 3:1–10; et al.). With Jesus' coming, *this* is the Year of Jubilee (Luke 4:19): after seven Sabbatical Years, debtors

are released from their obligations in the fiftieth year (Lev 25:8–12). *Today* God's salvation breaks through (Luke 4:21; cf. 2:11; 5:26; 13:32–33; 19:5, 9; 23:43). The most dramatic, albeit ironic, instance of release from captivity in Luke is Jesus' willing substitution of himself for Barabbas, freeing "a man thrown in prison for murder," and taking capital punishment upon himself (23:13–25). In no case does honor redound to the human wonder-workers who are the conduits of healing and release: praise of Jesus (4:41b; 5:25; 7:16; 8:39; 9:43) and of his apostles (Acts 2:47; 3:8–16; 14:11–18; 17:16–31) is redirected to God's glorification (Luke 2:13, 20; 5:25–26; 7:16; 13:13; 17:15, 18; 18:43; 19:37; 23:47). After all, "We are meritless slaves who have only done our duty" (17:10).

5. *The proclamation of universal salvation provokes outrage* (Luke 4:22–29). Nazarene plaudits sour when Jesus embraces the detestable. According to Scripture, as Jesus points out to his audience, the prophets Elijah and Elisha cast judgment on Israel by extending God's benevolence to Gentiles: a Sidonion widow (1 Kgs 17:1–16) and a Syrian commander (2 Kgs 5:1–15). This is precisely where Luke (24:47) and, in greater detail, Acts (1:8; 14:16) are headed. Without ultimately spurning Israel (Luke 1:16, 64, 68), God's mercy extends to Samaritans (irreligious half-breeds in pious Jewish eyes: 10:30–37; 17:11–19; cf. 2 Kgs 17:24–29). It embraces even Canaanites, whom Israel once dispossessed (Acts 7:45; 13:19–20a), and Gentile kings who had since taken Israel captive (Luke 21:24; 22:25) and had killed the Christ in collusion with Israel's leaders (22:63–23:48). As Simeon prophesied at Jesus' birth (Luke 2:29–32), no longer has Israel alone been called by God as a people for his holy name (Num 6:27; 1 Chr 17:21): "God had opened a door of faith to the Gentiles" (Acts 14:27; cf. 11:1; 15:7). This is the wondrous contradiction: God is never more faithful to the covenant established with Israel than when exercising sovereign freedom to extend salvation to whomever it pleases the Almighty. "When they heard this, all in the synagogue were as mad as hell, and they got up, threw [Jesus] out of the city, and dragged him to the edge of the hill on which their city was built, intending to hurl him down headlong" (Luke 4:28–29).

6. *An unimpeachable testimony to God's invincible will* (4:30): Jesus escapes death through mysterious means, walking through the murderous crowd, because a prophet cannot perish away from Jerusalem (13:33–34; 18:31). So it follows for all disciples: sinners though they be (5:8; 7:37, 39), their commission is to offer testimony, be it accepted or not, to "what you have seen and heard" (Acts 22:15; cf. Luke 9:5; 21:13). In spite of obstructions, refusal, and dire cost, God's "definite plan" (*hē boulē*) has predestined salvation for all "who trust in [Jesus] and receive forgiveness of sins through his name" (Acts 2:23; 10:43; cf. Luke 7:30).[12]

---

12. On "the purpose of God" in Luke, see Joel B. Green, *The Theology of the Gospel of Luke*, NTT (Cambridge: Cambridge University Press, 1995), 22–49.

Fig. 39. *The Return of the Prodigal Son* (1636), by Rembrandt van Rijn (1606–69). Housed in the Rijksmuseum, Amsterdam.

Need I add that Jesus' sermon at Nazareth two millennia ago raises the hackles of his followers to this day? What will they do with a Messiah who reminds them—from Scripture, no less—that God is terrifyingly faithful yet scandalously free to save people who aren't like them? That God won't be caged or abide by their standards of religiosity? Why, the next thing you know, Jesus will be telling us that the Most High is merciful to the ungrateful and the selfish (Luke 6:35), that pastors may leave their compliant flocks of ninety-nine to rescue one wayward lamb (15:3–7), and that are all invited to a jamboree for a wastrel who blew half the family's fortune on punts,[13] pot, and prostitutes (15:11–32). Everyone loves the parable of the prodigal son until they realize that God is racing down the road to hug someone other than themselves. It's no surprise that Jesus ended up crucified. The wonder is that he wasn't lynched in Nazareth at the start.

Would You Believe It?

Part II: Miracles

Behind the word "miracle" is *miraculum* (Lat.): "an object of wonder." That's one fair translation of the Greek term *dynamis*, which in the Gospels often refers to Jesus' "mighty works" (Matt 11:20–21//Luke 10:13; Matt 13:54//Mark 6:2; Luke 19:37). (That term's connotation of power is carried over into the English word "dynamite.") To think of a *dynamis* as "a breach of scientific laws" is anachronistic since such principles had not been formulated in the first century. Most modern readers of the Gospels are ignorant of the social and religious contexts in which the evangelists understood Jesus' exorcisms and healings.

That Jesus did such things cannot be doubted: they bubble up in every traditional stratum on which the Gospels relied. Even Josephus notes that Jesus was "a doer of startling deeds" (*A.J.* 18.3). By no means was Jesus antiquity's only itinerant miracle worker. But at least four things distinguish Jesus' mighty deeds—and all intersect with his preaching of the kingdom.

1. The beneficiaries of his healing were usually those on society's fringes: widows and children (e.g., Luke 7:11–17; Matt 17:14–21//Mark 9:14–29//Luke 9:37–48a), lepers and demoniacs (Matt 8:1–4//Mark 1:40–45//Luke 5:12–16; Matt 8:28–33//Mark 5:1–20//Luke 8:26–34), the blind and the deaf and the hungry (Matt 20:29–34//Mark 10:46–52//Luke 18:35–43; Matt 15:29–31//Mark 7:31–37; Matt 14:13–21//Mark 6:30–44//Luke 9:10–17). Cures and evangelism converged: "Jesus went all over Galilee, teaching in their synagogues, preaching the good news of the kingdom, and healing people from every kind of disease and sickness" (Matt 4:23 TEV; cf. Luke 4:40–43).

2. Jesus was remembered as linking his mighty works with the routing of the kingdom of God's enemies: demonic spirits (Mark 1:21–28//Luke 4:31–37; Mark 3:11//Luke 4:41a). When scolded by a synagogue officer for nullifying the Sabbath by curing a crippled woman, Jesus angrily reframed the issue: "You hypocrites! . . . Shouldn't this woman, a daughter of Abraham whom Satan tied

---

13. My editors fear that you, our readers, will not know that punters are stock-market speculators who gamble on high profits in volatile circumstances. If you were among the 54 percent of U.S. college students who majored in business during 2019–20, I'd bet you do. And if by now you are reading this book, you may have developed healthy interests other than making money.

up for eighteen long years, be liberated from this bondage on the Sabbath day?" (Luke 13:15a, 16).

3. Among ancient philosopher-healers, modesty was measly. Meet Empedocles (490–430 BCE):

> I sojourn among you as an immortal God, no longer mortal, venerated by all, adorned with holy diadems and blossoming garlands. I am praised by men and women and accompanied by thousands, who thirst for deliverance: some beseeching prophecies, others entreating my remedies for manifold disease. (*Pur.* 8.61)

By contrast, Jesus consistently turned attention away from himself: "And many followed him, and he cured them all, and he ordered them not to make him known" (Matt 12:15b–16; cf. Mark 7:36; 8:30; Matt 8:4//Mark 1:44//Luke 5:14). "Trust *God*" (Mark 11:22, emphasis added), for by such faith healing can occur (Matt 9:22//Mark 5:34//Luke 8:48; Matt 9:29//Mark 10:52//Luke 18:42).

4. Faith in God's power not only makes therapy possible; it also renders it intelligible. Jesus' deeds were celebrated but also dismissed (Matt 16:1–4//Mark 8:11–13//Luke 12:54–56), repudiated (Matt 9:3//Mark 2:6–7//Luke 5:21), or misattributed to Satan (Matt 12:24//Mark 3:22//Luke 11:15–16). Mighty works were equivocal acts. For the faithless, they proved neither the incursion of God's kingdom nor the credibility of their performer, Jesus. Yet in them the faithful found verification of both: "But if by the finger of God I cast out demons, then the kingdom of God has come upon you" (Luke 11:20).[14]

THE CASE OF THE WOEBEGONE WEALTHY

All the Synoptics present an encounter between Jesus and a man who asks him what he needs to do to secure eternal life (Matt 19:16–22//Mark 10:17–22//Luke 18:18–25). Luke's version stands out because, more than others, this Gospel constantly circles around its real subject: the danger of possessions and the necessity of their distribution among the needy.

The inquirer is denoted "a certain ruler" (*tis archōn*, Luke 18:18). Over what he rules we aren't told. "Rulers" in Luke are ambivalent. Some are admirable, like Jairus the synagogue ruler (8:41–42) or a humble centurion (7:2–10). Of the latter, Jesus says, "Not even in Israel have I found such faith" (7:9). Another ruler, a

---

14. On miracles, consult the perceptive analysis of Luke Timothy Johnson, *Miracles: God's Presence and Power in Creation*, IRUSC (Louisville, KY: Westminster John Knox Press, 2018).

Pharisee, is affronted by Jesus' working on the Sabbath, healing a man suffering edema (14:1–6). From Mary's Magnificat (1:51–52) we've learned that God is kicking the powerful off their thrones. In 18:18 we can't be sure of this ruler's character.

He asks, "Good Teacher, what must I do to inherit life eternal?" (v. 18). While the wording is identical with Mark's (10:17), it's noteworthy that the question is framed in economic terms: inheritance (*klēronomēsō*). "Eternal life" is mentioned in Luke only thrice: here; in the next passage, about recompense for those who have divested much for the kingdom (18:26–30); and in a quiz question put to Jesus by a certain lawyer in 10:25, in a setup for the parable of the good Samaritan (10:29–37), which shares similarities with 18:18–30. While the HB says little about eternal life (Job 19:25–26; Dan 12:2), the notion of indestructible life, transcendent blessedness as God knows it, gathers steam in Jewish literature written between the two Testaments (Wis 5:15; 4 Macc 15:3; *Psalms of Solomon* 3:16): "Since we die for his laws, the King of the universe will raise us up to a life everlastingly made new" (2 Macc 7:9 NEB).

Again deflecting any compliment for his goodness—"Why do you call me good?"—onto God alone (Luke 18:19), Jesus directs his questioner to the fulfillment of five of the Ten Commandments (18:20; Exod 20:12–16//Deut 5:16–20), which track with the imperative to live out complete devotion to God and love of one's neighbor in Luke 10:27–28 (Deut 6:5; Lev 19:18). There's no reason to suppose that Jesus' interlocutor is insincere in claiming he has kept God's commandments all his life (Luke 18:21). He should be home free, right? According to Jesus, "Yet you lack one thing. Everything—whatever you have—sell and distribute it among the poor, and you shall have treasure in heaven, and come, follow me" (18:22). In exactly twenty Greek words the Teacher has said a mouthful. (1) He's reminded us of "the good news preached to the poor" in Nazareth (4:18c). (2) His questioner has received a straight answer, which (3) entails discipleship to Jesus and (4) requires complete relinquishment of one's possessions for the benefit of those with none. Only in Luke's version of this story is the man required to divest himself of *everything* (*panta*; cf. Matt 19:21//Mark 10:21), just as Levi "leaves everything" at his tax office to follow Jesus (Luke 5:27–28) and the Samaritan of Jesus' parable opens a running tab to cover *all* of an injured stranger's expenses (10:34–35). Only in Luke are beatitudes for those now poor and starving (6:20–21) accompanied by woes leveled at the wealthy and those who now have it all (6:24–25). (Matthew's parallels make no indictments of the rich; the blessings are religiously and ethically curved away from tangible physical conditions: "the poor in spirit" [5:3]; "those who hunger and thirst for justice" [5:6]). Now comes the kicker: for the first time we learn that this fellow, pious though he be, is very rich (Luke 18:23b). "Sad" (NRSV) is an insipid translation of the ruler's response to Jesus' command (18:23a): *perilypos* suggests mournful grief. (Matt 26:38//Mark 14:34 use the same adjective to portray Jesus' distress in Gethsemane.) Jesus

Fig. 40. Relaxing atop the Mount of Olives, a camel regards with curiosity the needle held before it in the photographer's other hand. Photograph by Clifton Black.

concedes to the rich ruler grieving before him a sober fact, comically phrased: "How hard for those with wealth to enter the kingdom of God. For it's easier for a camel to come into the eye of a needle than for the rich to come into the kingdom of God" (Luke 18:25).

Luke is making two points: one moral, the other theological, both significant. Among the wretchedly poor of Luke's world were Jesus and his parents: the latter could afford only the most meager temple offering for their newborn (2:22–24; cf. Lev 12:8), who had been cradled in a trough perfumed by cattle turds (Luke 2:7). In another parable, unique to Luke (16:19–31), ulcerated Lazarus, slobbered by dogs, lies in wait of crumbs dropping from the lavish table of an opulent rich man, oblivious to the beggar's need. After death their stations are flipped: Lazarus nestles in Abraham's bosom; the plutocrat writhes in the fiery torment of Hades. Between them the chasm that in life should have been overcome is now unbridgeable: "If [the rich] do not listen to Moses and the prophets, neither will they be persuaded if someone should rise from the dead" (v. 31).

Equally sharp is the theological point in Luke 18:18–25. It's no accident that this exchange is prefaced by Jesus' paradoxical warning that entrance to God's

kingdom is impossible unless one receives it as does a child (18:17//Mark 10:15//
Matt 19:14; cf. Matt 18:2). The economy of God's kingdom overturns any known
in this world. The child's advantage is the helplessness to do what only God can do
for the child. "Who, then, can be saved? What is humanly impossible is possible for
God" (Luke 18:26–27). In the kingdom's ledger, acquisition of the whole world is a
net loss for those who have sacrificed their very selves (9:25). So it follows: the prosperous are paralyzed by their property. Unless they are surrendered, the possessions possess the possessors; the wealthy forfeit the permanence they seek (18:18).
At bottom the choice is between God and mammon[15] (16:13): In what does one
invest ultimate trust? Which deity is genuine? Which is phony? Which is adored?
Which is abhorred? Whom, or what, does one treasure more than all else (12:34)?

How does a would-be disciple of Jesus become so childlike to receive eternal
life? For Luke, the answer is as basic as it is ceaseless: human repentance, inviting
divine forgiveness. "Repentance" in this Gospel (and in Acts, as in 2:38; 5:31;
26:20) is not self-recrimination for being insufficiently religious. Nor is "forgiveness" carte blanche to do whatever one likes. Repentance, *metanoia*, literally refers
to the mind's reversal: instead of self-preoccupation, *one turns the mind Godward* in
the ways that Jesus teaches (Luke 13:3, 5; 24:47). Forgiveness is a religious metaphor drawn from economics: the release from captive indebtedness incurred by
the sin of human self-absorption: "Father, . . . forgive us our debts for we, too,
forgive everyone indebted to us" (11:4; see also 7:41–49; 23:34). "Just so, I tell
you, there is joy before the angels of God over one sinner who repents" (15:10).
The economy of repentance and forgiveness, which governs heaven, is not post-
poned to the afterlife: the angels are celebrating now. If, as Jesus preached in
Nazareth, *today* is the time of all captives' release (4:18), then *now* the hungry
must be fed (which entails repentance) and one's debtors released (forgiveness).
"Pay attention: if your brother sins, reprimand him; and if your sister repents,
forgive her; and if they sin against you seven times in a day yet turn to you seven
times and say, 'I do repent,' you have to forgive them" (17:3). "Don't judge, and
you won't be judged; don't condemn, and you won't be condemned; forgive,
and you'll be forgiven" (6:37). Luke 15:11–32 is a parable of not one but three
prodigals: the younger son; his incredibly compassionate father, who released
his ingrate child from staggering damages; and the elder brother, who despised
another's forgiveness and reckoned himself enslaved when in fact he had been
free all along (vv. 28–31).

Unlike Matthew (19:22) and Mark (10:22), Luke does not say that Jesus' well-
tailored inquirer slinks away, his tails between his legs (Luke 18:23). A few verses
later, another fat cat meets Jesus and voluntarily donates half his possessions to the

---

15. A late Middle English term, originally derived from the Aramaic word *māmōnā'*, referring to a
Syrian god of riches; hence, "wealth, riches."

poor and promises fourfold restitution to all from whom he has embezzled (19:1–10). Salvation, or restoration (*sōtēria*), has arrived "today" (v. 9). A camel *can* squeeze through a needle's eye—but that transit may be mighty rough on the camel.

Tough? Yes. Utopian? No. For twenty-nine years Anjezë Gonxhe Bojaxhiu (1910–97), an Albanian nun, ministered to the poorest of Calcutta's poor. In 1948 she began with a one-dollar sari and no money, persistently begging for food and medical supplies. By the 1960s Pope Paul VI gave her a limousine, which she raffled for her Missionaries of Charity. Accepting the Nobel Peace Prize in 1978, Bojaxhiu, now known as Mother Teresa, refused its gift and gala, redirecting Oslo's $192,000 to relieve India's impoverished. When the Nobel Committee asked her what others should do to promote peace, she replied, "Go home and love your family."

CAESAR VERSUS CHRIST

Lately scholars have worried over the Third Gospel's interaction with the Roman Empire. In Luke 2:1–5 Joseph and Mary comply with a census that supports imperial taxation and military operations (cf. Acts 5:36–37, about Jews who rebelled against such a census). Later (Luke 20:20–26) a trap is laid for Jesus over the question of paying imperial taxes. In 19:43–44 and 21:20–24, Jesus predicts a Gentile (Roman) military siege that will destroy Jerusalem and its temple. Does Luke mean to defend infant Christianity? Cooperate with the empire? Assail it?[16] Before addressing those questions, let's toss ourselves a Caesar salad.

Big Julie and the Imperials

Ancient Roman government was styled as SPQR: *Senātus Populusque Rōmānus*, "The Senate and People of Rome." In theory, authority was vested in the Senate: a council of elder aristocrats and freedmen among the military, judiciaries, and boroughs. Senatorial power enjoyed its zenith during the second and first centuries BCE.

1. But then **Gaius Julius** Caesar (100–44 BCE), commander of the Roman legions and temporary dictator, triggered a civil war that culminated in his assassination by senatorial conspirators on March 15 in 44 (*Jul.* 76–82), the withering of republican power, and the emergence of a Roman Empire under Caesar's

16. Favoring Luke as a defense against the Roman Empire is Henry Joel Cadbury, *The Making of Luke-Acts*, 2nd ed. (London: SPCK, 1958), 308–16; as détente, Robert Maddox, *The Purpose of Luke-Acts* (Edinburgh: T&T Clark, 1982), 91–99; as critic, Richard J. Cassidy, *Jesus, Politics, and Society: A Study of Luke's Gospel* (Maryknoll, NY: Orbis Books, 1978).

grandnephew and adopted heir, Octavian (63–14; reign, 27–14). Octavian took the humble name Augustus Caesar: "The Revered Emperor" (see Luke 2:1).

2. **Octavian**'s talent was tightrope walking. Rome had turned the corner toward one-man rule, but the Senate wouldn't tolerate another tyrant like Julius. Dazzlingly ambidextrous, Octavian extended with his right hand what he retracted with his left. He minimized popular elections while showering cash on thousands of plain folk. He made himself military *imperator* (triumphant commander-in-chief), hiring and firing his generals, overhauling legionaries' pensions so lavishly that he stymied their rebellious commanders. He restyled senators as administrators with enough honors, perks, and manipulable power so that they conferred on him the title of *Princeps* (first and foremost) and renamed a calendar month after Julius: July to August (*Aug.* 23–58). Basically, Augustus was a revolutionary masquerading as an establishment reformer. In his first-person funerary inscription *Res gestae* ("The Things I Did"), he wanted to be remembered for his largesse, rebuilding Rome, and doubling the empire's territories. His last words were, "Have I played the part well? Then applaud as I exit" (*Aug.* 99): a sly dog to the end.

3. Augustus's stepson **Tiberius** (42 BCE–37 CE) took over in 14 CE and ruled for the next twenty-two years (*Ann.* 1.10–13). Luke 3:1–2 synchronizes John the Baptist's preaching with Tiberius's fifteenth imperial year (ca. 29). Beginning with a rotten economy and a mutinous military, Tiberius's reign appears as bland as his predecessor's was splashy. Some senators had preferred other stepsons as the next Caesar. This did nothing to improve his disposition, which Pliny the Elder dubbed "the gloomiest of men" (*Nat.* 28.5.23). Having retired from politics in middle age before Augustus's death, Tiberius seems almost to have been dragged onto the throne and, once there, wanted the Senate to conduct the business of state and leave him alone (*Ann.* 3.32, 52). He was blasé about expanding the empire or being drawn into other potentates' skirmishes.

Occasional uprisings left Tiberius unfazed. About twenty-five convicts were executed for treason during his reign, which averages out to one victim per year. Some among these twenty-five, like Jesus, were innocent. Tiberius spent his last decade on the Isle of Capri, a virtual recluse. A lot of people asked, "What the hell is he doing over there?" Suetonius (*Tib.* 43–45, 60–64) cataloged salacious rumors of debauchery and abuse. After dying at age 77, the Senate did not deify him as they had Augustus, even Julius. Mobs demanded that his corpse be flung into the Tiber River (*Tib.* 73–75). It was respectfully cremated. He left the imperial treasury in the black by almost three billion sesterces (about 675 million U.S. dollars in 2022). Did this relieve Galileans, Judeans, and other Jews of tax burdens? To judge by Luke 20:20–26 and Romans 13:6–7 (ca. 56), of course not.

A. Julius Caesar. Archaeological
Museum, Turin, Italy. Photograph
courtesy of Ángel M. Felicísimo.

B. Augustus. Louvre, Paris.
Photograph courtesy of Carole
Raddato.

C. Claudius. Ny Carlsberg Glyptotek,
Copenhagen. Photograph courtesy of
Richard Mortel.

D. Nero. Glyptothek, Munich.

Fig. 41. A–I. Nine Caesars

E. Galba. Antiques Museum Royal Palace, Stockholm. Photograph courtesy of Wolfgang Sauber.

F. Otho. Houston Museum of Natural Science. Photograph courtesy of Ed Uthman.

G. Vitellius. Louvre, Paris. Photograph courtesy of Marie-Lan Nguyen.

H. Titus. Castello Barbacane, Island of Pantellaria. Photograph courtesy of Rabax63.

I. Domitian. Altes Museum, Berlin. Photograph courtesy of Richard Mortel.

4. Panting in the wings was **Gaius** (12–41), nicknamed **Caligula**: "Booties."[17] Already we know this won't end well. Rumor had it that Gaius, at the time visiting an imperial villa, first heard of Tiberius's death, then later that the emperor hadn't died but was recovering. Gaius sprang into action and, with a henchman's help, smothered the old man (*Ann.* 6.50; *Tib.* 73; *Hist.* 58.28). Once, at a palace banquet, Gaius burst out laughing. A magistrate beside him asked what was so funny. "Just thinking: I have only to nod and your throats would be slit on the spot" (*Cal.* 32). Here we must leave Caligula, who, reigning from 37 to 41, doesn't appear in the NT.[18] This is most unfortunate, because Booties was a real piece of work: power-grabber, spendthrift, showoff, carefree slayer of friends and family. Eventually three of his security detail hacked Gaius to pieces at home, then murdered his wife and her baby daughter. His uncle Claudius hid behind a palace curtain, was spirited away by sympathizers, and was quickly installed as the new emperor (*Cal.* 57–58).

5. Having barely managed to keep his trachea intact, **Claudius** (10 BCE–54 CE) ascended to the throne at the age of 50. His nearly fourteen-year reign (41–54) had its hiccups but, compared with his nephew's, was a Sunday afternoon at the library. Claudius enters Christian history indirectly. Trying to maintain a cohesive empire, he kicked Jews out of Rome around 49–50, owing to "constant disturbances at the instigation of Chrestus" (*Claud.* 25.4). Suetonius seems to have confused "Chrestus," a common Greek name, with "Christus," Christ Jesus, executed two decades earlier but now the nub of conflict between Jews and Jewish Christians. According to Luke (Acts 18:2), Paul's colleagues Prisca (Priscilla) and Aquila were among those expelled (see also Acts 18:18, 26; 1 Cor 16:19) but were allowed to return to Rome after Claudius's death (Rom 16:3; cf. *A.J.* 19.5.3).

6. So we come to one of history's prodigious thugs, **Nero** (37–68), about whom we can say little here because the NT says nothing.[19] Two chapters ago you may recall my mentioning a horrendous fire that erupted in Rome (June

17. Get your mind out of the gutter. Here the term "booties" refers to infant slippers: baby booties. According to Suetonius (*Cal.* 9), soldiers under the command of his father, General Germanicus (15 BCE–19 CE), gave Gaius this moniker because the three-year-old tyke was shown off wearing a child's army costume.

18. At least not explicitly. Commentators note that "the lawless one" in 2 Thessalonians in 2:3–4 could be a veiled reference to Gaius, who aspired to divine recognition and planned to install statues of himself in the Jerusalem temple (*B.J.* 2.184–86, 192–97). As noted by Victor Paul Furnish, *1 Thessalonians, 2 Thessalonians*, ANTC (Nashville: Abingdon, 2007), 156, there are other nominees for this mysterious figure, in a letter that cannot be dated with confidence (anytime from the early 60s to the mid-90s).

19. At least not explicitly. Here we go again. In Revelation 13:18 the beast whose number is six hundred and sixty-six may be a heavily camouflaged allusion to "Neron Qaesar." The sum of the Hebrew letters N (= 50) + R (= 200) + V (O = 6) + N (= 50) + Q (= 100) + S (= 60) + R (= 200) is 666. For further discussion, see Brian K. Blount, *Revelation: A Commentary*, NTL (Louisville, KY: Westminster John Knox Press, 2009), 261–62.

64). It blazed for over a week, consuming countless shops, mansions, and temples, wiping out ten of the city's fourteen districts. The rumor mill ground out blame upon Nero himself for starting the fire. In turn, he scapegoated Christians, arresting and setting them afire as living tiki torches (*Ann.* 15.44). Another curious factoid: if Paul's case went to Caesar (Acts 25:11–12; 28:19), that would have been Nero.[20]

Amid civil turmoil, economic hemorrhaging, military uprisings, and the usual household homicides,[21] Nero affected a weird insouciance: singing, showboating in athletic games, and generally making an ass of himself in ways that only the powerful can do really well. By 68 CE the empire's provincial governors were in open revolt. The Senate declared him a public enemy. True to form, the head of Nero's security detail threw in his lot with Galba, a Spanish governor. At a friend's villa outside Rome, Nero took his own life or had someone help him do so, sighing, "What an artist dies with me" (*Nero* 48–49). Thus ended the Julio-Claudian dynasty, and not a moment too soon.

After Nero died, the empire was convulsed by ghastly civil war. Between June of 68 and December of 69, three emperors flew by in such fast succession that none was in the palace long enough to unpack his bags.

7. After seven months **Galba** (3 BCE–69 CE) was assassinated—you guessed it—by his security detail.

8. **Otho** (32–69) lasted only three months until stabbing himself in the heart.[22]

9. **Vitellius** (15–69) warmed the throne for eight months before being killed by his successor's soldiers.

10. The last emperor standing was **Vespasian** (9–79), who had distinguished himself as Nero's commander in quashing the First Jewish Revolt in Judea (66–73), to which the Synoptics allude but never describe (Matt 22:7; 24:1–3//Mark 13:1–4//Luke 21:5–7; Luke 19:41–44; 21:20–24). What we know of Vespasian's reign (69–79) is generally positive. He reorganized the military to stymie revolts, began rebuilding a war-ravaged Rome, secured shipments of grain from Egypt to stem famine, and reformed the financial system. His most famous tax was on human urine, whose ammonia was used for processing fabric (*Vesp.*

20. Carl R. Holladay, *Acts: A Commentary*, NTL (Louisville, KY: Westminster John Knox Press, 2016), 461. To tie down some other loose ends: Felix, the Roman procurator (or prefect) of Palestine (52–60) who heard Paul's case after his removal from Jerusalem to Caesarea (Acts 23:23–24:27), was a freed slave from Claudius's family (*Claud.* 28; see above in this chapter). Festus, procurator of Judea (ca. 59–62), consulted with Herod Agrippa II before granting Paul's appeal that his case be tried before Caesar (Acts 24:27–26:32; see "A Horde of Herods" in chap. 3).

21. Claudius died by poisoning, perhaps by his fourth wife, Agrippina (15–59), Nero's mother (*Claud.* 44.23). In 59 Nero orchestrated matricide after beginning an affair with Poppaea Sabina, whom he married and may have killed after executing his first wife. Be sure to read Suetonius's heartwarming life of Nero. It may put some of your family's troubles in perspective.

22. It's too bad that this is a historical summary, not an opera. When all these sovereigns were knifed, they could have burst into song instead of spurting blood all over the place.

23.3). Dying of severe diarrhea at age 69, he sighed, "Dear me, I think I'm becoming a god" (*Vesp.* 23.4). He was the first emperor to provide an orderly succession by his biological sons, Titus (39–81) and Domitian (51–96). For all his even-tempered competence, this Caesar is best remembered for lending his name to Italian and French urinals (*vespasiano, vespasienne*). Life is unfair.

11. Despite a brief reign (79–81), **Titus** (39–81), Vespasian's elder son, was a chip off the old granite: valiant in battle (*B.J.* 5.1–6.6),[23] diplomatic (*Hist.* 69.19),[24] a builder (the Colosseum: the most famous venue for popular entertainment ever seen [*Hist.* 66.25]),[25] and beneficent (*Hist.* 66.22–24). Evidently he died from natural causes. Reportedly his last words were, "I have made but one mistake" (*Titus* 10): an allusion, historian Dio Cassius believed, to Titus's failure to crisp his brother as toast on a plate after Domitian was implicated in a conspiracy against him (*Hist.* 66.26). Nobody's perfect.

(12) The reign (81–96) of **Domitian** (51–96) remains controversial. Ancient biographies are damning but dodgy. Early Christians loved Domitian as little as Jews adored Titus. During Domitian's reign, Christians were targeted as enemies of the state, and the guardedly subversive book of Revelation was written (*Haer.* 5.30.3).[26] The Gospels of Matthew and Luke were probably composed during his ruthless, efficient autocracy. He governed with a hand so high you'd need binoculars to see his fingers. Suetonius (*Dom.* 13.2) and Dio (*Hist.* 67.4.7) claim that he entitled himself *Dominus et Deus*, "Lord and God," behaving as though he were. He executed three vestal virgins who had violated their sacred vows of chastity and buried alive the chief vestal virgin, Cornelia (*Dom.* 8.3–4). It's no surprise that the evangelists never mention him: who wants to dice with the devil? On September 18 in 96, when 44 years old, he was assassinated by court conspirators (*Dom.* 14–17). The Senate, which he had enfeebled, damned his memory. His coins were melted, his statues reduced to rubble, his arches torn down, his name erased from all public record.

---

23. Valor depends on one's point of view. While Pop (Vespasian) was on the throne (70), Titus oversaw the sack of Jerusalem, which climaxed with demolition of Herod the Great's (= the second) temple. For that he was immortalized in the Arch of Titus at the Forum's southeastern entrance. Tens of thousands of Jews, captured and enslaved, felt differently. The million or so slain were left incapable of feeling anything. The Babylonian Talmud (b. Giṭṭin 56b) portrays Titus fornicating with a prostitute on a Torah scroll inside the temple as it burned to rubble.

24. Criticized by leading Romans, fearing a mini-Cleopatra, he ended an affair with Herod Agrippa II's sister, Bernice/Berenice, whom he intended to marry but quietly sent away (*Hist.* 65.15). See chap. 3, above.

25. Overseen by Roman architects and engineers, the Colosseum's builders were for the most part Jewish slaves, who found the enterprise less than pleasurable.

26. See n. 19. When an early Christian book, written in Greek, uses a Hebrew numeronym to hide a reference to Nero when in fact it may be pointing to Domitian, we're talking "guarded."

Little wonder that scholars find it hard to get a fix on Luke's presentation of Jesus, his followers, and the imperial order. No evangelist is more sensitive than he to the savage political world in which the ministry of Jesus and his followers was carried out, and none is more cautious in engaging it. Luke may have adopted a strategy of "quiet subversion" that, for him, was the only viable alternative that reconciled the undeniably explosive potential of the good news and the equally irrefutable threat of imperial backlash against a fledgling religious movement with an inbuilt missionary propellant. Among the Synoptic evangelists, Luke is most explicit about Jerusalem's demolition by military siege (19:43–44; 21:20–24)—and Titus's troops made that happen. Likewise, Luke is clearest that Jesus' death resulted from collusion between specific Jewish and Roman officials (22:66–23:25). This evangelist knows of violent Jewish insurrection against Rome (Luke 23:18–19; Acts 5:36–37) and goes to great lengths to prove that the Jesus movement is not in that league. Roman centurions are portrayed as positive figures (Luke 7:1–10; cf. Acts 10:1–48; 21:31–32; 22:22–29; 23:16–22; 24:23; 27:31, 41–44), including the one at Skull Place, who pronounces the crucified Jesus *dikaios*: "just" or "upright" (Luke 23:47). That coheres with Luke's consistent portrayal of Roman governors' exoneration of the Christian movement in Acts, dismissing it as an imperial threat (18:12–17; 24:1–27; 25:1–26:32).

On the other hand, the canticles that embellish Luke's infancy narrative overflow with declarations that God's sovereignty—by implication, not Caesar's—has triumphed in the coming of Jesus, the *sotēr*, "Savior": obvious pilferage of imperial propaganda (1:47–55, 68–79; 2:10–11, 29–32). To Israel's God belongs highest glorification, for that true God is the only hope for human peace and the only ruler who will never be deposed (2:14). The classical Roman virtues of beneficent reciprocity are undermined in Jesus' teaching (6:22–36; 14:7–33): "When you throw a banquet, invite the poor, the crippled, the lame, the blind, and you will be blessed, because they cannot repay you. You will be repaid when the righteous are raised" (14:13–14). Even as Jesus refused the diabolical temptation of ruling over all the world's kingdoms by worshiping only "the Lord your God" (4:5–8), his disciples in Luke are challenged to repudiate this world's ideologies: "So, then, whoever among you who does not renounce all that he has"—not only worship of wealth, but every activity that contradicts the constitution of God's reign—"cannot be my disciple" (14:33). Luke's Jesus is no revolutionary (23:47). Neither are his emissaries (Acts 4:19–20). But Caesar has his limits. God's kingdom outweighs human empires.

"Then render to Caesar the things that are Caesar's, and to God the things that are God's" (Luke 20:25). That dictum, appearing in all the Synoptics (Matt 22:21//Mark 12:17a), acquires in Luke a peculiar irony. Mary and Joseph complied with an Augustan decree to be enrolled in a census, which assessed imperial taxation (2:1–2). By rendering to Caesar they fulfilled prophecy that the Davidic king par excellence, carried in Mary's womb, would be born in Bethlehem (Mic

5:2; cf. 1 Sam 17:12). Likewise, in Acts, the spread of the gospel is unwittingly expedited by Caesar's functionaries (25:21; 26:32; 27:24; 28:18, 31). Of Christ's kingdom there will be no end (Luke 1:33), even though Caesar had no idea that his decisions would buttress it.

Ambiguous Yet Powerful

A Conversation with Barbara E. Reid, OP

Barbara E. Reid (PhD, Catholic University of America), a Dominican Sister of Grand Rapids, Michigan, is the Carroll Stuhlmueller, CP, Distinguished Professor of New Testament Studies at Catholic Theological Union (CTU) in Chicago. In November 2020, she was appointed the first woman president of CTU, where she had served as vice president and academic dean. Esteemed for her research in feminist interpretation of the Scriptures, she is general editor for the Wisdom Commentary Series, a new 58-volume feminist commentary on the Bible (Liturgical Press). Her many honors include her election to the presidency of the Catholic Biblical Association (2014–15), the Yves Congar Award for Theological Excellence (Barry University, 2017), and a doctorate honoris causa *conferred by the University of Graz, Austria (2019).*

CCB: Barbara, although your scholarship spans the entire Bible, much of your work has been dedicated to Luke. Are certain aspects of this Gospel especially attractive or intriguing for you?

BER: When I was first attracted to Luke, it was because of the many parables; some of my favorites are only in the Third Gospel. Also, the women characters attracted me. However, as I began to study Luke with a more critical feminist approach, I realized that Luke is really not much of a friend to feminists. After the Infancy Narratives, his female characters never speak except to be corrected or disbelieved.

CCB: No less than that of the other Synoptics, Luke's presentation of Jesus seems to me distinguishable yet complex. Do you agree? If asked to sum up what Luke believes about Jesus, what would you say?

BER: Yes, the Lukan Jesus is complex. One of the things that Luke emphasizes more than the other evangelists is that Jesus is a prophet. Prophets always experience a double reaction from people: those who are being "lifted up" (what Mary sings about in the Magnificat) love what he is saying and doing;

those whose power, privilege, and status are threatened want to do away with him. Thus, a Lukan explanation for the death of Jesus is that he is a rejected prophet. I find this a much more helpful way to understand Jesus' death than as atonement for sins.[27]

CCB: In your opinion, does the life of discipleship look much the same in all three Synoptics, or does Luke's characterization distinctively stand out?

BER: There are some commonalities in all the Gospels. All four feature women and men disciples, but Luke shows a bias toward the male disciples. For him, the apostles, whom he equates with the Twelve, have the prime role, even though Luke notes that some women like Mary Magdalene, Joanna, Susanna, and many others (8:1–3) were supporting him financially and followed him to the cross (23:27–31, 49, 55–56).

CCB: As you've suggested, Luke's Gospel uniquely contains some of Jesus' most vivid and memorable parables, such as the good Samaritan (10:29–37) and the Prodigal Son (15:11–32). Is there a theological line that runs through most of this Gospel's parables, or are they so varied that they resist such reduction?

BER: I wouldn't try to reduce them. One notable thing is that Luke is the only Gospel that presents three parables with women as the central character: the woman hiding yeast in dough (13:20–21), the woman searching for a lost coin (15:7–10), and the widow who confronts an unjust judge (18:1–8). All are powerful images of how God acts and how we can envision God in female form.

CCB: Let's turn to some controversies that have lately swirled around Luke's interpretation. One is the reception of Jesus' ministry within Israel. How would you characterize Luke's presentation of fledgling Christianity and its Jewish parentage?

BER: Luke, unfortunately, has an anti-Jewish bias, and any Christian reading his Gospel today needs to take great care to read against the grain and not to foment anti-Judaism.

CCB: I interpret Luke differently. While some fellow Jews turn against Jesus (4:16–30), violently so against his apostles in Acts (9:23; 23:12, 27), the Gospel

---

27. This interpretation jibes with Luke's version of Jesus' words to the Twelve at the Last Supper. In Mark (14:22–24) and Matthew (26:26–28), Jesus refers to his blood as "the covenant . . . poured out [for forgiveness of sins]." Luke omits this sacrificial characterization and substitutes Jesus' presence "among [them] as one who serves" (22:27).

begins and ends with pious Jews in Judaism's religious heart, the temple. Even in Acts, some Jews side with the apostles (6:7; 14:1, 4; 21:20); others offer them the benefit of doubt (5:33–42). Where do you see Luke's bias coming most clearly to the fore?

BER: Certainly at the end of the Gospel (Luke 22–23) there is a clear divide between "the people" and the Jewish leaders, but most stark is Luke's painting the Jewish leaders as tools of Satan (22:3–6, 53). And Acts makes repeated accusations that Jews killed Jesus (3:12–15; 5:30; 7:52; 10:39), and they continue to be portrayed as enemies of Jesus' followers.

CCB: Another dispute among Luke's interpreters relates to the Gospel's stance toward the culture of imperial Rome. Does Luke intend to placate the empire? Subvert it? Respond in some other way?

BER: I think Luke wants his Gospel to show that Jesus' followers are not a threat to the empire. He shows centurions in a favorable light, for example (7:1–10; 23:34; Acts 10:1–48).

CCB: Yet another disputed issue, which you have investigated at length, is Luke's portrait of women, particularly Jesus' female disciples. Do you believe that depiction is positive, hazardous, or irresolvably ambiguous? Does Luke promote or hinder equality among women and men? Is a question so modern fair to ask of a late first-century document?

BER: I think Luke presents us with an ambiguous portrait of women. Luke would not have understood what we mean by equality among women and men, nor would anyone in his day. We have to understand the patriarchal culture in which he wrote and then in many cases read against the grain of the direction he would go.

CCB: Whether the reader be Christian or not, why is Luke still worth reading? What does this Gospel help us to understand about Jesus and his followers that is distinctive and remains important?

BER: This is still a powerful story from the beginnings of Christianity, which helps us reflect on the compassion of God as revealed in Jesus, a strong theme in Luke. It must be reinterpreted for our context, but that is well worth the effort.

CCB: Many thanks, Professor Reid, for an invigorating conversation.

IN THEIR END IS THEIR BEGINNING

Perhaps owing to Zoroastrian influence, exerted while Israelites were in exile,[28] belief in resurrection from death is characteristically Jewish, sparsely evidenced in the HB (Isa 26:19; Dan 12:1–3), and espoused in apocalyptic works of the era between the Testaments (2 Macc 7:11, 28; *1 Enoch* 61:2, 5; *2 Baruch* 50:2; 51:5). It should be differentiated from two other ideas. One is resuscitation of someone who was dead but will again die: Jairus's daughter (Matt 9:18, 23–25//Mark 5:35–52//Luke 8:49–55), the only son of the widow at Nain (Luke 7:11–15), Tabitha and Eutychus (Acts 9:36–42; 20:7–12), and most famously but beyond the Synoptics, Lazarus (John 11:1–44; 12:9–11). By contrast, in Plato's *Phaedo* (69e–104c), Socrates argues for the *soul*'s immortality: the body decays, but human beings possess souls that are impervious to death. While some ancient theologians, both Jewish (Wis 3:1–4; *B.J.* 2.8.14; *A.J.* 8.14–15) and Christian (Gregory of Nyssa [ca. 335–395], *On the Soul*), endorsed that belief, the NT moves in a different direction: resurrection is God's bestowal of an utterly new creation of life to one who has truly died, and of that life there will be no end (1 Cor 15:1–58). "In a very crude and inadequate analogy, the software running on our present hardware will be transferred [by God] to the hardware of the world to come."[29] The unprecedented aspects in budding Christian beliefs were two: (1) *one and only one would first be raised*, meaning the Messiah, with others to follow (as opposed to all the righteous, or both the just and the wicked, being raised for reward or punishment);[30] (2) *the linkage of resurrection with messiahship*, since, until the writings of the NT, one could believe in the one without inferring the other.

Among the Synoptics, Luke's Gospel concludes with the most elaborate stories of the risen Jesus' postmortem appearances to his disciples: (1) the women's discovery of Jesus' empty tomb and their "vision of angels," testifying about his resurrection to "the eleven and all the rest," who refuse to believe it (24:1–11, 22–24); (2) Jesus' accompaniment of disciples on the road to Emmaus (24:13–33a); (3) a second report by those disciples, confirming Jesus' resurrection and appearance to Simon Peter (24:33b–35); (4) Jesus' appearance to his disciples en masse, in Jerusalem, with instructions (24:36–49); and (5) in Bethany, his ascension into heaven and his followers' return to Jerusalem (24:50–53). Recurring themes bind these five passages and draw this Gospel to apposite closure.

---

28. See Benjamin Studevant-Hickman, "Mesopotamian Roots for the Belief in the Resurrection from the Dead," *RC* 3 (2009): 524–36; John Granger Cook, "Resurrection in the Mediterranean World," *ANET* 8 (2020): https://www.asor.org/anetoday/2020/04/resurrection-mediterranean.

29. John C. Polkinghorne, *The Faith of a Physicist: Reflections of a Bottom-Up Thinker* (Princeton, NJ: Princeton University Press, 2014), 164.

30. The latter belief crops up in some Jewish intertestamental texts, as well as in the Talmuds of the third and fourth centuries.

1. *God* still *intervenes in human history, still creating something out of nothing that upends everything, with an outcome outrunning dull comprehension.* Even though his disciples have been thoroughly primed for Jesus' resurrection from brutal death (Luke 24:6–7; cf. 9:22; 17:25; 18:31–33), they repeatedly dismiss its reality as nonsense (24:11, 25–26, 37–38). So Zechariah scoffed at Gabriel's promise of Elizabeth's pregnancy at an extreme age (1:18–20).

2. *The female ministers are faster on the uptake than their male counterparts.* Having conceived a child, Elizabeth offers nothing but thanksgiving and blessing (1:24–25, 42–45). "How happy is she"—Mary, and perhaps Elizabeth herself—"who has had faith that the Lord's promise would be fulfilled!" (1:45 NEB). Mary accepts Gabriel's impossibility as possible, with piety ("Here I am, the Lord's servant; as you have spoken, so be it"; 1:38 NEB) and an outpouring of praise ("Sing out, my soul"; 1:46–55). Finding the tomb empty, Mary Magdalene, Joanna, Mary the mother of James, "and the other women with them" (cf. 8:2; 23:49) are at a loss, then terrified. Prompted by interpreting angels, *they* remember Jesus' predictions—something Luke never says of the male disciples—and report to the Eleven and all the others what was announced to them (24:2–9; cf. 1:26–32). Later Luke emphasizes that others had gone to the tomb and found things just as the women had attested (24:24).

3. As throughout this Gospel, so also in 24:1–53: the braided motifs of *travel and testimony.* Whether for Elizabeth, Mary, the shepherds, the apostles (9:1–6; 10:1–17), or Jesus himself (9:51–19:27), the good news is never static nor lacking verification through attestation. Having gone to the tomb on the Sabbath, many women are given good reasons to return to Jesus' apostles with a substantiated report (24:6–10). That very day two of those disciples are discussing these events while going (*poreuomenoi*) to a village, Emmaus, some seven miles from Jerusalem (vv. 13–14). A fellow traveler, the risen Jesus himself, accompanies (*syneporeueto*) them (v. 15). If his disciples are prevented from recognizing him (v. 16), it's because this story is unfolding as God arranges it, not as they choose it. In a lovely yet poignant stroke of irony (vv. 19–24), Cleopas and his fellow disciple—still en route—testify *to* Jesus, believing him to be "the only visitor to Jerusalem ignorant of the happenings in recent days" (v. 18), a summary of Luke's Gospel: that Jesus of Nazareth—God's prophet powerful in word and deed (7:16), beloved of Israel's people (2:10; 4:42; 5:1–3; 6:17; 7:1, 16, 29; 8:4; 13:17; 18:43; 19:48; 21:38; 23:27), their hope for Israel's redemption (1:68; 2:38; 21:28), slain by their chief priests[31] and rulers three days previously—had afterward been declared alive (22:67–24:11). The risen Jesus' first act of ministry to his dimwitted followers is *not* to identify himself. Instead, he readies them for that revelation by interpreting to

---

31. Luke maintains that "the people" (*ho laos*) didn't turn on Jesus. Instead, they were misled by their leaders, who were intimidated by the people's embrace of him (13:17; 19:47–48; 20:19, 26; 22:2, 66; 23:35).

them everything in their Scriptures that, properly understood, signaled the divine necessity of the Messiah's suffering for his glorification (24:25–27). This directs them, and Luke's readers, back to the intricate mosaic of scriptural testimony that Luke aligns with John and Jesus at their births (1:5–2:52), as well as to Jesus' tumultuous testimony in Nazareth's synagogue, pronouncing his mission as the fulfillment of Isaiah (Luke 4:16–30). It also points them forward to 24:46, where Jesus urges Cleopas and the other disciple to understand the Law, the Prophets, and the Psalms with hindsight, as pointing to himself, the Christ. Further on, he urges the Eleven to testify: "You are witnesses of these things" (24:48). And further still, to travel in order to do so: "You shall be my witnesses in Jerusalem and in all Judea and Samaria and to the end of the earth" (Acts 1:8).

4. Upon arrival in Emmaus, the two disciples invite their still unrecognized Lord to dine with them (Luke 24:28–30a). In this Gospel, particularly in traditions drawn from its special source (L), *suppers are occasions for dramatic disclosures*: not only by Jesus, but also of other characters' true selves (Simon the Pharisee, 7:36–50; Simon Peter and other disciples, 12:41–48; a father's two sons, 15:21–32; one man rich, another poor, 16:19–21; a servant and his master, 17:7–10; Zacchaeus, 19:1–10; the Twelve, 22:1–38). In Luke 14:1–24 alone, banquets figure in no fewer than four passages, recounted in rapid succession. You can't get more dramatic than 24:30–32, when Jesus takes, blesses, breaks, and gives bread to these two disciples who have been walking with him, whose eyes are opened to the Lord who has ministered to them in the same way as to others twice before (9:16–17; 22:14–19). In a second appearance, to the Eleven, Jesus' resurrection is again confirmed by eating (24:36–43). "They told what happened on the road, and how he was made known to them by breaking bread" (v. 35). Any resemblance to Christian experience of their Lord in celebrations of his Supper is not in the least coincidental (cf. 1 Cor 10:15–17): before and after his resurrection, Jesus is recognized as Lord when his disciples gather at suppertime.

5. At both Emmaus and Jerusalem (24:33), *a jumble of emotions resolve into joy*. Jesus' mother struggled to make sense of all that was happening to her (1:29; 2:19, 48–51). So did the disciples after his death (24:22–24, 32–37): "They were still unconvinced, still wondering, for it seemed too good to be true" (24:41 NEB). Eventually, Jesus' servants surrender themselves to joy at what has been done for them (10:17; 15:7; 24:41, 52). God's news is too good to be false.

6. Luke's Gospel ends where it began: in *Israel's center, Jerusalem's temple, with blessing and praise*. Just as the stories of John's and Jesus' births and Jesus' boyhood revolve around the temple, Jesus' disciples are authorized to await their empowerment in Jerusalem to testify to God's continuing forgiveness of sins (24:47–48, 52; cf. 1:5–21; 2:22–52). That will occur after Jesus' departure from them (24:51), when the Holy Spirit launches apostles into the next phase of God's saving history: proclamation of Jesus' name and his benefactions to all nations (v. 47; cf. Acts

1:6–2:42). Until then the sensible things to do are to receive their Lord's "blessing"
and to reciprocate it by "praising God" (Luke 24:50–53). That's what

♦ Elizabeth had done:
  Blessed are you among women, and blessed is the fruit of your womb! (1:42);
♦ and her kinswoman Mary had done:
  My spirit rejoices in God my Savior (1:47);
♦ so also Elizabeth's husband, Zechariah:
  Blessed be the Lord God of Israel,
    for he has visited and redeemed his people (1:68);
♦ and the heavenly host,
  praising [and] giving glory to God in the highest (2:13–14);
♦ then, too, the shepherds, having seen an infant in a manger,
  glorifying and praising God for all they had heard and seen,
    as it had been told them (2:20);
♦ and old Simeon,
  who took [the child] up in his arms and blessed God (2:28);
♦ and the angel, presenting
  a Savior, who is Christ the Lord (2:11); who later announces:
  ■ *Blessed are you poor, for yours is the kingdom of God.*
  ■ *Blessed are you that hunger now, for you shall be satisfied.*
  ■ *Blessed are you that weep now, for you shall laugh.*
  ■ *Blessed are you when people hate you. . . .*
  ■ *Rejoice in that day, and leap for joy* (6:20–23; cf. 7:23; 11:28; 12:37–38, 43);
♦ and a woman, cured of an eighteen-year spinal curvature, who
  praised God (13:13);
♦ and a Samaritan, cured of leprosy,
  praising God with a loud voice (17:15);
♦ and a blind beggar, recovering his sight,
  glorifying God (18:43);
♦ and a Roman centurion, eyes opened to a crucified yet righteous innocent,
  praised God (23:47);
♦ alongside an array of witnesses to God's loving mercy (11:27; 14:15; 19:38).

The words on which Luke's Gospel ends are *eulogountes ton theon*, "praising God"
(24:53). And for good reason: with Jesus, God broke the biggest of all boundaries—
that between death and life. There could be no better conclusion for this Gospel,
for the Synoptics overall, for the Bible in general, and for all of God's creatures.

THE CONVERSATION CONTINUES

"I Invited the Christ Spirit to Manifest in Me"

A Conversation with Anna Marley about the Gospels
in the Art of H. O. Tanner

Anna O. Marley (PhD, University of Delaware), is the Kenneth R. Woodcock Curator of Historical American Art and Director of the Center for the Study of the American Artist at the Pennsylvania Academy of the Fine Arts in Philadelphia. Her volume, Henry Ossawa Tanner: Modern Spirit,[32] *is widely acclaimed as the most substantial scholarly study of that artist's life and work. She has curated over sixteen national exhibitions, chaired the international Association of Historians of American Art (2014–16), and in 2020 was selected among a dozen international scholars as a Fellow of the Center for Curatorial Leadership for her "demonstrated curatorial achievements, commitment to expanding audiences, and openness to creative and entrepreneurial thinking." Currently she is an Advisory Board member of the Smithsonian* Archives of American Art Journal.[33]

CCB: Anna, although Henry Tanner (1859–1937) has achieved iconic status, he may not be as well known as some of his contemporaries in the world of art. Could you sketch a thumbnail biography of Tanner?

AOM: Henry Ossawa Tanner was born in Pittsburgh and raised in Philadelphia, the firstborn son of Benjamin and Sarah Tanner, prominent members of the Black middle class in Philadelphia in the years after the American Civil War. Tanner wanted to become an artist at a young age, and his mother supported him in this, though his father wanted him to follow him in the ministry. Eventually Tanner was able to study at the Pennsylvania Academy of the Fine Arts, where Thomas Eakins was his exacting teacher. After the PAFA, like Eakins before him, he traveled to Paris to study, and in 1894 he had his first painting accepted by the prestigious Paris Salon. Tanner became famous for his modern religious paintings and had patrons in Europe and the United States. He lived in France for the rest of his life, in part because he married a white American woman, Jessie Olsson, and his marriage would have been illegal in

32. Philadelphia and Berkeley, CA: Pennsylvania Academy of the Fine Arts / University of California Press, 2012.
33. "I Invited the Christ Spirit to Manifest in Me" is quoted by Marcia M. Matthews, *Henry Ossawa Tanner: American Artist* (Chicago: University of Chicago Press, 1969), 73.

many parts of the United States. Yet he often returned to the United States and never relinquished his citizenship. He served with the American Red Cross in France during World War I and after the war served as an elder statesman to many African American artists who made pilgrimages to meet him in France.

CCB: Tanner's father became a bishop in the African Methodist Episcopal Church. Is his father's vocation purely coincidental with his son's gravitation toward religious subjects in much of his art, or do you think the reasons for that lie elsewhere?

AOM: Tanner was always deeply religious, and I believe he felt a great moral and spiritual responsibility to his father for not having become a minister. When Tanner began his career, he wanted to be an animal painter; even his early paintings of lions have a depth and gravitas to them that would appear in his first major religious painting *Daniel in the Lions' Den* (exhibited 1896; this 1895 original has been lost). I think that he wanted to make his parents proud, and he was deeply religious, but he was also a smart businessman—and religious paintings had a large audience at the Paris Salon and in American museums and private collections. His European contemporaries, like Pascal Dagnan-Bouveret (1852–1929) and Jacques Joseph Tissot (1836–1902), were deeply influential on his practice as a religious painter, and one of his major patrons was department store scion Rodman Wanamaker (1863–1928), who commissioned Tanner to make large religious paintings for his flagship stores in Philadelphia and New York.

CCB: Let's move to Tanner's representations of scenes described in or suggested by the New Testament's Gospels. What sets his oeuvre apart from other religious paintings of his era?

AOM: Tanner starts out very much under the sway of Dagnan-Bouveret, whose naturalist *Last Supper* created a sensation at the Paris Salon of 1896. Tanner responded to this painting with *The Resurrection of Lazarus* (1897), which was the first of three paintings by him to be purchased by the French government and is now held in the collection of the Musée d'Orsay in Paris, along with his paintings *Christ and His Disciples on Their Way to Bethany* (ca. 1902–03) and *The Pilgrims of Emmaus* (1905). What seemed to strike critics about his works at the time is how personal and modern his religious paintings were. Additionally, his use of light was unique. Light sources seem to radiate from the canvases themselves, from the tomb of Lazarus, from the heart of Christ speaking with Nicodemus, or from the angel Gabriel abstracted as a beam of electric light, which we'll examine momentarily.

Fig. 42. *The Disciples See Christ Walking on the Water*, by Henry Ossawa Tanner. Housed in The Des Moines Art Center, Iowa. For full color version, see https://emuseum .desmoinesartcenter.org /search/tanner.

CCB: Let's consider a few specimens of Tanner's art. Here, for example, is his depiction of The Disciples See Christ Walking on the Water *(ca. 1907). Could you comment on this painting?*

AOM: This is the painting that has always spoken to me since I first saw it in person. The painting itself is composed of layer upon layer of blue, green, and purple pigments. Often these nocturnal scenes are painted in what some have labeled "Tanner blue." He dearly loved shades of blues, and he worked and worked at his canvases, using between nine to as many as nineteen layers of paint and varnish to create his ideal effect. He worked in a number of techniques throughout his career, from quickly conceived impressionist sketches on board, to highly finished academic paintings on canvas. Tanner continued experimenting with application of paints—oil, tempera, and watercolor—until the end of his life.[34]

---

34. I regret that figures 42–46 cannot be rendered in color, as Tanner intended. Using the internet links, readers are strongly encouraged to visit webpages for those museums where the original paintings are housed.

Fig. 43. *The Banjo Lesson*, by Henry Ossawa Tanner. Collection of the Hampton University Museum, Virginia. For full color version, see https://home.hamptonu .edu/msm/.

When seen in the flesh, *Christ Walking on the Water* shimmers like the tiles that Tanner brought back with him from his travels to the Near East. Notice that Christ is abstracted: he is no more than a beam of light levitating above the water; his reflection in the water is none other than the moon. This suggests to me that if you looked away too quickly, you would miss him, miss the Christ, and only see the moon. I feel like this is a painting that is about looking, about seeing, about believing what you can't always see. It is remarkable to me that a painter was able to convey this using pigment and canvas.

CCB: It astonishes me. One of Tanner's most celebrated paintings is The Banjo Lesson *(1893, fig. 43). I am struck by its resonance with* Christ and His Mother Studying the Scriptures *(ca. 1909, fig. 44). What impresses you in these oils?*

AOM: In both these paintings, Tanner is focusing on the transmission of knowledge between generations. In *The Banjo Lesson* a young boy learns to play the banjo from an older man, perhaps a grandfather. It is the polar opposite of

Fig. 44. *Christ and His Mother Studying the Scriptures*, by Henry Ossawa Tanner. Image courtesy of Dallas Museum of Art. For full-color version, see https://dma.org/art /exhibitions/focus-henry -ossawa-tanner.

the racist images of minstrelsy that dominated American visual culture in the late nineteenth century. In *Christ and His Mother Studying the Scriptures*, Tanner uses his wife and son, Jesse, as models for Mary teaching her son to read. While *The Banjo Lesson* is by far the more famous painting now, more people may have seen *Christ and His Mother* during Tanner's lifetime since it once hung in the Wanamaker Department Store in Philadelphia.

CCB: Among Tanner's paintings, the one I find most arresting is his breathtaking portrayal of The Annunciation *(1898; fig. 45). Can you help us understand the genius of this work, which, with the brush of a hack, would have resulted in miserable kitsch?*

AOM: This is one of Tanner's most spectacular paintings, one of his most daring. My colleague Hélène Valance has made the convincing argument that Tanner's depiction of the angel Gabriel was influenced by Nikola Tesla's display of electric light in Paris in the 1890s.[35] In addition to being strikingly modern and

35. Hélène Valance, "The Dynamo and the Virgin: Henry Ossawa Tanner's Religious Nocturnes," in Marley, *Tanner: Modern Spirit*, 127–34.

Fig. 45. *The Annunciation*, by Henry Ossawa Tanner (1898). Housed in the Philadelphia Museum of Art. Purchased with the W. P. Wilstach Fund, 1899, W1899-1-1. For full color version, see https://philamuseum.org/learn/educational-resources/the-annunciation.

abstract, like the abstracted *Christ Walking on the Water*, the abstracted angel is more universal for not being an angel in recognizable human form. Tanner's Mary is the opposite of abstract but is probably based on very real Palestinian girls that Tanner saw on his travels to Palestine and Egypt in 1897. The combination of abstracted spirit with humble humanity, based on detailed study and observation, is what gives this painting its unique power.

CCB: That's it: the juxtaposition of ineffable spirit with unpretentious humanity. In all of Tanner's artistry, I respond, not as though I'm observing a narrative, but as one being drawn into the tableau itself. Do you experience something of the same? If so, can you articulate how Tanner achieved that?

AOM: Yes, Tanner often composes his paintings so as to erase the boundaries between the scene in the painting and the viewer. For example, in *The Resurrection of Lazarus* (1896), we feel as if we are in the tomb with Lazarus, standing on his shroud; and in the *Annunciation*, the carpet that Mary rests her bare feet

Fig. 46. *The Resurrection of Lazarus* (1896). Photograph courtesy of Rama. Housed in the Musée d'Orsay, Paris. For full color version, see https://www.musee-orsay.fr/en /artworks/la-resurrection-de-lazare-9241.

on stretches into our space, so that we feel again as if we are standing in the room with her.

CCB: In this case I shall deviate from my publisher's assignment and direct our reader's attention to an episode narrated, not in the Synoptics, but in the Gospel of John (11:1–44). Tanner's genius justifies it.

Anna, what is Tanner's legacy, as both artist and interpreter of Jewish and Christian Scriptures?

AOM: I think his legacy as an artist is complex. For many he is seen in an almost hagiographic light as the father figure of African American art. But he never wanted to be seen in this particular way; he stated that he wanted to be seen as he believed he was in Paris, as simply Monsieur Tanner, an *artiste américain*. Even though he was taken to task by Black intellectuals like Alain Locke (1885–1954) in the 1920s for refusing to privilege a West African aesthetic, Tanner was always esteemed by African American artists and communities in particular. I have found his legacy as a religious painter to transcend race. When our exhibition was open in Philadelphia (2012), my colleague Jeffrey Richmond-Moll provided traveling lectures for churches of all denominations, and religious groups of many faiths came to see the exhibition. I think Tanner as an artist and human being is a transcendent figure.

CCB: Long after this book and others produced by my colleagues in the biblical guild have turned to dust, Tanner's interpretations of the Bible will endure. We are grateful to you, Dr. Marley, for helping us better to appreciate them. Thank you!

COURSE SYLLABUS

The Sermon on the Plain

by R. T. M'Gordon

Sometime after the turn of the twenty-first century, standardized templates were created and enjoined, if not mandated, for replication by instructors throughout the United States to satisfy agencies that accredit colleges and universities. What might such a syllabus for Luke 6:20–49 have looked like had the evangelist been required to submit one?

*Component Required by Accrediting Agencies.

*Course Number/Title: No number/no title.

Semester/Year: For all time.

Class Day/Time: One day. 30 min.

*Professor Contact Information and Office Hours:

Jesus. On a level place. Catch him when you can.

*Course Description:

~~This course will provide a conceptual framework for students who wish to ponder deeply in relation to the complexities of the God–human human–human dynamic. Students in the course will be invited to consider a range of philosophical perspectives (with special attention to phenomenology, epistemology, and metaphysics).~~

Blessings and responsibilities of Jesus' disciples.

*Course Objectives:

~~1. This course will supply a comprehensive survey of milestones in the philosophy of discipleship in antiquity.~~

~~2. Participants will be supplied a survey of primary concepts of philosophy: phenomenology, epistemology, and metaphysics.~~

~~3. The objective of the course is to assist students in penetrating critical components to constructive Christian behavior.~~

To learn to love unconditionally, forgo judgments of others, bear good fruit, and do as Jesus commands.

*Student Learning Outcomes:

As a result of this course, students will be able to:

1. ~~Demonstrate a working knowledge of basic conceptual dimensions of the phenomenological, epistemological, and metaphysical approaches to philosophies of behavior encountered in the course.~~

2. ~~Think critically and constructively about the primary assumptions pertaining to behavior, especially in relation to aims, contexts, curricula, and the complementarity of roles in the teacher/learner(s) relationship.~~

3. ~~Articulate a competent critique for each approach to the philosophy of behavior encountered in the course.~~

For those by the wayside, the devil cometh and taketh the word out of their hearts. Those on the rock for a while believe and in time of temptation fall away. Those among the thorns are choked with cares and riches and pleasures of this life and thus bring no fruit to perfection. Those on the good ground, with an honest and good heart, hear the word, keep it, and bring forth fruit with patience.

*Course Requirements:

~~Essential Bibliography including Required Textbooks and Other Readings~~

If anyone will come after me, let him deny himself, and take up his cross daily, and follow me. No woman, having put her hand to the plow and looking back, is fit for the kingdom of God.

Assessment of Student Learning

1. ~~Three essays, each 20–30 pages in length: each 10 percent of the final grade.~~

2. ~~Mid-Term Examination: 30 percent of the final grade.~~

3. ~~Final Examination: 40 percent of the final grade.~~

After dying, beggars will be carried by the angels into Abraham's bosom; the rich who die will lift up their eyes in hell, being in torments, and see Abraham afar off, with the poor in his bosom.

Decision of the Dean of the College

SYLLABUS UNACCEPTABLE. COURSE UNAPPROVED.

Instructor's Response

Woe unto you, lawyers! For ye have taken away the key of knowledge: ye entered not in yourselves, and them that were entering in ye hindered.

For Further Study

All of the following are generally recognized as trustworthy works of scholarly merit.

These suggestions are itemized under three categories. *Basic Works* are just that: elementary tools for studying the Gospels. Studies of *Intermediate Difficulty* proceed at a level about a notch above what the reader has encountered in this book. They will stretch your intellectual muscles but are accessible if read carefully and with patience. *Technical Studies* are written by scholars for scholars. Presupposing knowledge of the biblical languages, they open vast veins of historical and literary information. However, one needn't be a professional scholar to derive benefit from them. All those indicated here are clearly written. All raise interesting questions and open angles of vision on the Synoptics that the present volume could touch only lightly, if at all.

1. The Gospels: A Curtain-Raiser

Basic Works

Attridge, Harrold W., ed. *The HarperCollins Study Bible: Fully Revised & Updated*. San Francisco: HarperOne, 2006.

> An indispensable resource, produced by members of the international Society of Biblical Literature, providing up-to-date introductions and concise annotations of all biblical books, maps, charts, diagrams, and a wealth of background information.

Barrett, C. K., ed. *The New Testament Background: Writings from Ancient Greece and the Roman Empire That Illuminate Christian Origins*. Rev. ed. San Francisco: HarperCollins, 1989.

> First published in 1956 and updated in successive editions, this is among the finest one-volume collections of primary Greek, Roman, and Hellenistic Jewish sources that locate the Gospels in their cultural contexts.

Barton, Stephen C., ed. *The Cambridge Companion to the Gospels*. Cambridge: Cambridge University Press, 2006.

Throckmorton, Burton H., Jr. *Gospel Parallels: A Comparison of the Synoptic Gospels, New Revised Standard Version.* 5th rev. ed. Nashville: Thomas Nelson, 1992.

> Another standard tool. The Synoptics are arranged in parallel columns, allowing the reader to recognize immediately their similarities and differences in wording.

Intermediate Difficulty

Green, Joel B., and Lee Martin McDonald, eds. *The World of the New Testament: Cultural, Social, and Historical Contexts.* Grand Rapids: Baker Academic, 2017.

> An invaluable compendium of research in early Christianity, authored by thirty-seven distinguished scholars.

Sanders, E. P., and Margaret Davies. *Studying the Synoptic Gospels.* Philadelphia: Trinity Press International, 1989.

Technical Studies

Beard, Mary. *SPQR: A History of Ancient Rome.* New York: Liveright & Norton, 2015.
Sanders, E. P. *Judaism: Practice and Belief, 63 BCE–66 CE.* Minneapolis: Fortress Press, 2016.

2. Jesus according to Mark: A Veiled Unveiling

Intermediate Difficulty

Black, C. Clifton. *Mark.* Abingdon New Testament Commentaries. Nashville: Abingdon Press, 2011.
Boring, M. Eugene. *Mark: A Commentary.* New Testament Library. Louisville, KY: Westminster John Knox Press, 2006.

Technical Studies

Marcus, Joel. *Mark 1–8* and *Mark 8–16.* Anchor Yale Bible Commentaries. New Haven, CT: Yale University Press, 2002–9.
Yarbro Collins, Adela. *Mark: A Commentary.* Hermeneia. Minneapolis: Fortress Press, 2007.

3. Jesus according to Matthew: Torah Incarnate

Intermediate Difficulty

Culpepper, R. Alan. *Matthew: A Commentary.* New Testament Library. Louisville, KY: Westminster John Knox Press, 2022.
Senior, Donald. *Matthew.* Abingdon New Testament Commentaries. Nashville: Abingdon Press, 1998.

Technical Studies

Davies, W. D., and Dale C. Allison Jr. *Matthew 1–7, Matthew 8–18,* and *Matthew 19–28.* International Critical Commentary. Edinburgh: T&T Clark, 2004 in paperback..
Luz, Ulrich. *Matthew 1–7, 8–20,* and *21–28.* Translated by James E. Crouch. Hermeneia. Minneapolis: Fortress Press, 2007, 2001, 2005.

4. Jesus according to Luke: Joyous Boundary Breaker

Intermediate Difficulty

Carroll, John T. *Luke: A Commentary*. New Testament Library. Louisville, KY: Westminster John Knox Press, 2012.
Tannehill, Robert C. *Luke*. Abingdon New Testament Commentaries. Nashville: Abingdon Press, 1996.

Technical Studies

Fitzmyer, Joseph A. *The Gospel according to Luke I–IX* and *The Gospel according to Luke X–XXIX*. Anchor Bible 28 and 28A. Garden City, NY: Doubleday & Co., 1982–85.
Green, Joel B. *The Gospel of Luke*. New International Commentary on the New Testament. Grand Rapids; Wm. B. Eerdmans Publishing Co., 1997.

Miscellaneous Investigations

The Gospels in Art

Drury, John. *Painting the Word: Christian Pictures and Their Meanings*. New Haven, CT, and London: Yale University Press in association with the National Gallery, London, 1999.
MacGregor, Neil, with Erika Langmuir. *Seeing Salvation: Images of Christ in Art*. New Haven, CT: Yale University Press, 2000.

The Gospels in Classical Music

Minear, Paul S. *Death Set to Music: Masterworks by Bach, Brahms, Penderecki, Bernstein*. Atlanta: John Knox Press, 1987.
Steinitz, Paul. *Bach's Passions*. Masterworks of Choral Music. New York: Charles Scribner's Sons, 1978.

The History of the Gospels' Interpretation

Blowers, Paul M., and Peter W. Martens, eds. *The Oxford Handbook of Early Christian Biblical Interpretation*. Oxford: Oxford University Press, 2019.

The Gospels Interpreted in Literature and Life

Price, Reynolds. *Three Gospels: The Good News according to Mark; The Good News according to John; An Honest Account of a Memorable Life*. New York: Scribner, 1996.

Index of Scripture and Other Ancient Sources

Index of Subjects

vision, 58
Vitellius (Roman emperor), 148 fig., 151

Wagner, Richard. 122
"Wake Up, Little Susie" (song), 89n4
Wanamaker, Rodman, 62, 165
water, walking on, 103, 104 fig.
wealth, 34–35, 142–46, 153
Weiss, Johannes, 25
will of God, 139
Willimon, William H., 79–83
wise men. *See* Magi
wives, in Roman Empire, 35–36, 36 fig.
women
    in birth and infancy narratives, 131
    Blickenstaff on, 133–36
    as church leaders, 134
    as disciples of Jesus, 133–35, 134n11
    as financial supporters of Jesus, 138, 155
    in genealogy of Jesus, 89, 91

in Hebrew Bible vs New Testament,
    133–34
Lukan, 154–56, 158
Markan, 76–77
in ministry of Jesus, 133
portrayal of, 135–36
in Roman Empire, 35–36
World War I, 162
Wrede, William, 56n11

Xanthus, 37
Xenophon, 57

Yale University, 118
Yiddish, 51n5

Zadokites, 27
Zealots, 30
Zechariah (husband of Elizabeth), 131,
    137–38